IMAGES
of America

LANESVILLE AND FRANKLIN TOWNSHIP

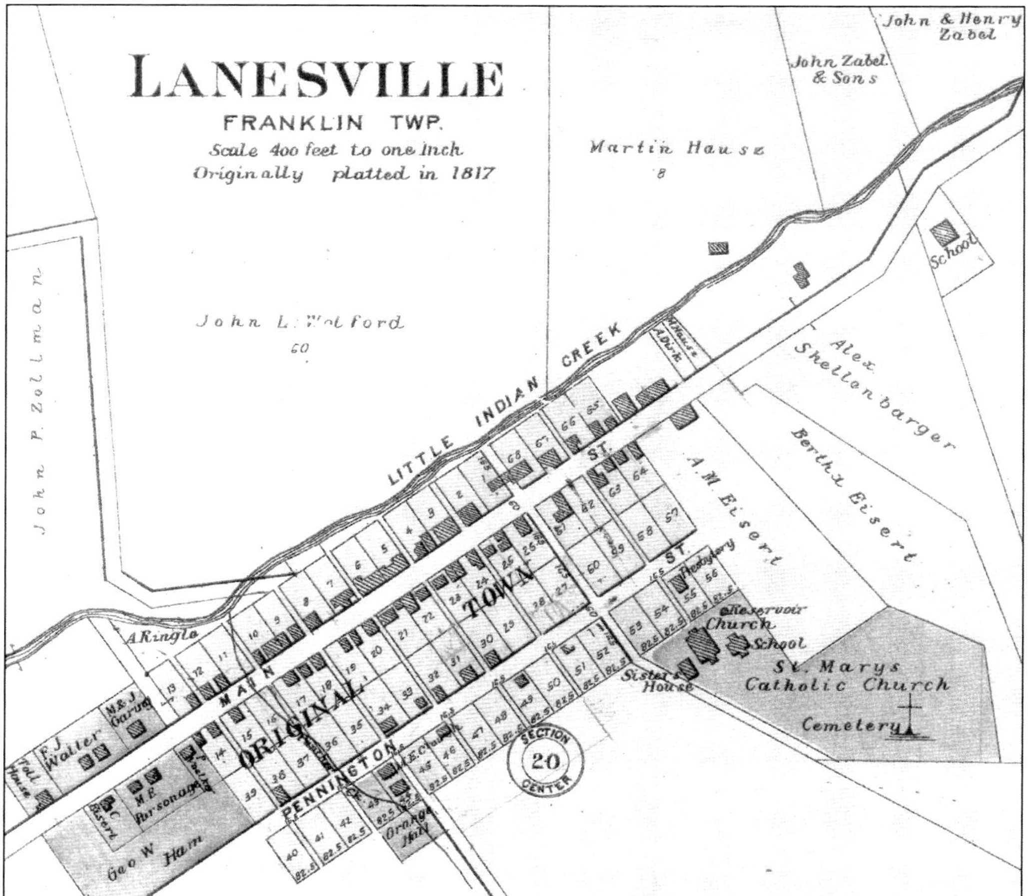

This Lanesville map is from the 1882 Harrison County Atlas. Note how the town was platted at the time, with various numbered lots referencing homes and businesses. (Courtesy of the Lanesville Library.)

On the Cover: The Voelker family enjoys watermelon on a hot summer day in 1897. Christina Gehlbach Voelker is the woman holding the knife with her youngest daughter, Emilie, in front of her. Christina's husband, Anton, is standing in the straw hat. Note the man at the far right, kneeling with a face full of watermelon; that is Ed Voelker, who took the picture. Notice the string in his hand that he used to pull the shutter to take the photograph.

IMAGES
of America

LANESVILLE AND FRANKLIN TOWNSHIP

Tim Bridges

ARCADIA
PUBLISHING

ISBN 978-0-7385-9411-8

Published by Arcadia Publishing
Charleston, South Carolina

Printed in the United States of America

Library of Congress Control Number: 2012942211

For all general information, please contact Arcadia Publishing:
Telephone 843-853-2070
Fax 843-853-0044
E-mail sales@arcadiapublishing.com
For customer service and orders:
Toll-Free 1-888-313-2665

Visit us on the Internet at www.arcadiapublishing.com

I must dedicate this book to the late Bruce Green. He was my teacher, my colleague, and my friend. He started this project some 40 years ago but never completed it. I hope that Bruce would be proud of this book.

Contents

Acknowledgments		6
Introduction		7
1.	Working in Lanesville and Franklin Township	9
2.	The Schools	37
3.	The Churches	63
4.	The Farms and the Farmers	75
5.	Memorable Faces and Stories	103

ACKNOWLEDGMENTS

Writing this book took many hours of searching and visiting people in their homes and on street corners to gain access to the photographs and stories that make up the history of our town and the surrounding area. I must give thanks to those who helped me with this project.

First, thank you to my wife, Rhonda Bridges, who put up with me being away for many evenings talking to people and working on this project at both school and home. Thank you to Kathy Fisher from the Porter-Griffin Center in Corydon; Paul Hancock, the Lanesville Community Schools technology coordinator, for his patience with some really dumb computer-related questions; and Martha Beckort, the Lanesville Community Schools media specialist, for her guidance and help whenever I asked.

Thanks to Michelle Scarber, a Lanesville High School English teacher who proofread the countless pages of text, and Steve Morris, superintendent of Lanesville Community Schools, for allowing me the use of school facilities and anything I needed to make this book possible.

I must thank all those at Arcadia Publishing for allowing this book to be published. My editor, Sandy Shalton, has been a great help and I want to thank her for everything she has done to make this book happen.

The biggest thanks go to the people of Lanesville and Franklin Township. Without their kindness, photographs, and memories, this book would have never been written; it was truly a community project. Many people shared their families' history with me, and now I will share that history with the readers of this book. Those people are too numerous to mention but will receive credit throughout the book for the images they submitted. Everyone I talked to was very kind and very open to allowing me to share a bit of their lives with you.

INTRODUCTION

After the Revolutionary War, settlers began streaming into the land west of the Appalachian Mountains, pouring into southern Indiana in the late 1780s and early 1790s. A small group settled in what would become Lanesville in 1792.

James Harbison, a Revolutionary War soldier originally from Pennsylvania and part of Kentucky's Lincoln County Militia, first came into the area in the 1780s. William Henry Harrison, Indiana's first territorial governor and later the ninth president of the United States, settled on the land in and around Little Indian Creek, which runs down the middle of the settlement, in about 1807. Ed Pennington and his wife, Nettie, came from Virginia, had nine children, and settled in the village of Lanesville. One son, William Pennington, stayed in Lanesville, making a living and raising his family, while his brother Dennis Pennington went west about eight miles and helped start the city of Corydon.

James Armstrong, a Methodist minister, came and set up business along the creek where a small salt lick was located. Salt came bubbling up from the creek bed below, supplying salt for many of the local animals. The land was good and the salt lick meant two things: there was plenty of food from animals needing salt, and there was plenty of salt to preserve that food. The creek also provided a means to power machines later on in Lanesville's history.

Harbison started a small gristmill early in the 1800s, and Lanesville became a small but thriving settlement in a growing Indiana territory. Indiana became a state on December 11, 1816, locating its capital in Corydon, just eight miles to the west. Lanesville's population grew, more shops and business sprang up, and it became time to have the town platted and surveyed properly. Government surveyor Gen. Thomas Lane surveyed and platted the town. On December 11, 1817, one year to the day after Indiana became a state, Lanesville became a town, named for its surveyor.

In the 1830s and 1840s, immigration to the United States increased and Lanesville welcomed and absorbed new people, many of whom were German. Early families who came and settled the town and the surrounding farmlands are well known today with names like Blank, Voelker, Reinhardt, Gleitz, Zollman, and Gresham. Many came from Mendenhall, Hesse Darmstadt, and Baden, Germany, and others came from places in France via New Orleans and Vincennes, Indiana, because Lanesville's rolling fields and woods reminded them of their homeland.

The early settlers were very industrious, using what God gave them to build their town and their businesses and work the land. From quarrying stone to milling flour, the people found niches in which they could contribute to the development of the area. Star Mill was one of the first enterprises established in Lanesville, erected and operated by Philip Zabel and John Foreman in 1865. It has gone through some changes, but still stands in its original spot and is a landmark in town. There was a strong sense of pride in the town and surrounding farms, which is still evident today throughout the township. Many of the farms are still worked by the same names as those first settlers.

An early "ridge road" was built about three miles north of Lanesville in about 1851. Called Corydon Ridge Road, it connected the capital of Corydon with Oatman's Ferry in New Albany and was a main link from the Ohio River to the early state capital. Later, a few miles to the south of the ridge road, another road was built through the town of Lanesville, known as a plank road or a corduroy road.

Roads like these were built all over the newly settled state. William Henry Harrison owned some of the land the corduroy road was built on as well as land along the Little Indian Creek, near what would be the center of Lanesville. The corduroy road was a toll road, collecting at certain points in the town as people passed through. It remained a toll road until 1911.

In the 1870s, the Air Line Railroad was laid, connecting St. Louis, Missouri, to Lexington, Kentucky. On its way to Lexington, the line passed through north Franklin Township. In 1901, the Southern Railroad Line bought the Air Line Railroad. In the early 1990s, it became Norfolk Southern, and it continues to run trains through the township today. Railroads and roads connected all parts of Lanesville and Franklin Township with the rest of the ever-changing country.

The people of Lanesville and Franklin Township saw a need to have their children learn beyond what the farm taught them and there has always been a strong sense of pride in the education of children. Early on, there were 10 one-room schoolhouses scattered throughout the township so none of the township children would be denied an education.

Early settlers also built churches in which to worship. There remains a strong faith in God in the community, which has sustained the people through good times and bad. Catholics, Lutherans, and Methodists all had a strong presence early on, and while they differed on theology, they all joined together when it came to the needs of the town. Many of the churches were built between the late 1840s and the 1870s, with one exception: Pfrimmer's Chapel United Methodist Church in west Franklin, which was built in 1812. It was the first United Brethren (Methodist) Church in the state of Indiana. It still has services to this very day. The Baptists came much later, not until 1975, but have become an important part of the town and township's people.

Lanesville has a rich history, and I will only be able to show you a portion of its history in images I have collected from townspeople, which is part of what makes this book so special. It is a collection of family histories and memories and community happenings. It will take a look at the schools, churches, businesses, farms, and people that have made Lanesville and Franklin Township important to me. It must be noted that many of the captions that are included with the images are based on the memories of the people who supplied them. I have tried to be as accurate as possible in chronicling those memories.

One

Working in Lanesville and Franklin Township

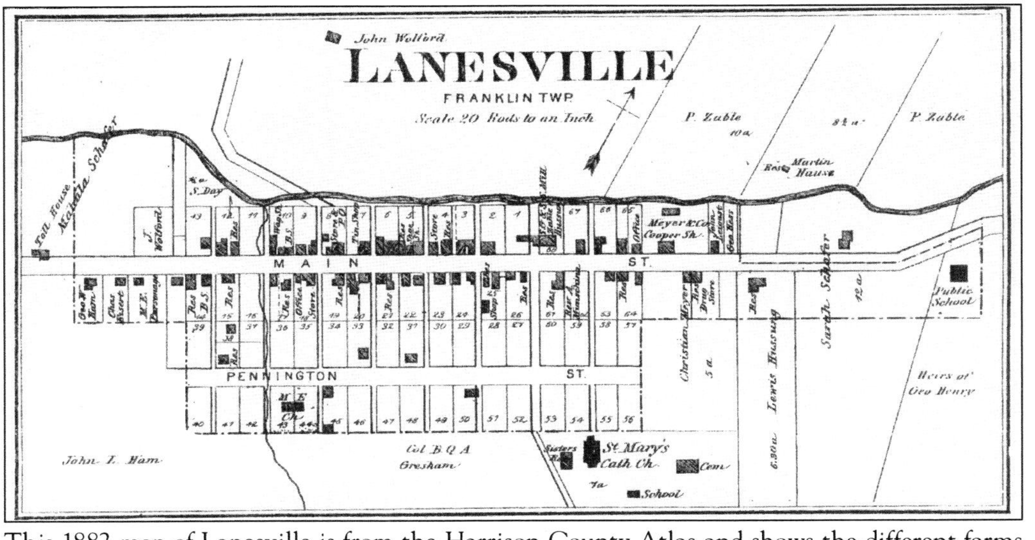

This 1882 map of Lanesville is from the Harrison County Atlas and shows the different farms and properties laid out in Franklin Township. (Courtesy of the Lanesville Library.)

LANESVILLE BUSINESS REFERENCES.

EDWARD WALTHER, Commissioner of Harrison Co.

PETER ENDRISS, Ex-Sheriff of Harrison Co.

MICHAEL GEHLBACH, Trustee of Franklin Township.

A. M. EISERT, Assessor of Franklin Township.

WM. BENSON, Justice of the Peace and Ex-Co. Treasurer.

ALPHONSE MUNSCHINA, Catholic Priest.

COL. B. Q. A. GRESHAM, Notary Public.

LOUIS STIEGEMEYER, Lutheran Minister.

HENRY C. FOUTS, M. D., Physician and Surgeon.

JACOB S. HORNER, M. D., Physician and Surgeon.

IVERSON LYNN, Veterinary Surgeon.

GEORGE SCHAFER, Blacksmith. All kinds of Blacksmithing done with neatness and accuracy. Machinery repaired and parts manufactured. Run two forges. Work solicited, and done cheap for cash.

WM. C. YEAGER, Blacksmith. All kinds of fancy and rough blacksmithing done with neatness and accuracy. Repairing of all kinds of machinery with care. Shop on Main street.

A. M. EISERT, Manufacturer and dealer in all kinds of cooperage. Also agent for Phœnix, Hartford, and German Fire Insurance Companies, of Indianapolis. Book and Paper Agent.

JOHN REDICK, Dealer in Dry Goods, Groceries, Hats, Caps, Boots, Shoes, Ready-made Clothing, Wooden ware, Hardware, Queensware, Cutlery, Candies, Pickles, Cigars, Tobaccos, Toilet Soaps, Fancy Articles, Notions, &c., and all goods usually kept in a first-class country store. Country produce taken in exchange for goods.

C. MEYER, Dealer in Dry Goods, Groceries, Hats, Caps, Boots, Shoes, Hardware, Queensware, Wooden ware, Notions, Toilet Soaps, fancy articles, &c. Also dealer in drugs, medicines, patent medicines, Paints, Oils, Varnishes, Dye-stuffs, &c. Cigars, Tobacco, School Books, Stationery, &c. Prescriptions carefully compounded day or night. Store on Main St.

JOSEPH SCHUMANN, Dealer in Dry Goods, Groceries, Hats, Caps, Boots, Shoes, Hardware, Tinware, Queensware, Glassware, School Books, Notions, Patent Medicines, Toilet Soaps, Fancy Articles, &c. Mrs. Maggie Schumann, Post-mistress. Store and Post Office at Breckenridge, on New Albany turnpike.

PETER A. DAY, Carpenter, Contractor & Builder. Contracts solicited and promptly executed. House and Sign painting done. Graining and all kinds of fancy painting neatly done.

JOHN WRIGHT, Carpenter, Contractor & Builder Res. Sec. 2.

AUGUST JUNGBLUTH, Dealer in Fine Liquors, Brandies, &c. Proprietor of Saloon on Main Street.

JOHN MILLER, Grower and dealer in Peaches, Pears, Plums, Cherries and Apples of all varieties Choice varieties furnished at all proper seasons. All parties desiring any kind of fruit will find a choice variety by addressing me by letter or calling at my farm and residence, Sec. 8, near Georgetown, Ind.

LEROY JENKINS, Grower and dealer in peaches, pears, apples, plums, raspberries, gooseberries, strawberries, currants, and all varieties of small fruits. All varieties above mentioned are of the finest quality. Also gardener and dealer in garden products generally. Dealer in all articles found in the markets. All persons having any thing in my line will find a ready sale by calling upon me. My farm is for sale cheap for cash. Situated in a good fruit growing region, and within thirty-five rods of St. L. & N. A. R. R., and contains sixty acres. P. O. Georgetown, Floyd Co.

J. E. WILLIAMS, Grower of apples, pears, peaches, plums, cherries, raspberries, strawberries, gooseberries, grapes, &c. A first-class variety grown and for sale in proper season at my residence—Sec. 4.

JOHN ARNOLD, Stiller and manufacturer of fine peach and apple brandies. Highest cash price paid for fruits. Fruit wanted at my distillery—Sec. 18, Franklin twp. Brandies for sale at all times.

HENRY BACHMAN, Stiller and manufacturer and dealer in fine peach and apple brandies, vinegar, &c. All kinds of whiskies and brandies for sale at my residence—Section 21, near Lanesville.

J. J. SIMLER, Teacher of Public Schools.

J. E. WILLIAMS, " "

JOHN T. GEHLBACH, Dealer in all kinds of Dry Goods, Groceries, Hats, Caps, Boots & Shoes, Notions, Toilet Soaps, and Fancy Articles. Will fill all orders that may be made. Having had considerable experience in dealing and delivery of goods, I am prepared to furnish from my wagon any of the above articles cheap. All kinds of hucksters' stock taken in exchange for goods, or cash paid for same. Will be in the country Tuesdays, Wednesdays, and Thursdays, and Fridays in Louisville. My wagons will make regular trips—trade solicited.

WM. MEYER & CO., Wholesale manufacturer and dealer in all kinds of cooperage. Highest cash price paid for coopers' materials. Orders for work solicited and promptly filled. Selling cheap for cash. Also proprietors of steam circular saw mill.

ZABLE & HUSSUNG, Owners and proprietors of new and elegant flouring and saw mill. Having recently rebuilt, we are now prepared to and do manufacture a first-class brand of Family Flour. Custom work done on Tuesdays, Thursdays and Saturdays. Highest cash price paid for wheat. Manufacturers and dealers in all kinds of hard and soft lumber. Custom sawing also done. We pay highest cash price for logs. Orders for lumber and plastering laths solicited and promptly filled, cheap for cash.

PHILIP L. HIRT, Manufacturer and dealer in all kinds of boots and shoes. All work warranted and fits guaranteed. Orders promptly filled.

STEPHEN DAY & BRO., Carpenter, Contractor & Builder. Contracts solicited and promptly executed. Mills, churches, schools, and house buildings of all kinds. Also undertaker and cabinet maker. Also all kinds of house and sign painting done, graining and rough painting, &c.

This list of businesses is from the 1882 Harrison County Atlas. It is amazing to see the varied occupations taking place in the town as early as 1882. (Courtesy of the Lanesville Library.)

FRANKLIN TOWNSHIP.

Arnold, John	Lanesville.	Farmer & Distiller	Hesse Darmstadt, Ger.	1854
Allstott, Thomas	"	"	Harrison Co., Ind	1826
Burkett, Caroline	"	"	Kentucky	1829
Benson, Wm.	"	" J P & Ex Co Treas	Jefferson Co., Ky	1834
Benson, R. T.	"	"	Harrison Co., Ind	1848
Bachman, H.	"	" & distiller.	Baden, Ger.	1848
Benson, Jas. H	"	"	Harrison Co., Ind	1835
Benson, Jas. E.	"	"	" "	1854
Carter, Wm. L.	Breckenridge.	Cooper.	" "	1823
Cox, Elizabeth M	Georgetown.	Farmer	" "	1850
Day, Stephen	Lanesville	Carpenter.	Germany.	1848
Day, Peter A.	"	Carpenter & Painter	"	1848
Deutsch, J. T.	"	Farmer	France.	1836
Endris, Peter	"	Ex-Sheriff.	Germany.	1848
Eisert, A. M., Sr.	"	Assessor	"	1843
Fouts, H. C.	"	Physician & Surgeon.	Harrison Co., Ind	1843
Green, Jas. T.	"	Farmer & Ex. J. P	Rockbridge Co., Va	1811
Gresham, Col. B. Q. A.	"	Notary Public.	Harrison Co., Ind	1826
Gehlbach, John T	"	Huckster.	" "	1847
Gehlbach, M	Breckenridge.	Twp. Tru-tee	" "	1843
Horner, J. S.	Lanesville	Physician & Surgeon.	Clark Co., Ind	1826
Hauz, M.	"	Cooper.	Germany.	1853
Hussung, L.	"	Miller	New York City	1837
Hirt, P. L.	"	Boot & Shoe Manuf.	New Albany, Ind	1848
Harbison, Jas. A.	Breckenridge.	Farmer	Harrison Co., Ind	1844
Jungbluth, A.	Lanesville	Saloon Keeper	Germany	1870
Jenkins, L.	Georgetown	Gardener & Fruit Gwr.	Clark Co., Ind	1861
Lynn, I.	Lanesville	Farmer and Vet. Surg	Harrison Co., Ind	1830
Munschina, A.	"	Catholic Priest.	France.	1839
Meyer, C.	"	Druggist.	Harrison Co., Ind	1844
Meyer, Wm.	"	Cooper.	" "	1842
Miller, J.	Georgetown	Farmer and Fruit Gwr.	Jefferson Co., Ky	1856
Miller, C. L.	Lanesville	"	Harrison Co., Ind	1854
Pfrimmer, J. S.	Breckenridge.	" and Music Teacher	" "	1831

This reference from the 1882 atlas gives quite a bit of information about those who lived and worked in the township. The chart includes an individual's post office address, occupation, "nativity" or place of origin, and date of settlement in Franklin Township. (Courtesy of Lanesville Library.)

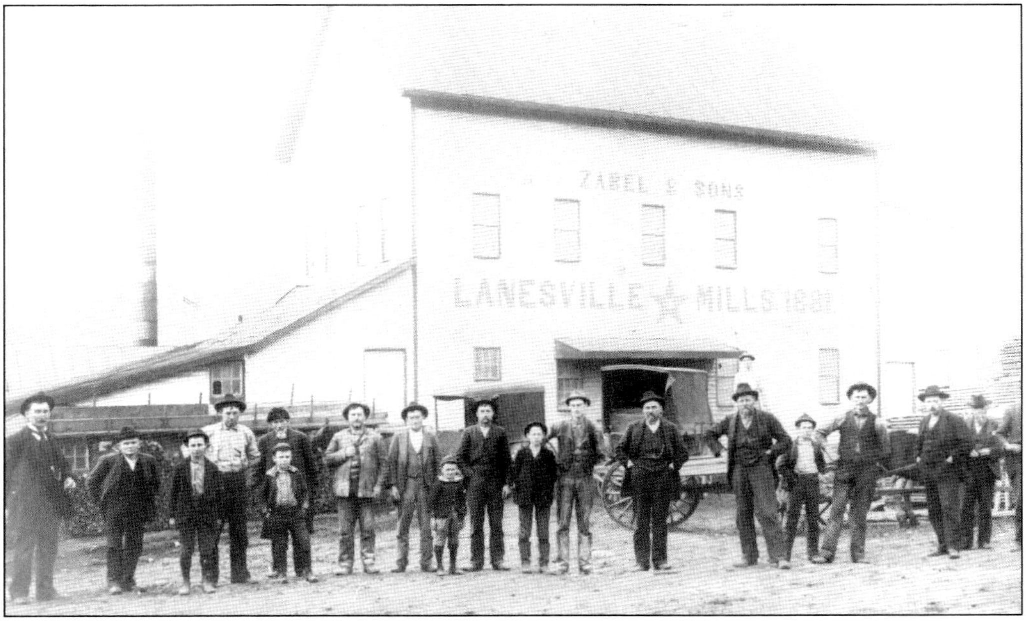

The Lanesville Star Mill is seen here around 1881. It was originally built by Philip Zabel and John Foreman in 1865. When the mill burned later in 1881, it was immediately rebuilt at a cost of $8,000. In 1892, the mill was equipped with a roller system to help produce flour. It produced the brands Flour X and Lanesville Star, which was the best-known flour of that day, selling to markets in Louisville, New Albany, and Jeffersonville. The mill was considered one of Harrison County's most substantial manufacturing plants. (Courtesy of Terry Zabel.)

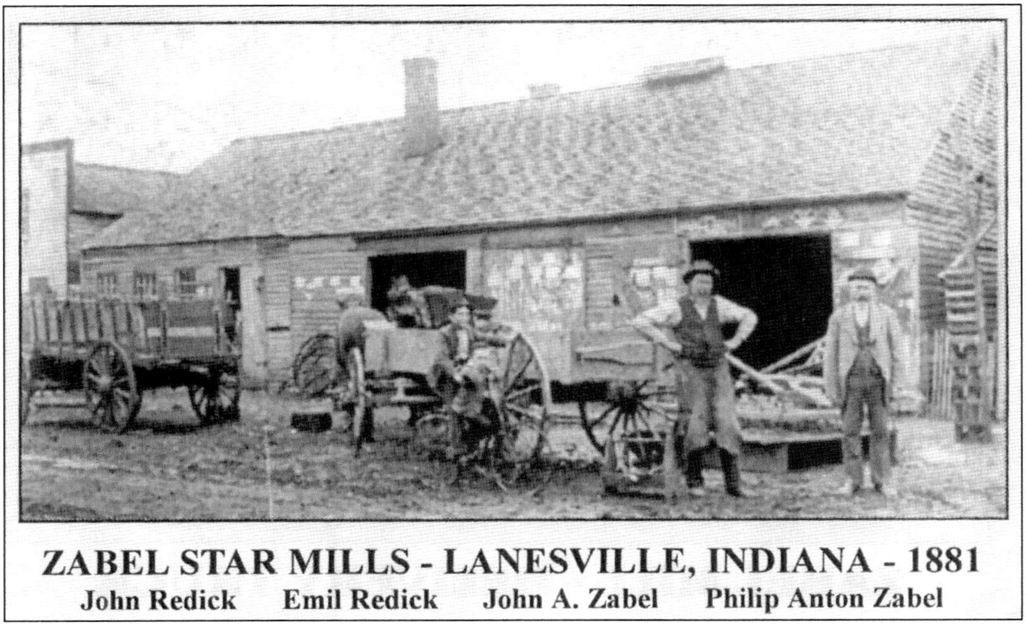

The Lanesville sawmill seen here was attached to the Lanesville Star Mill. From left to right are John Redick, Emil Redick, John Zabel, and Philip Zabel. The sawmill, one of several in town, was a first-class mill, turning out all kinds of lumber cut to order. (Courtesy of Terry Zabel.)

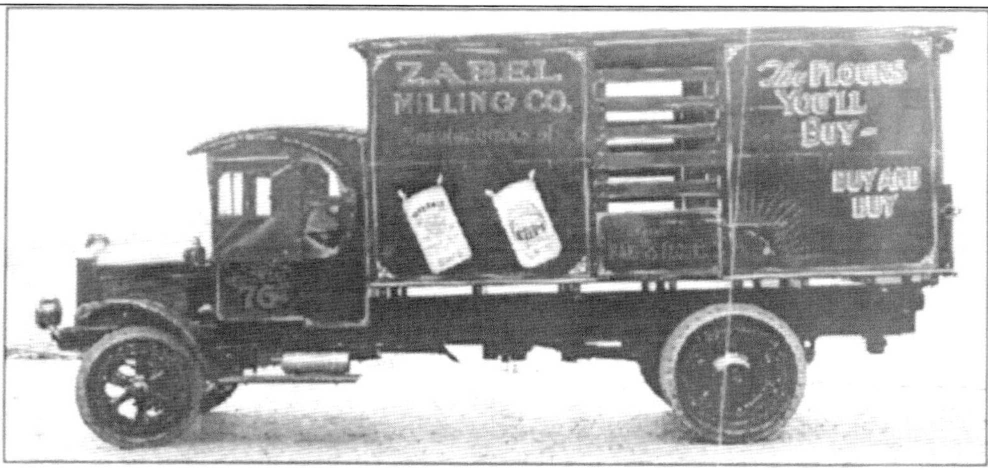

ZABEL MILL - DELIVERY TRUCK

The Zabel Milling Company delivery truck is seen here around the 1910s. In 1921, the Zabels sold the mill to Tony Kochert, dismantling parts of the mill and moving the operation to Budd Road in New Albany. The Zabels continued to make flour in their new mill, delivering it to stores in Louisville and southern Indiana in this truck, which they also used to make deliveries to the Southern Railroad in New Albany and move their flour products to various parts of the region. (Courtesy Terry Zabel.)

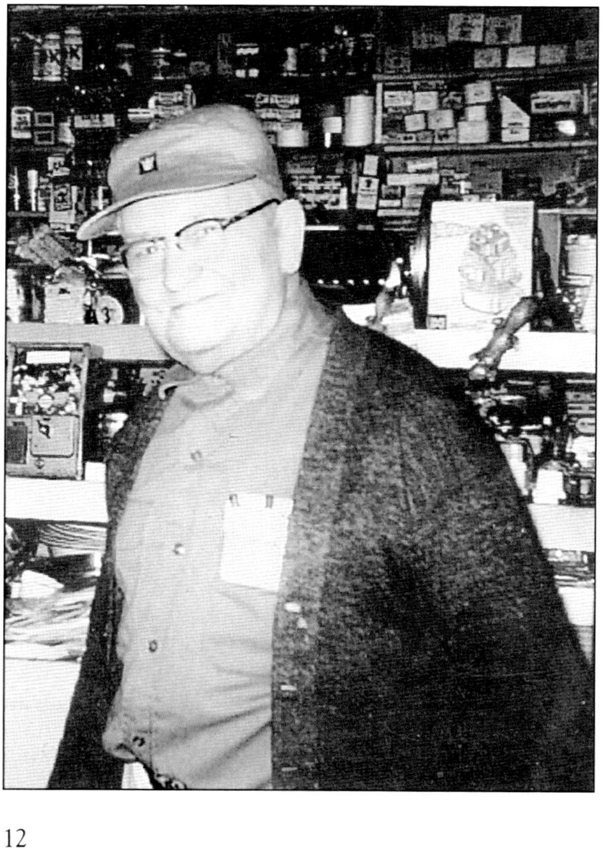

Julius George "J.G." Zabel was the owner and proprietor of J.G. Zabel's Hardware, which has been a staple in Lanesville for about 100 years. Zabel obtained the store from his uncle Louis Zabel around 1916, about five years after he started working there, and ran the store until his death in 1969. At its height, the business had 17 employees on the payroll. It sold John Deere tractors, Willys-Knight cars, and a variety of other products, including gas pumps and oil products for the cars and tractors sold. The store is still operated by J.G.'s grandson Terry Zabel. (Courtesy of Terry Zabel.)

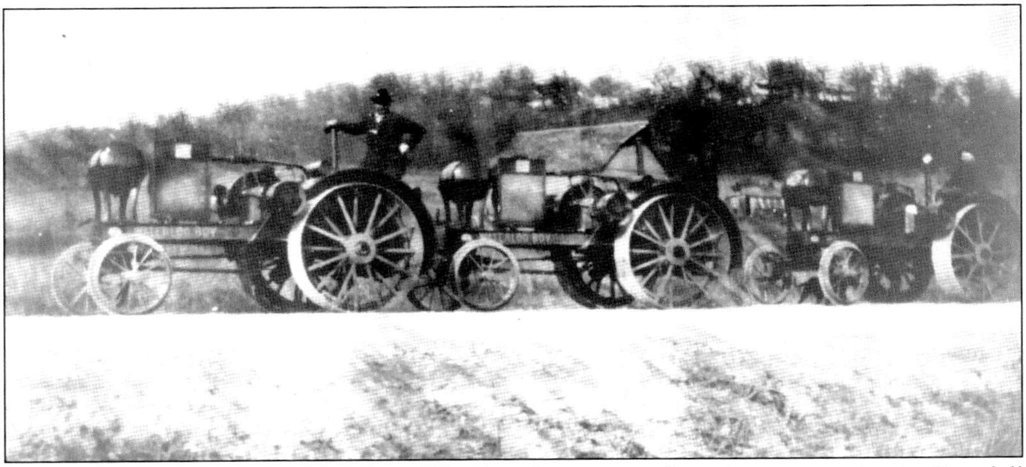

J.G. Zabel and Robert F. Walther drive Waterloo Boy tractors from the train station in Crandall to the store in Lanesville. The tractors were built between 1916 and 1924, and the company was bought out by John Deere in 1918 and slowly phased out. Zabel maintained a full line of parts and service for the Waterloo Boy and John Deere tractors he sold. (Courtesy of Terry Zabel.)

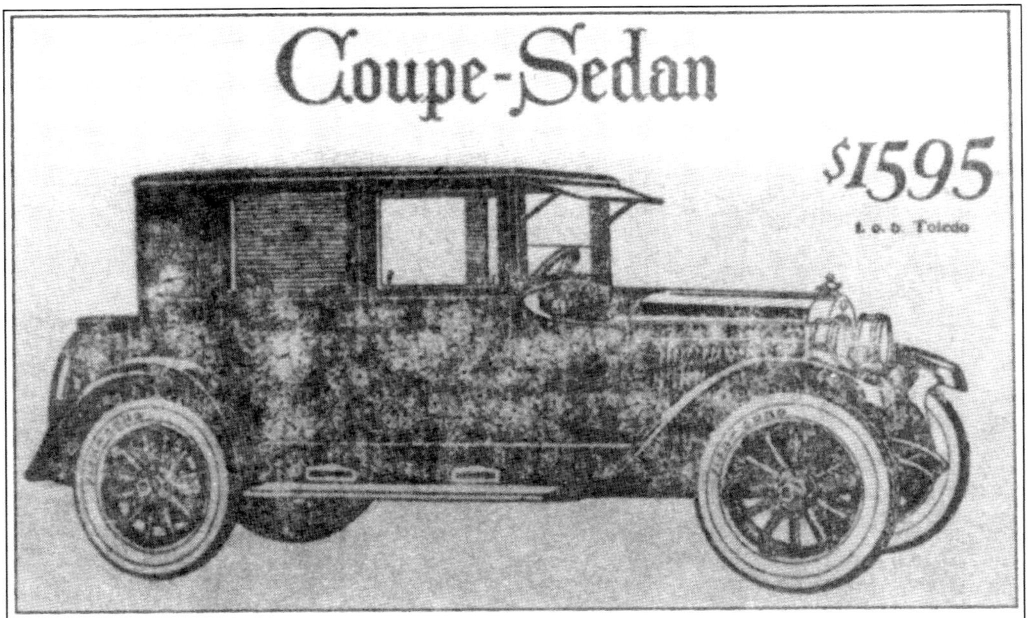

RAILROADERS' GARAGE CO. - Julius G. Zabel, Lanesville 1923.
The latest model of the Willys-Knight Coupe-Sedan at one low price $1595.

J.G. Zabel and Robert F. Walther advertised the Willys-Knight Coupe-Sedan at the low price of $1,595.00. These cars were sold at Zabel's Hardware from 1926 to 1931. Even though the car was advertised at a low price, the average worker in 1926 would probably have a hard time buying the car outright, as the average yearly salary of a worker at that time was not far from the advertised price. Walther and Zabel set up payment plans to accommodate both buyer and seller. (Courtesy of St. Mary's Church, Lanesville.)

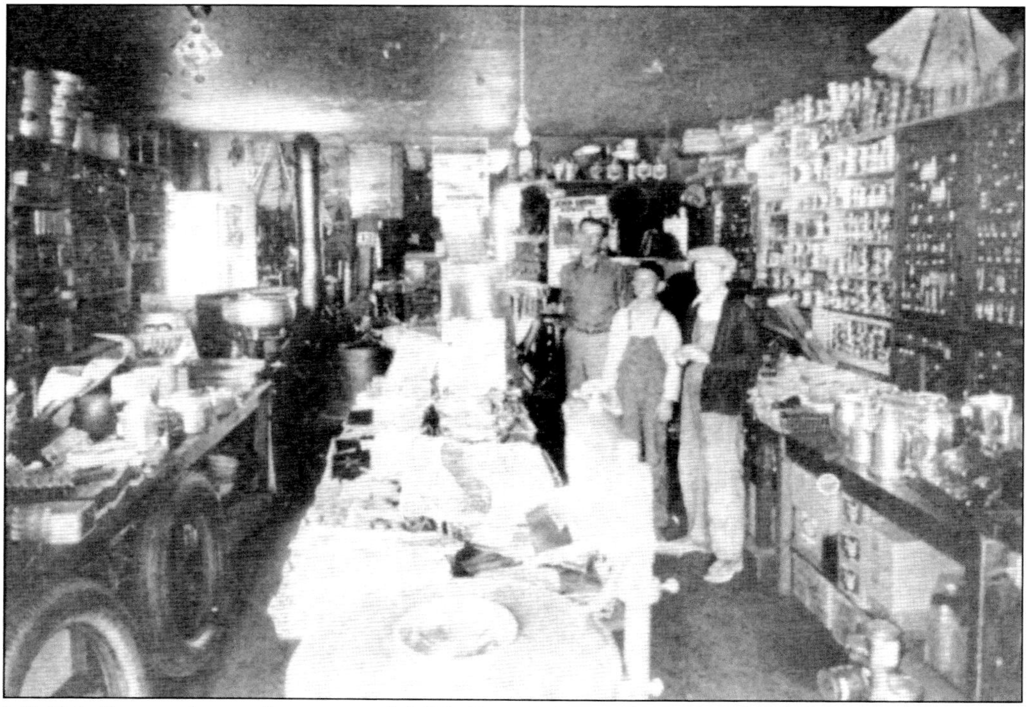

J.G. Zabel's store is seen here around 1928. From left to right are Paul Baker, Walter Zabel, and Robert Walther. The store supplied many products needed by the residents of the town and township, and it was also a place to catch up on the news from around town, as it still is today. (Courtesy of Marvin Zabel.)

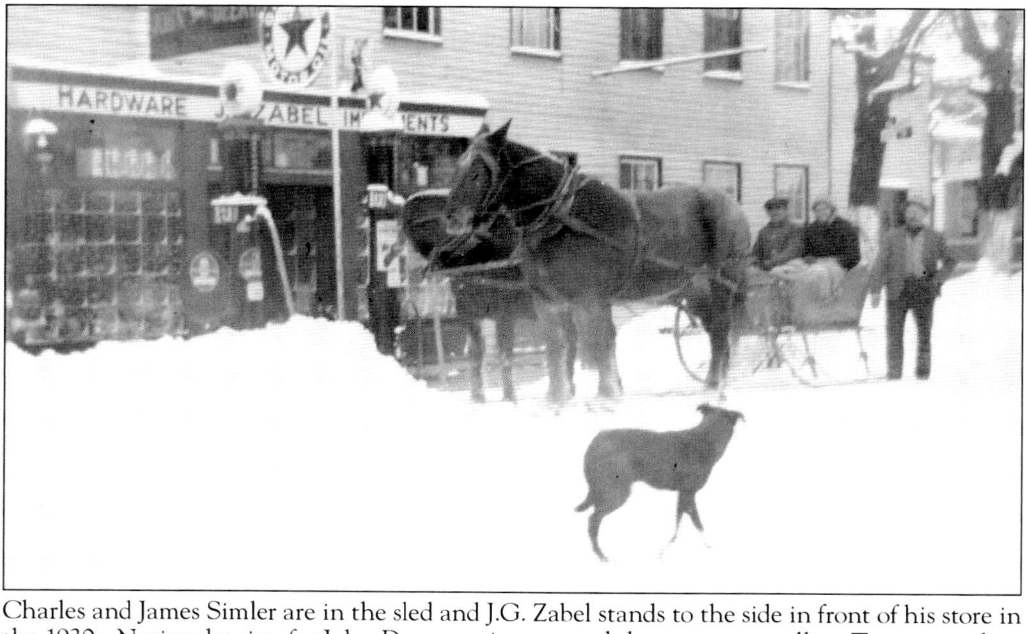

Charles and James Simler are in the sled and J.G. Zabel stands to the side in front of his store in the 1930s. Notice the sign for John Deere equipment and the gas pumps selling Texaco gasoline and motor oil products. (Courtesy of Marvin Zabel.)

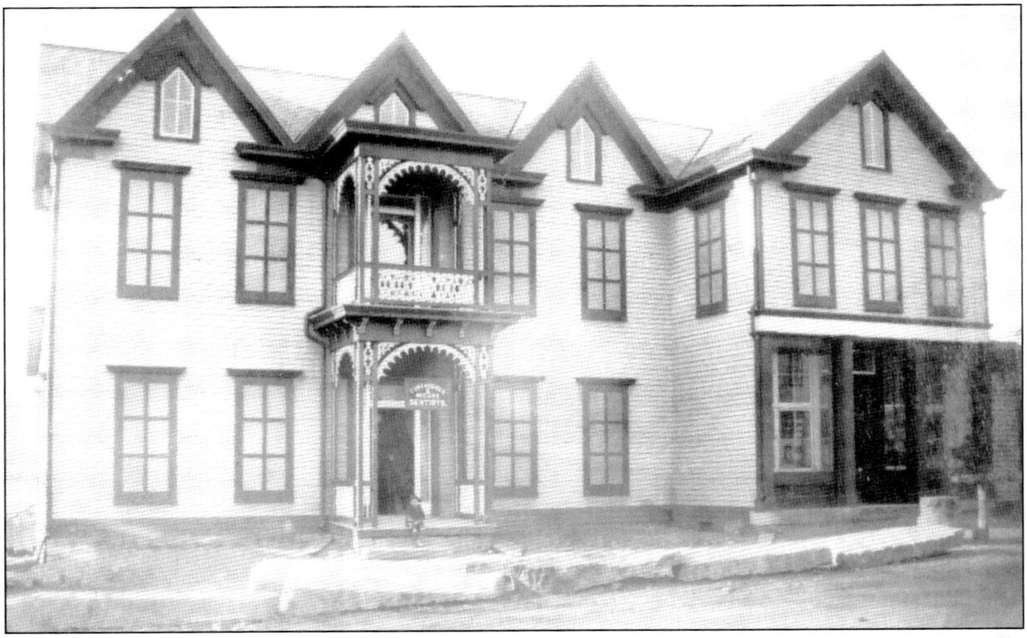

This house was built in downtown Lanesville in 1887–1888 by Christian Meyer. It was originally his house and store as well as his son Oscar's medical practice. At the time of this photograph, it was office space for dentists Funkhouser and McCord. Notice the chiseled rocks along the street are not quite set in place yet. This building is currently used as the town hall. (Courtesy of Byron Baker.)

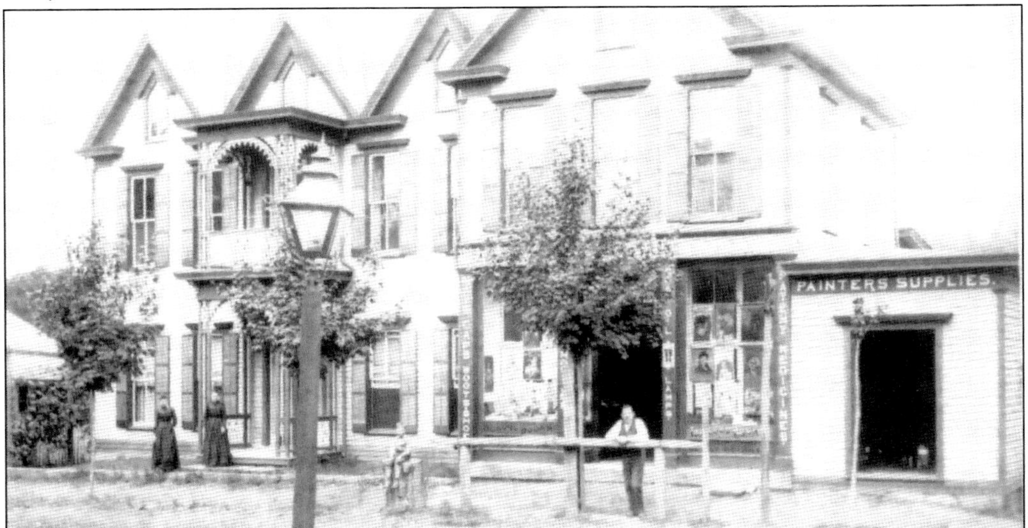

This image of the Christian Meyer house was taken just a few years later in about 1910. The building was a dry goods store and drugstore and later Oscar Meyer's doctor's office and pharmacy. When Julius Green became postmaster in 1933, the section that says "painters supplies" became the post office. Notice the street lamp in front. Dave Schnell, a German immigrant, was the town's lamplighter and would cuss the neighborhood boys in German when they threw snowballs at him. (Courtesy of Byron Baker.)

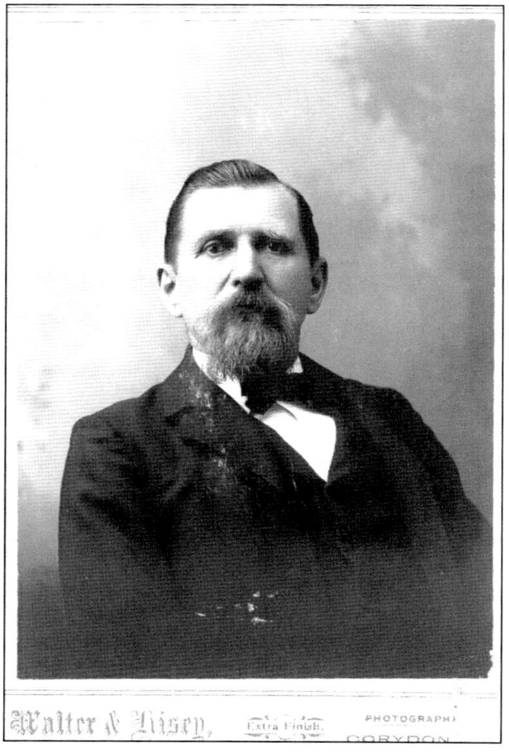

Christian Meyer (1844–1917) is seen here. He was a dealer in dry goods, groceries, shoes, hats, caps, wooden stoves, notions, toilet soaps, medicines, paints, oils, varnishes, tobacco, stationery, and prescriptions. His home and business was on the main street; it now serves the town as Lanesville Town Hall. (Courtesy of Marydee Meyer.)

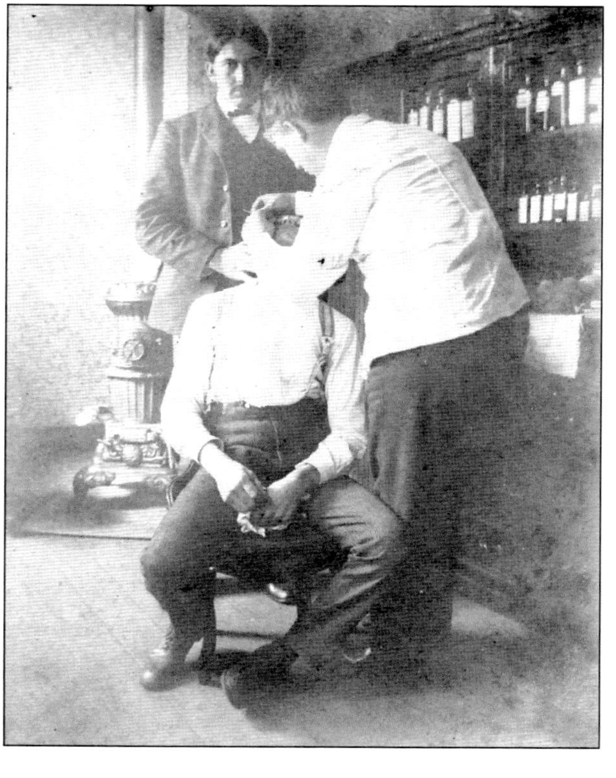

This photograph shows the inside of the doctor's office around 1900. Notice the potbellied stove and bottles of medication on the shelf. This image gives great insight into the early doctor's office and the way patients in town were cared for. (Courtesy of Sharon Gleitz.)

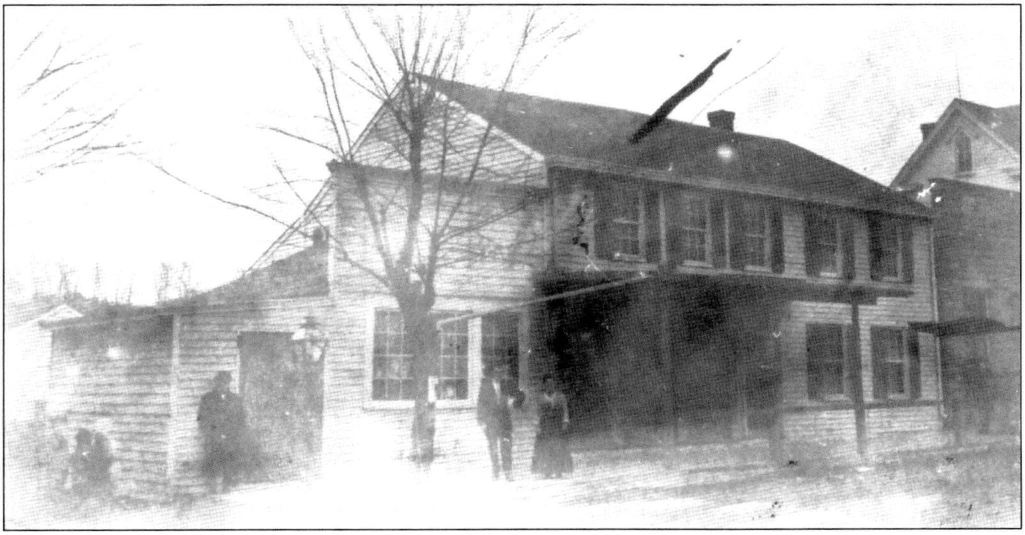

The John Garing store is seen in this 1913 postcard. John Geis bought the store from Garing and sold it to Morris Baker in 1916. Baker then sold it to Urban Zollman in 1921. The narrow building at the right is Farmer's State Bank, built in 1910. (Courtesy of Lanesville archives.)

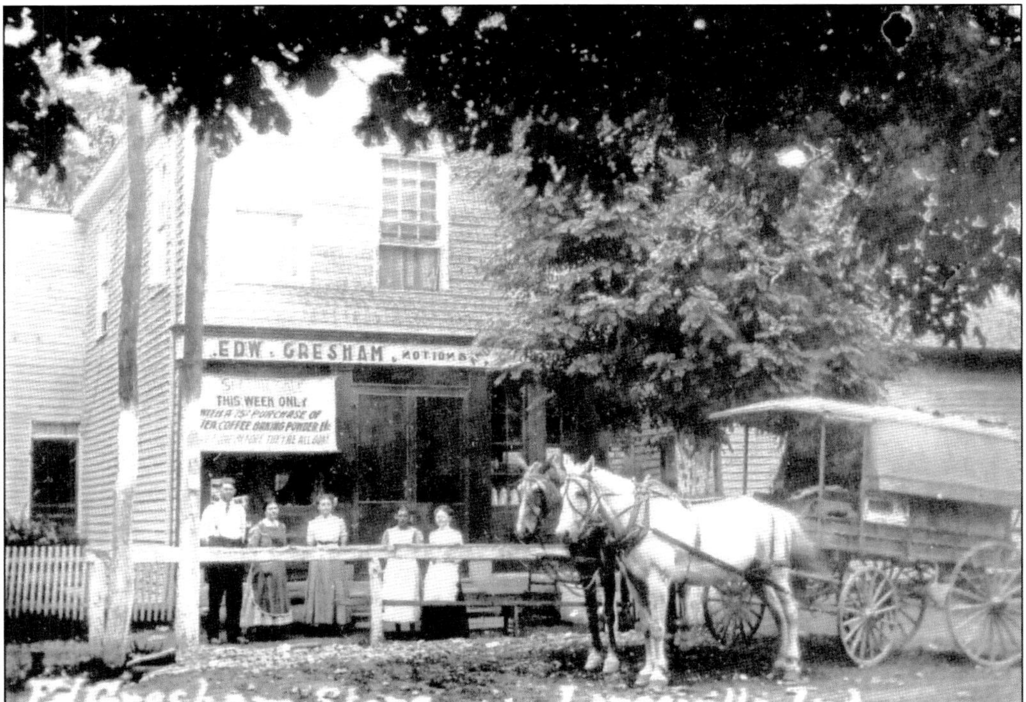

Across the street from where Farmer's State Bank would be built, Ed Gresham's store opened on August 12, 1908. In front of the store are, from left to right, Ed Gresham, Ruth Thomas, Laura Thomas, Marie Simler, and Katie Gresham. Notice the "special sale" advertisement in the background. Ed Gresham eventually sold the store to Willard Stoner, who sold out to Jerry Walter. Walter sold it to Morris Baker in the early 1920s. (Courtesy of Lanesville archives.)

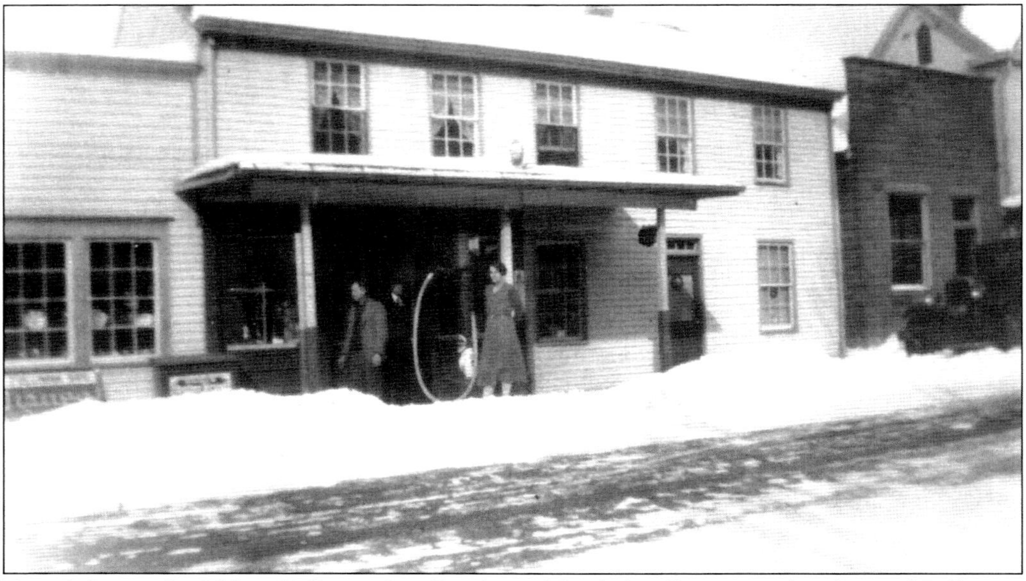

From left to right, Urban Zollman, Ray Resch, and Rachel Zollman stand in front of Zollman's store after a 1936 snowstorm. Urban Zollman bought the store in 1921 from Morris Baker, who opened Baker's General Store in 1924. Zollman's store sat where the First Federal Bank's parking lot is today. The Zollmans ran the store from 1921 until the early 1950s, when Farmer's State Bank bought the property and tore down the building to expand the bank in the 1960s. (Courtesy of Bernice Barnickle.)

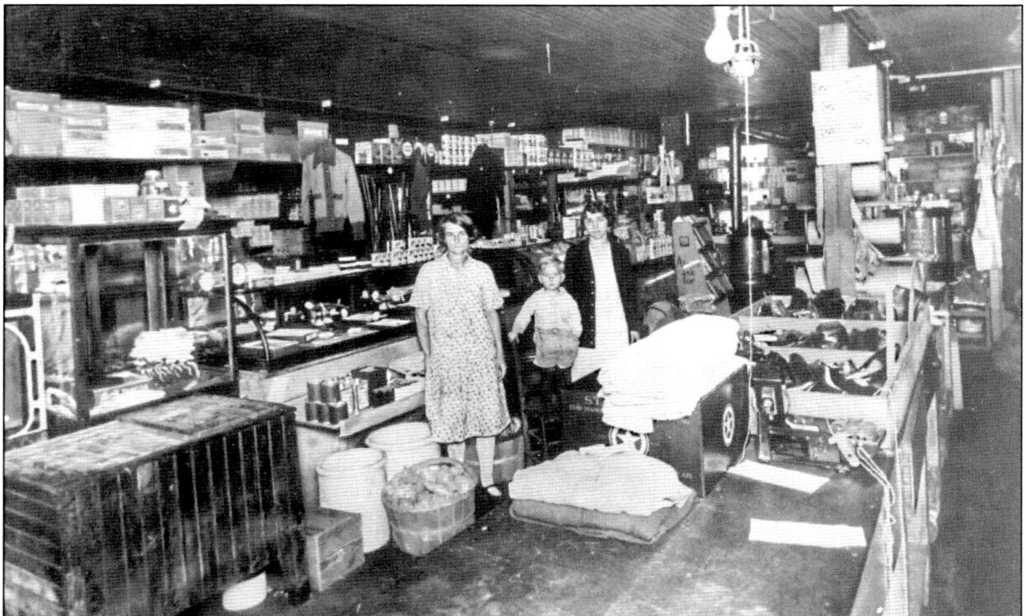

This image was taken inside Zollman's store in the late 1920s or early 1930s. Rachel Zollman and her little boy, Cletus, pose along with Rella Berg, who worked at the store for many years. Zollman's served the people of Lanesville with items they needed every day for many years. For a small town, Lanesville was blessed with many dry goods stores. (Courtesy of Bernice Barnickle.)

Baker's General Store is seen here around late 1923 or early 1924 when construction was nearing completion. Standing in front of their new store are the Bakers, from left to right, Byron, Paul, and dad Morris. The Baker family operated the store from 1924 to 1988, and it became an icon in town. The store has had different owners since then and is now the Lanesville Food Mart, owned and operated by Gary Blank. The building has changed very little and still features the original wood floors. (Courtesy of Carolyn Baker.)

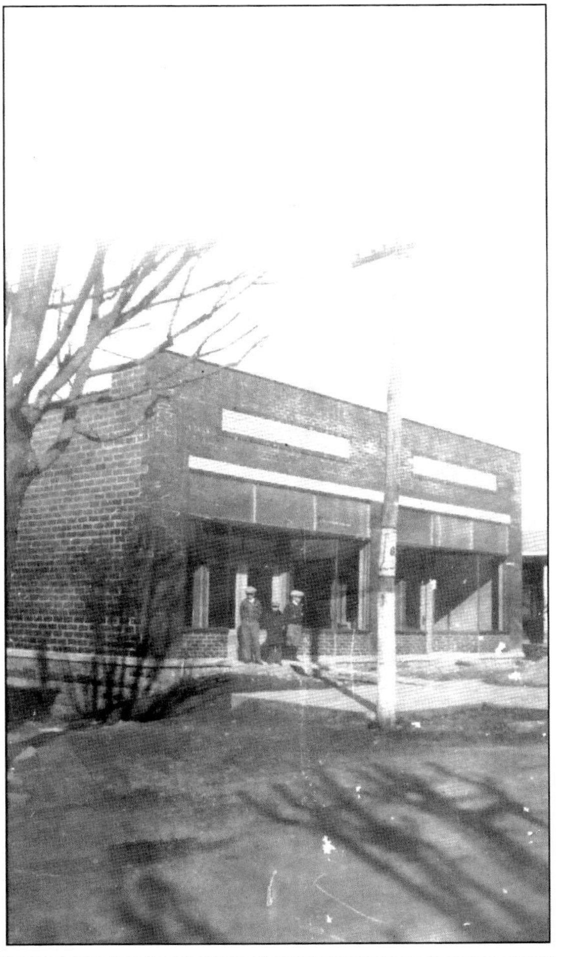

Baker's General Store is seen here around the early 1930s. Notice the sponsorship from Dr. Pepper on the side of the building. Early on, Morris Baker sold farm supplies like feed and wire on the west side of the store and sold groceries on the east side. They also had gasoline pumps and oil products for your car. The store still sells gasoline today. (Courtesy of Carolyn Baker and Bill Baker.)

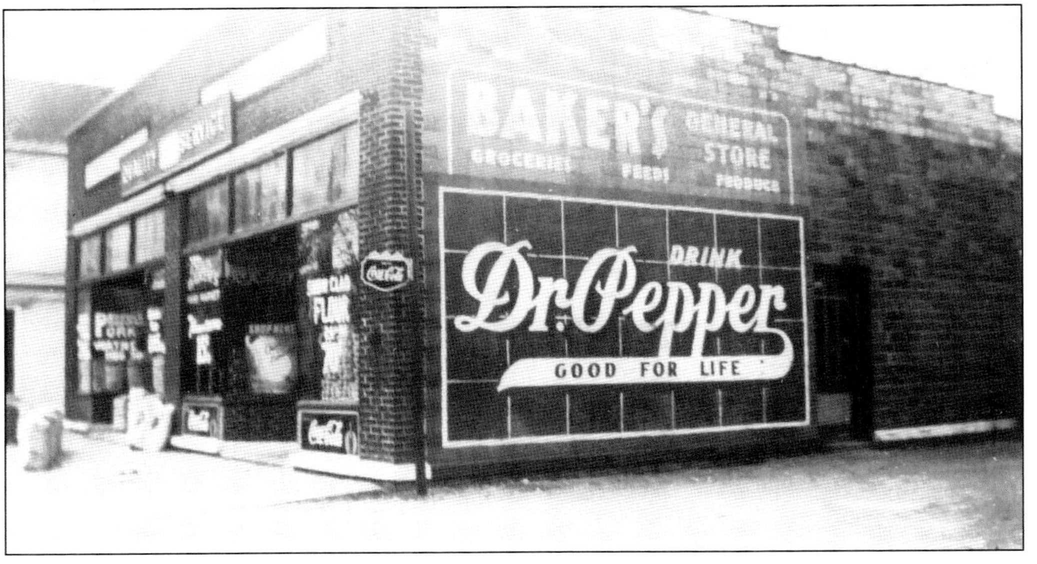

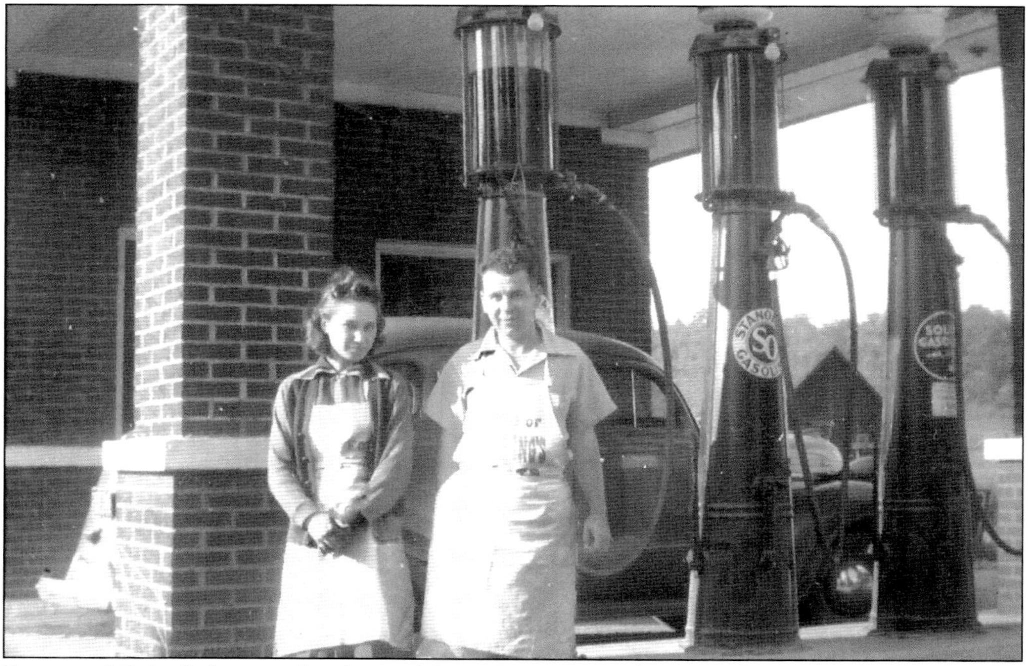

Byron and Ruby Baker stand in front of the gas pumps at Baker's General Store in the late 1930s. Note the glass bulbs showing the amount of gas being pumped into a car. Hand pumps were used at this time, and people liked to see how much gas was going into their car when Byron would pump it. Gas at that time was usually between 23¢ and 29¢ per gallon. (Courtesy of Bill Baker.)

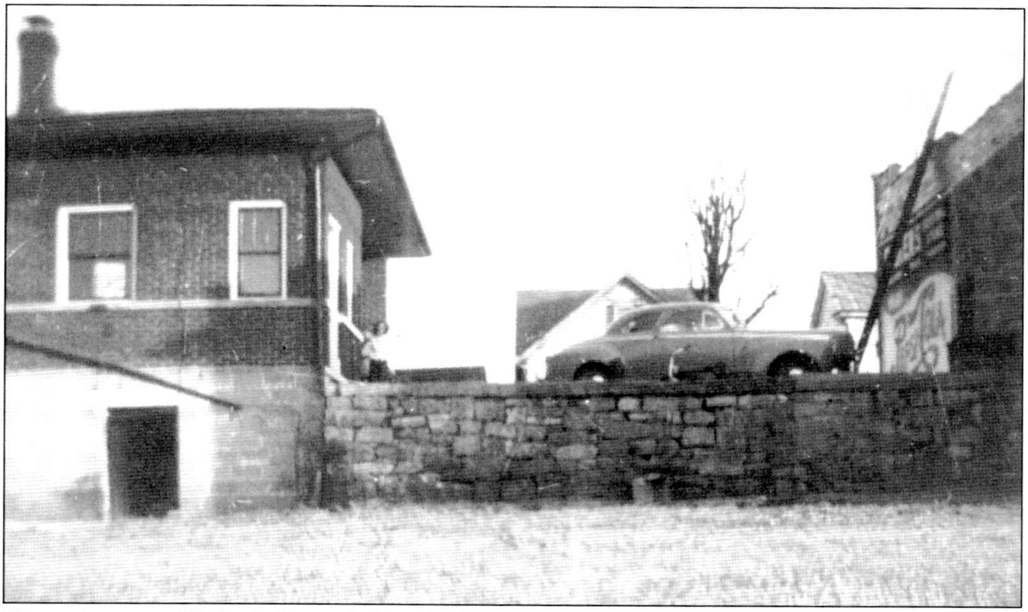

This side view of Baker's General Store looks south. To the left is the gas pumps area, and there is a rock wall at the end of the parking lot. Even though the store still exists, this rock wall no longer is there. Even though Lanesville Food Mart still sells gasoline today, the configuration is different. (Courtesy Bill Baker.)

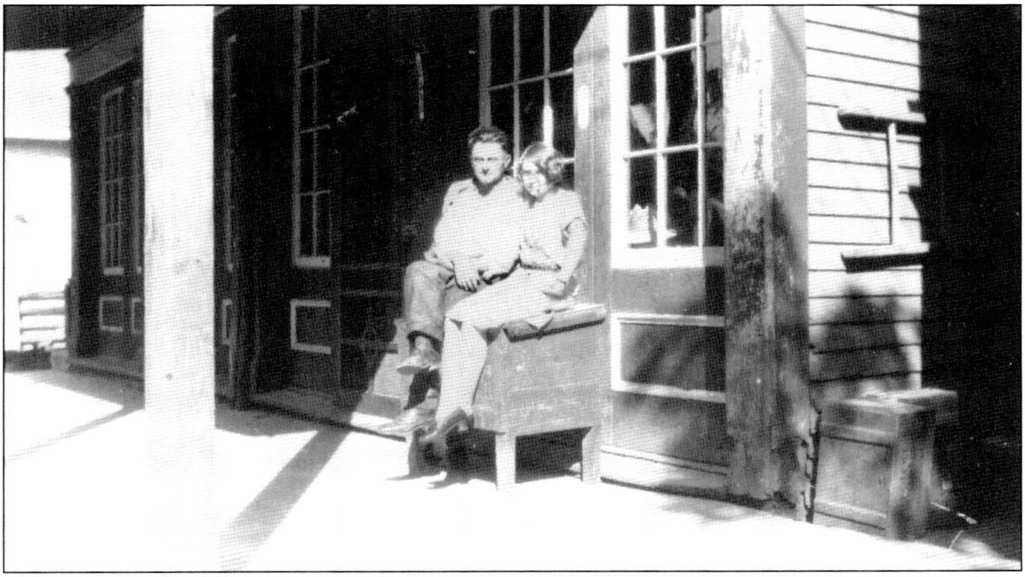

Elmore Ott sits with an unidentified young lady on the bread box in front of Louis Ott's store in the early 1930s. The store sat on the site of the old K&H Tavern, where Hog's Tavern is today. Apparently, the bread box was a popular meeting place for young couples to talk and get acquainted. Louis and Sophie Ott ran the store for several years. (Courtesy of Oneda Ringle.)

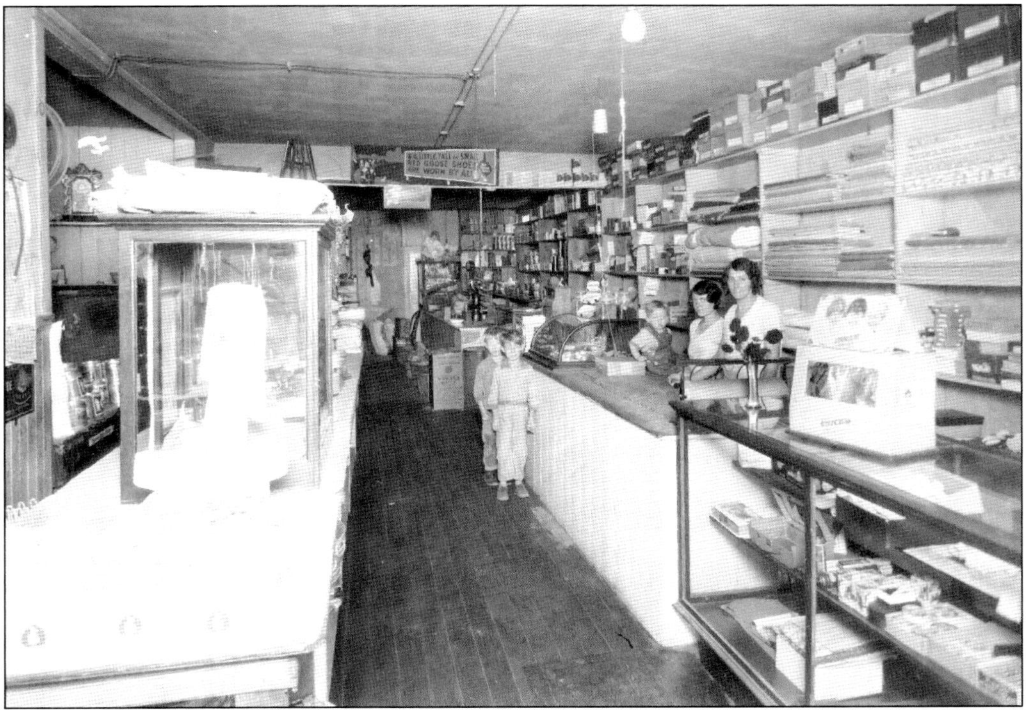

Julia Ott stands behind the counter beside young Oneda (Ott) Ringle in Louis Ott's store around 1925. (Courtesy of Oneda Ringle.)

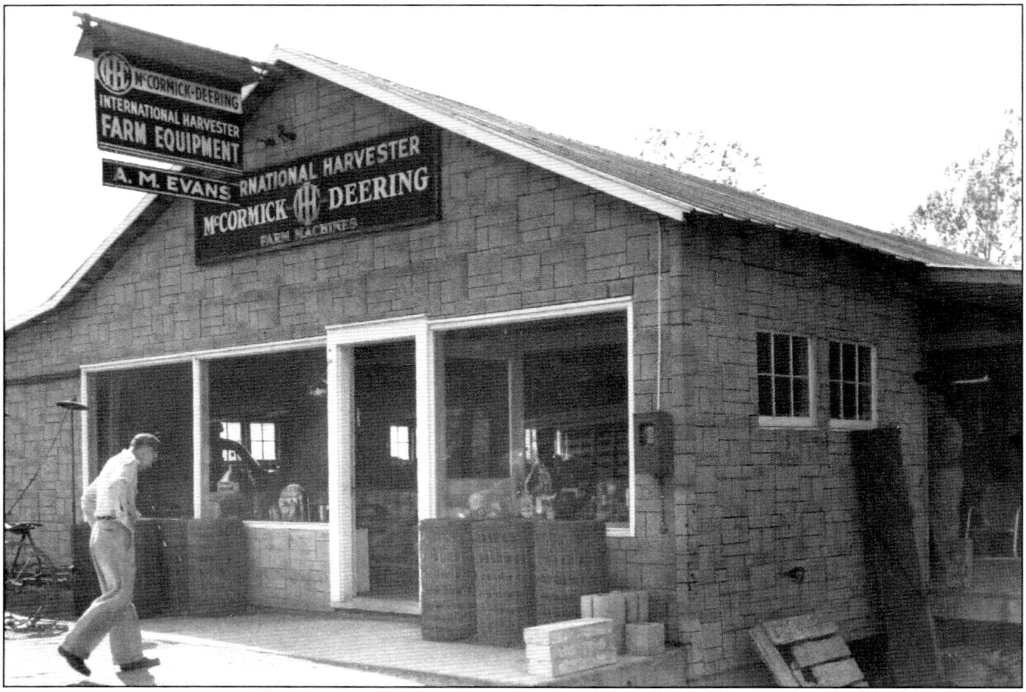

A customer walks into Asa Evans's store around the late 1940s or early 1950s. Evans ran the store on the east end of town in the building that now houses Creekside Furniture Store, selling International Harvester equipment and parts as well as farm supplies from the mid-1930s to the mid-1950s. (Courtesy of Carolyn Baker.)

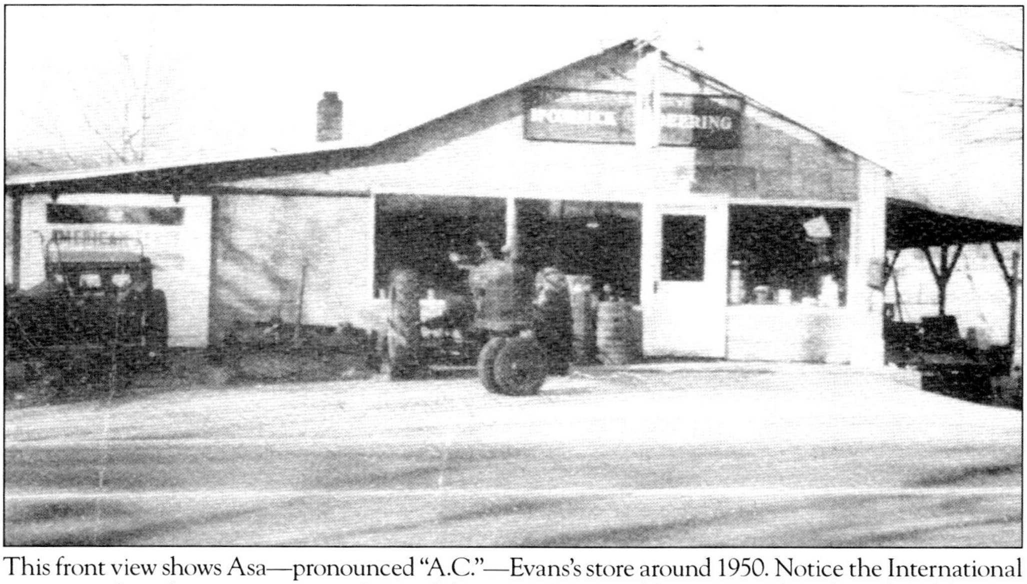

This front view shows Asa—pronounced "A.C."—Evans's store around 1950. Notice the International tractor and implements sitting in front of the store. Evans sold a variety of products local farmers in the area needed on a daily basis. (Courtesy of Carolyn Baker.)

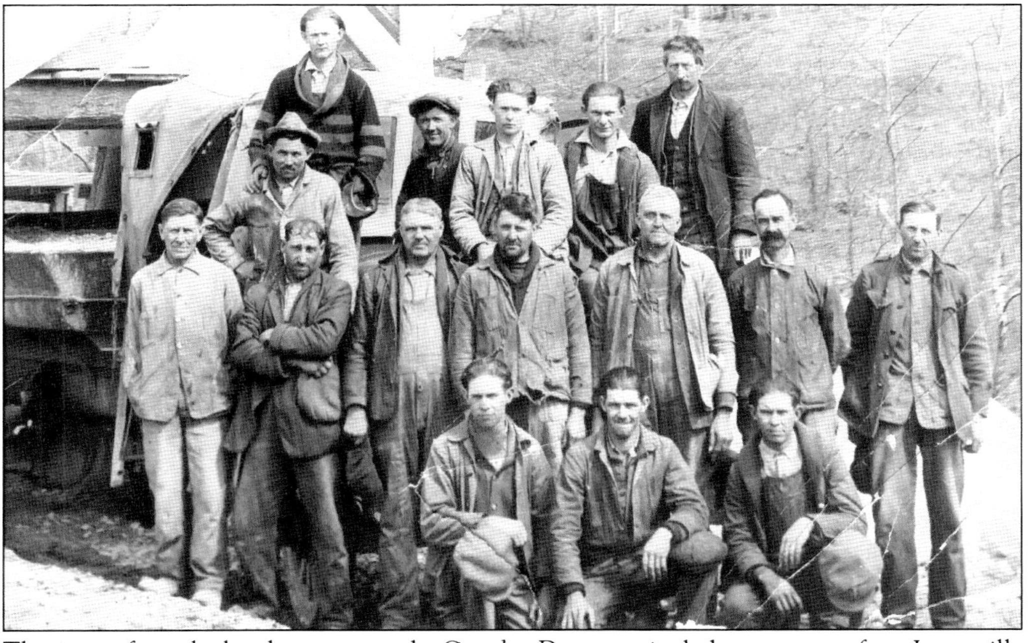

This image from the local newspaper, the *Corydon Democrat*, includes many men from Lanesville who worked in the quarries. Although it was taken at Louis Knable Quarry in Edwardsville, the early-1920s photograph includes Severin Bachman (middle row, third from right), a Lanesvillian who ran several quarries in the area, in Lanesville, Elizabeth, Laconia, Corydon, Byrneville, and this quarry in Edwardsville. Bachman's son Joseph was later the owner and operator of Corydon Crushed Stone in the late 1950s. (Courtesy of Russell Bachman.)

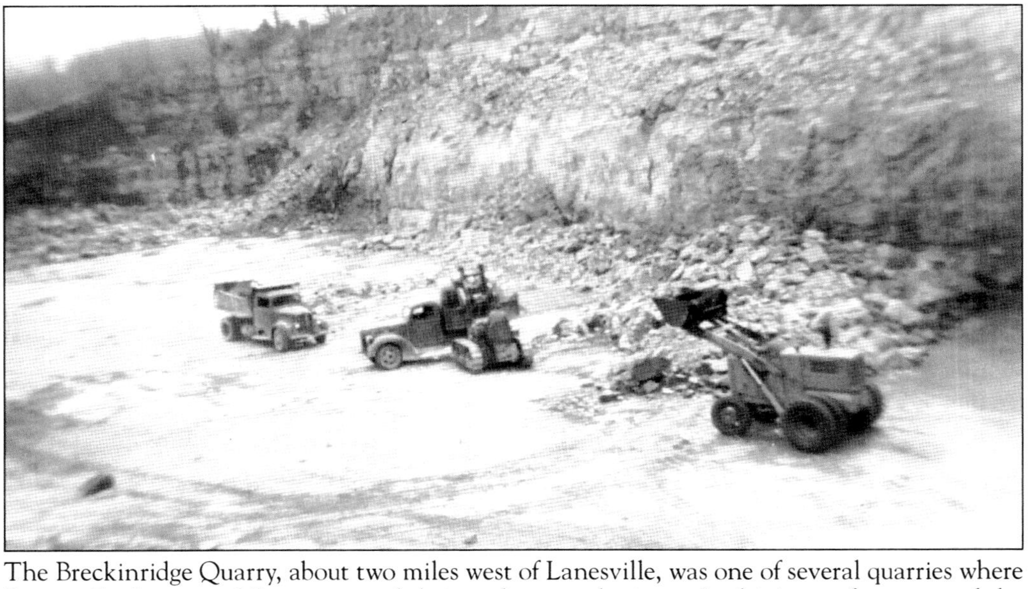

The Breckinridge Quarry, about two miles west of Lanesville, was one of several quarries where Severin Bachman and Sons operated their rock quarry business. In this image from around the mid-1940s, rock is being loaded onto trucks by loader operator Earl Allen; it is then hauled to the rock crusher, which will crush the rock into various sizes. This quarry closed down in the late 1940s but is still seen on the drive west of Lanesville. (Courtesy of Russell Bachman.)

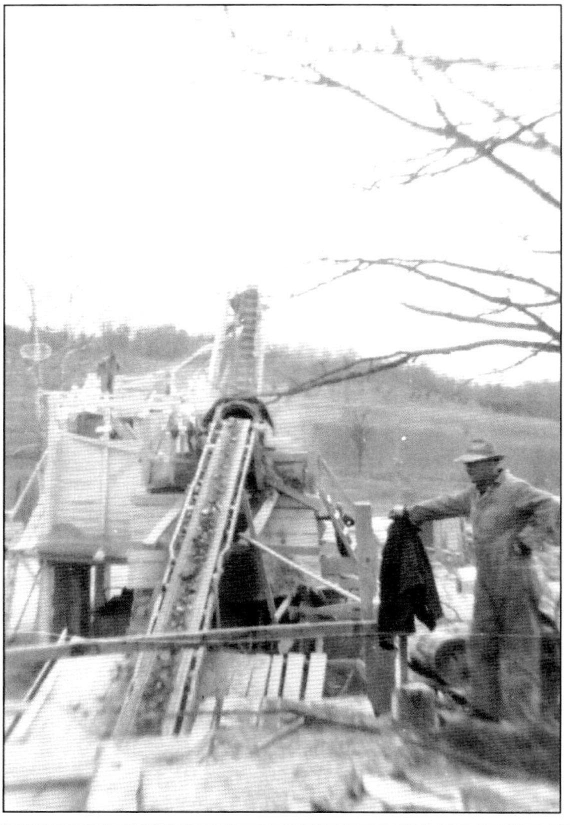

Joe Bachman is seen here running an early rock-crushing machine that is taking rock from the Breckinridge Quarry up the conveyor into the crusher. The Breckinridge Quarry was closed down in the late 1940s, just a few years after this photograph was taken. (Courtesy of Russell Bachman.)

The Lanesville Milling Company is seen here in the early 1920s. Tony Kochert bought the mill from the Zabels in 1921 and continued to mill flour there. Charlie (center) and Tony Kochert (right) are seen outside the mill. The mill supplied flour not just to locals but to larger cities in the area as well. Already producing Flour X and Lanesville Star, the Kocherts added Snow Clad flour in the 1930s, and it was sold to Louisville and southern Indiana until the 1960s. (Courtesy Dolores Dotson.)

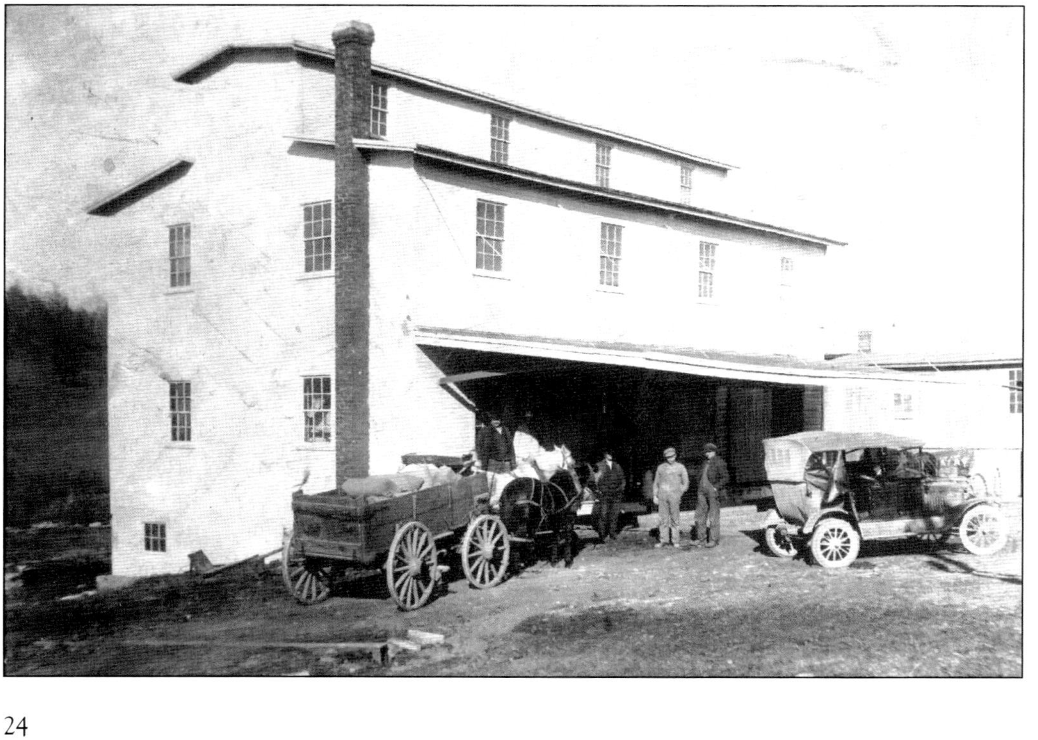

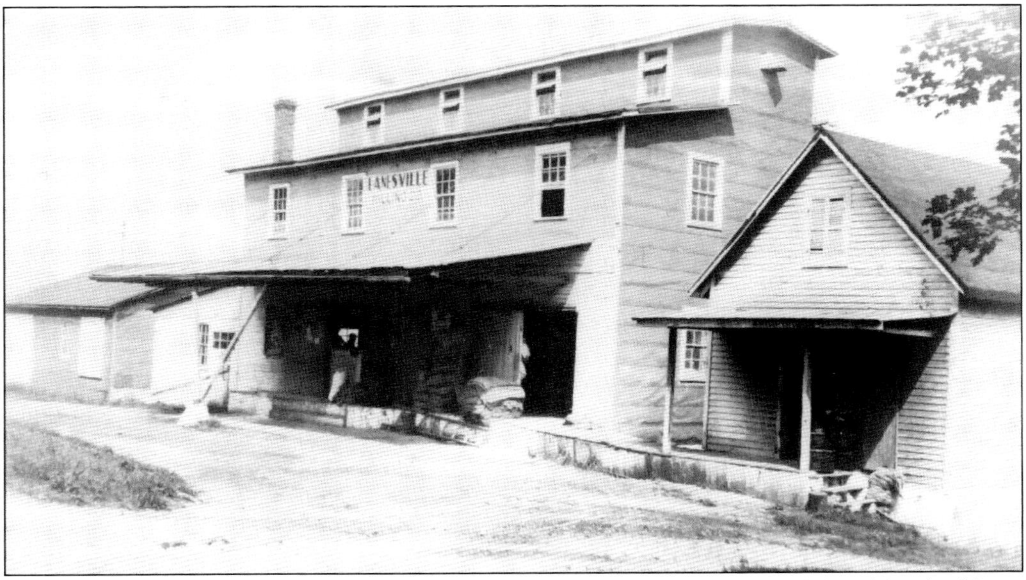

There have been a few changes to the Lanesville Milling Company, one of the oldest buildings in town, since this photograph was taken around 1945. The Kochert family ran the mill from 1921 until 1976. Tony Kochert's sons, Maurice and Jim, ran it after their father did before selling it in 1976. It was made into a restaurant but now sits vacant in town and is owned by Mark Bush. (Courtesy of Jim Kochert.)

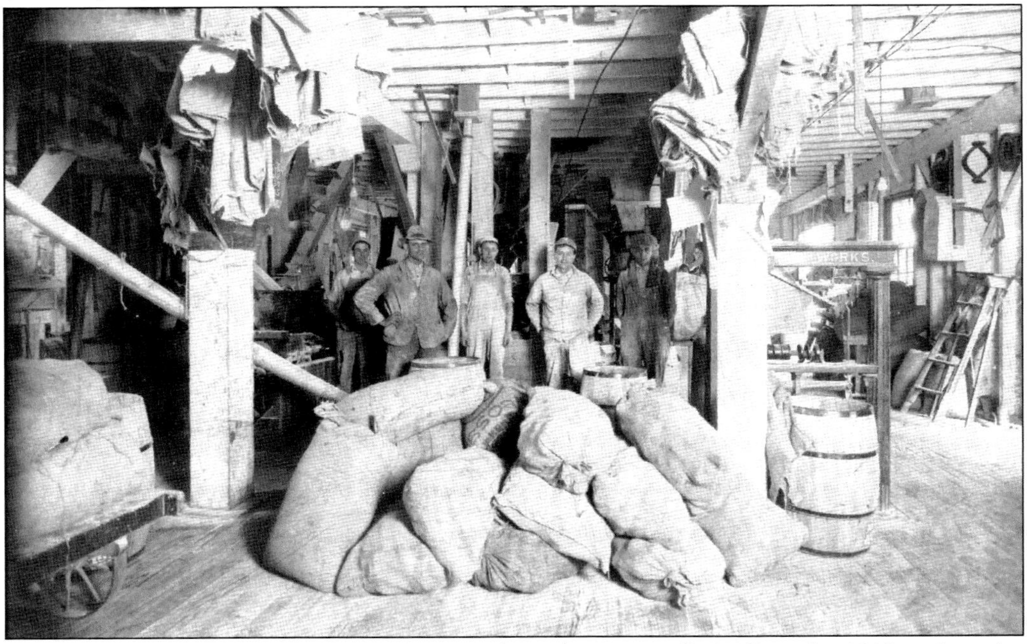

Workers take a break to pose for a photograph at the Lanesville Mill in the 1930s, when the mill was owned by the Kochert family. These men are, from left to right, Wilferd Day, George Richmer, Charlie Lape, Paul Kochert, and Maurice Kochert. The mill continued to produce baking flour up into the 1960s but produced livestock feed and feed supplies for several years until 1976. (Courtesy of Dolores Dotson.)

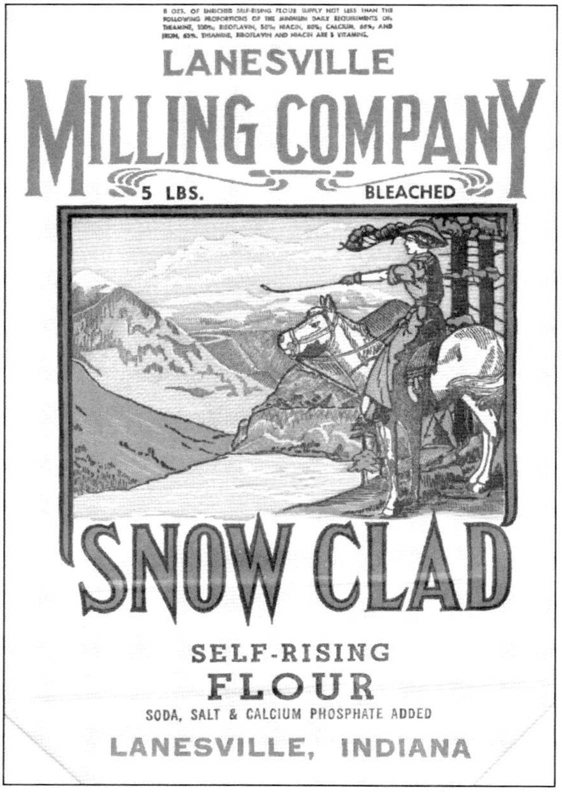

This Snow Clad flour bag was seen in many homes in Lanesville and Franklin Township. Flour was produced in the Lanesville Mill first from the Zabels and then by the Kocherts, two families who played a critical part in meeting the basic needs of the people of Lanesville for over 100 years. This flour bag was a staple and remains a keepsake in many homes today. (Courtesy of Jim Kochert.)

George Schafer ran this blacksmith shop, pictured around the first decade of the 20th century, for many years. The shop sat at the corner of what is now Crestview Avenue South and Highway 62 until the early 1930s, providing for the needs of the early farming community. Blacksmith shops were common in the late 1800s and early 1900s, and Lanesville had several. (Courtesy of Bill Baker.)

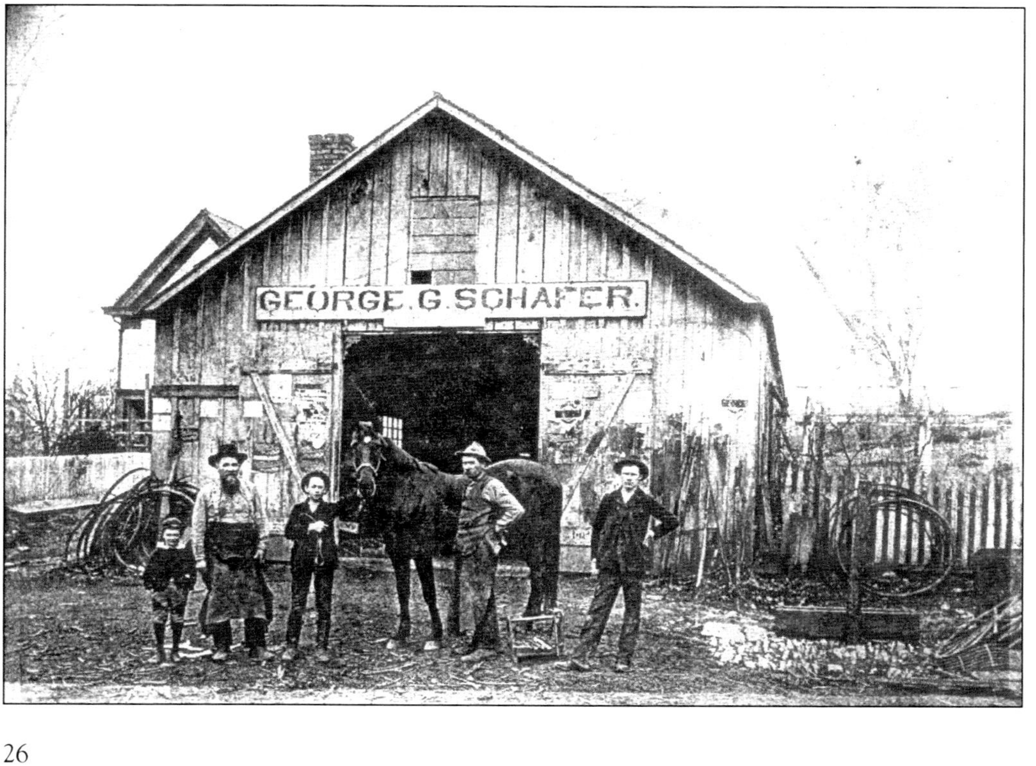

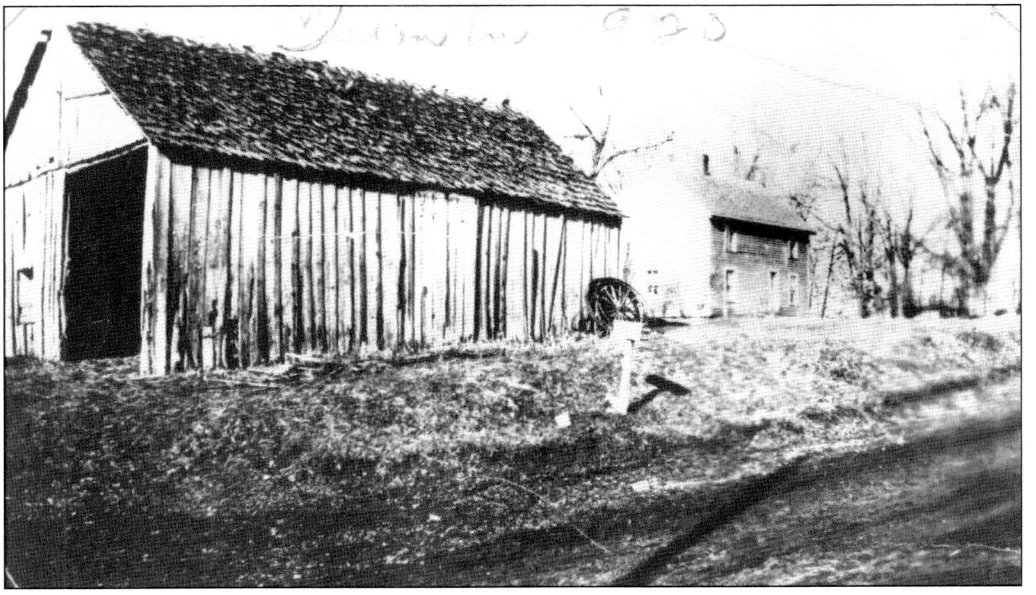

Joseph Stark's blacksmith's shop is seen here in 1920. The shop sat on the west corner of Corydon Ridge Road and what is now the Interstate 64 interchange. It was the home place of Herman, Bob, and Earl Stark. Though the blacksmith shop was torn down long ago, the house in the background was still standing until just a few years ago. (Courtesy of Kathy Stark.)

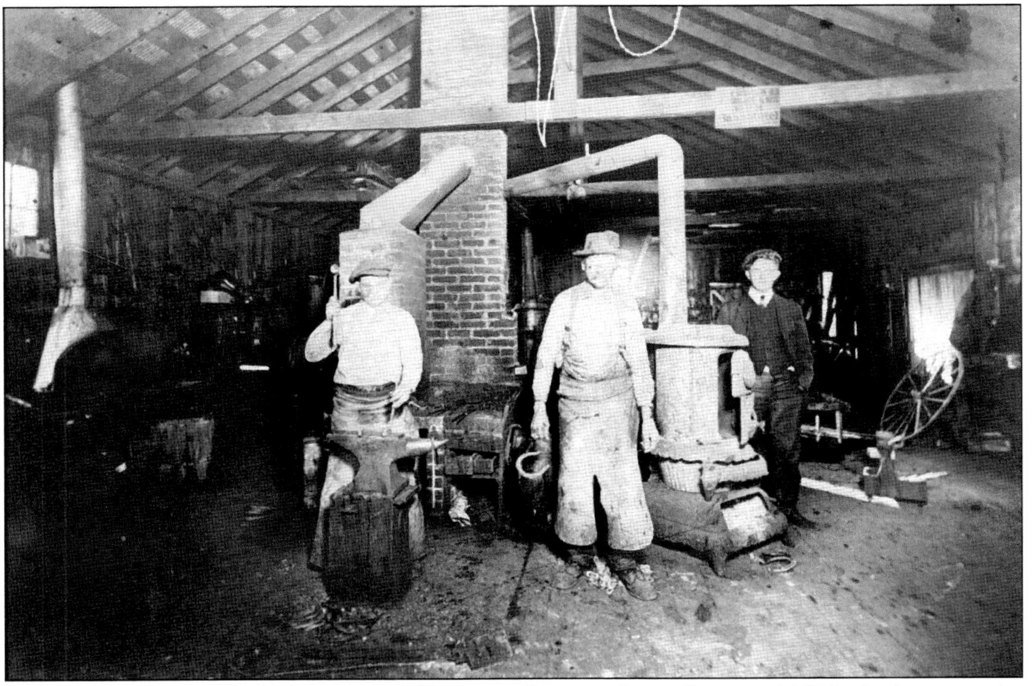

Ed Lieber's blacksmith shop in Lanesville is seen here in the early-to-mid-1920s. Lieber is in the center and his son Orlin is to the left holding the hammer. The fellow next to the potbellied stove is unidentified. Ed Lieber owned the shop from the early 1900s until his death in 1939. (Courtesy of Don Schickel.)

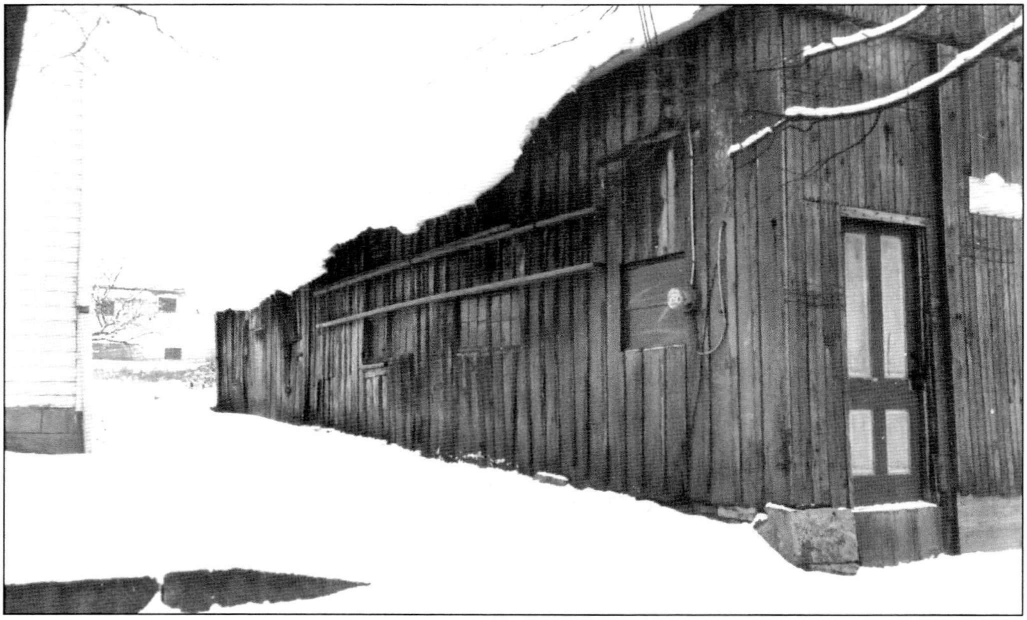

Ed Lieber's blacksmith shop sat almost in the middle town, where the firehouse sits today, across from Lanesville Food Mart. (Courtesy of Marvin Zabel.)

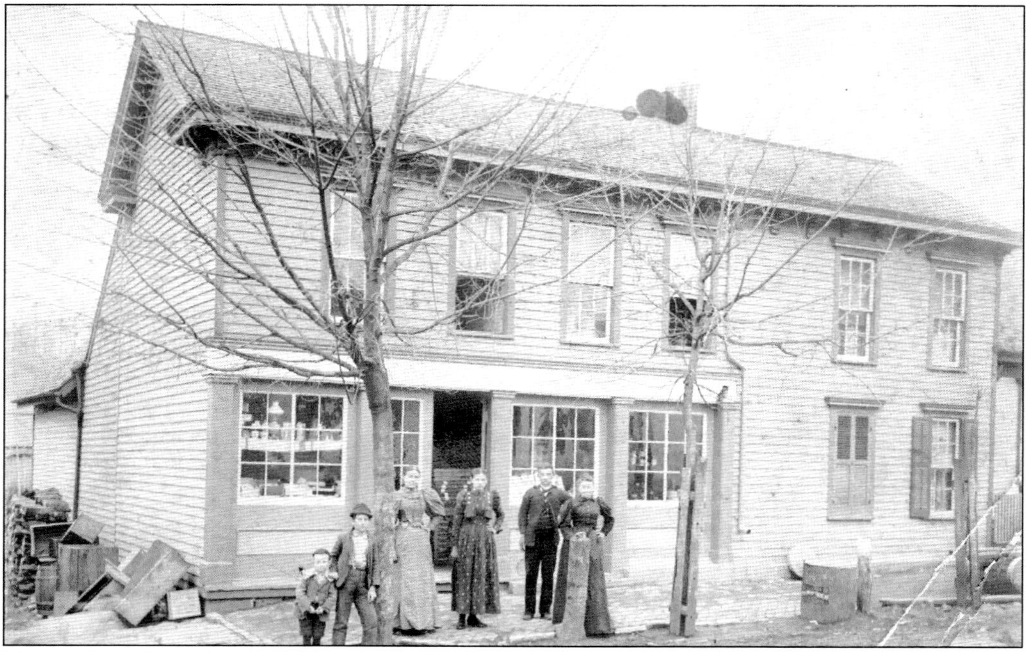

To the far right, John Redick and Christina Redick pose with their family in front of their dry goods store in 1893. The family included, from left to right, sons John and Emil and daughters Anna and Clara. This house still exists, now housing the Lanesville Liquor store. This building has quite a past; after being a dry goods store, it was home to the Wonderland restaurant in the 1940s and 1950s and was the Circle Bar from 1963 to 1994. The building has changed very little over the years and it is still identifiable when passing through town. (Courtesy of Mark Strauss.)

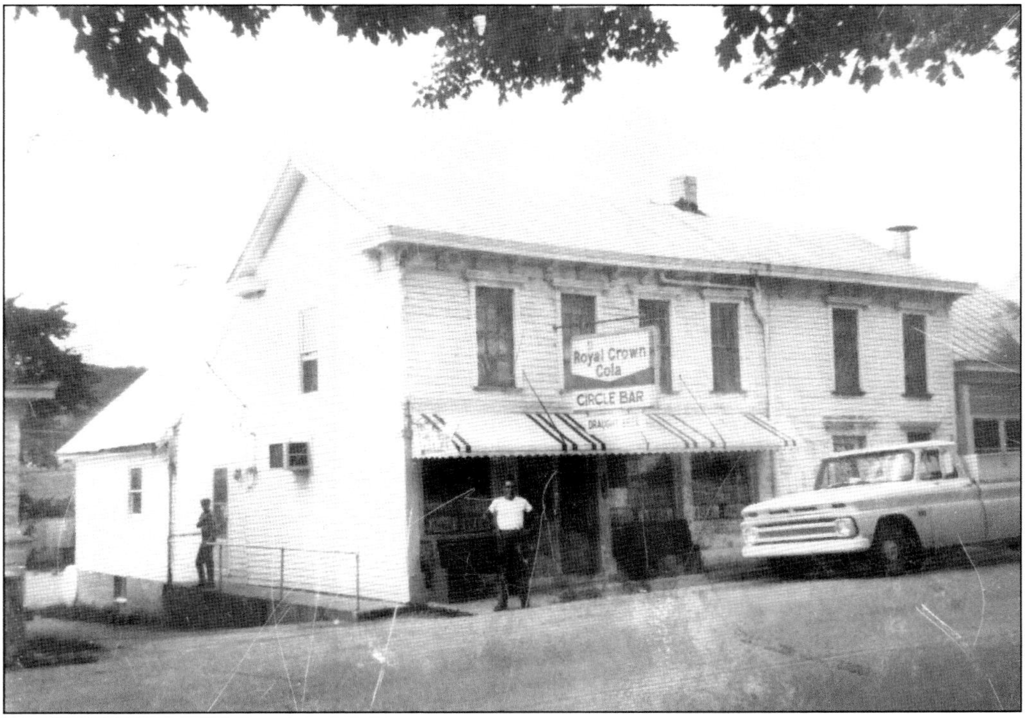

The Circle Bar is seen here around 1968. At the time, the bar was owned and operated by Charles "Pat" Strauss and his wife, Marie. They bought the place in 1963 and ran it until 1975, when John Hubert bought it, keeping the name Circle Bar until it closed in 1994. (Courtesy of Mark Strauss.)

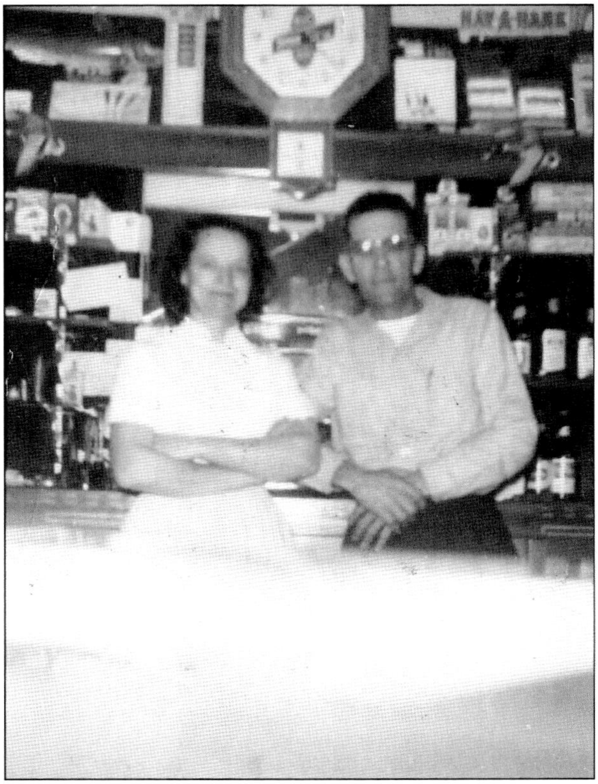

Marie and Charles "Pat" Strauss pose inside the Circle Bar in 1965. The bar was a mainstay in Lanesville for the next 30 years, continuing on after it was sold to John Hubert, who kept the name and traditions. (Courtesy of Mark Strauss.)

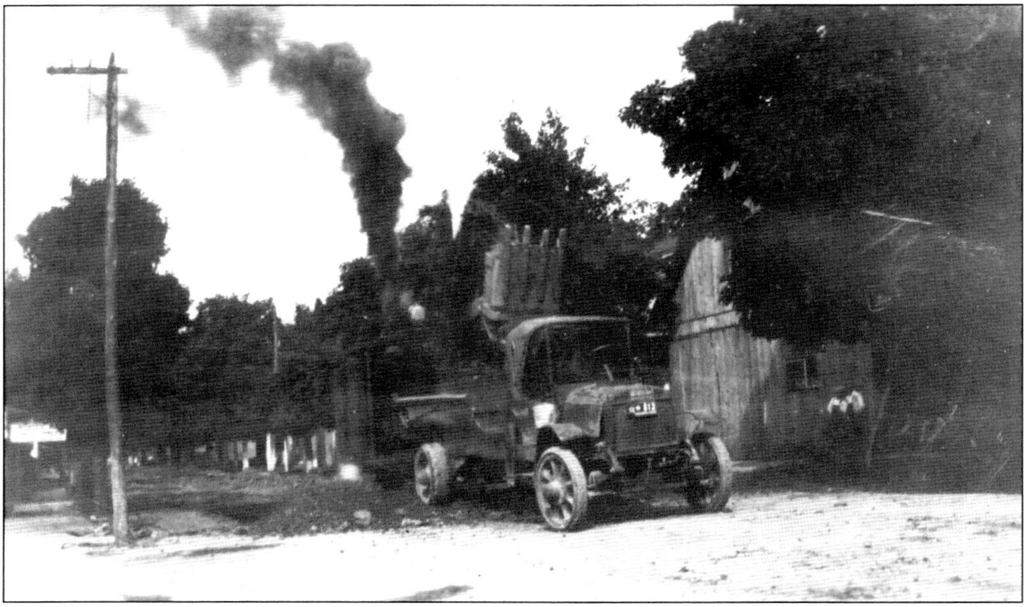

A steam shovel digs up and levels what was Main Street around the mid-1920s during the construction of State Highway 62 and US 460. State Highway 62 and US 460 ran through the middle of town and connected Evansville to Louisville. Here, a steam engine blows black smoke, and also seen is the solid-wheeled dump truck common in the 1910s. To the right of the truck is Ed Lieber's blacksmith shop in the middle of town. (Courtesy of Norbert Walther.)

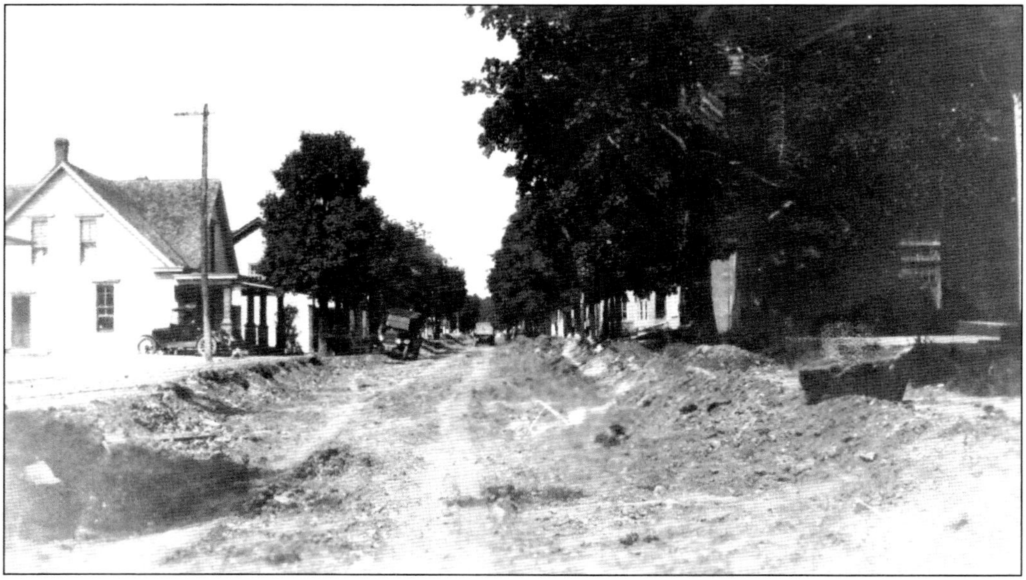

In this construction photograph, the roadbed has been dug out and is getting packed for a better surface. This was the old plank road for a long time but as more cars were on the road, motorists needed better roads to meet the larger amount of daily travel. The gravel base was taken from the small quarry still visible from the road near the Breckinridge Quarry just west of town. State Highway 62 and US 460 later became Highway 62; it is still the main road through Lanesville. (Courtesy of Norbert Walther.)

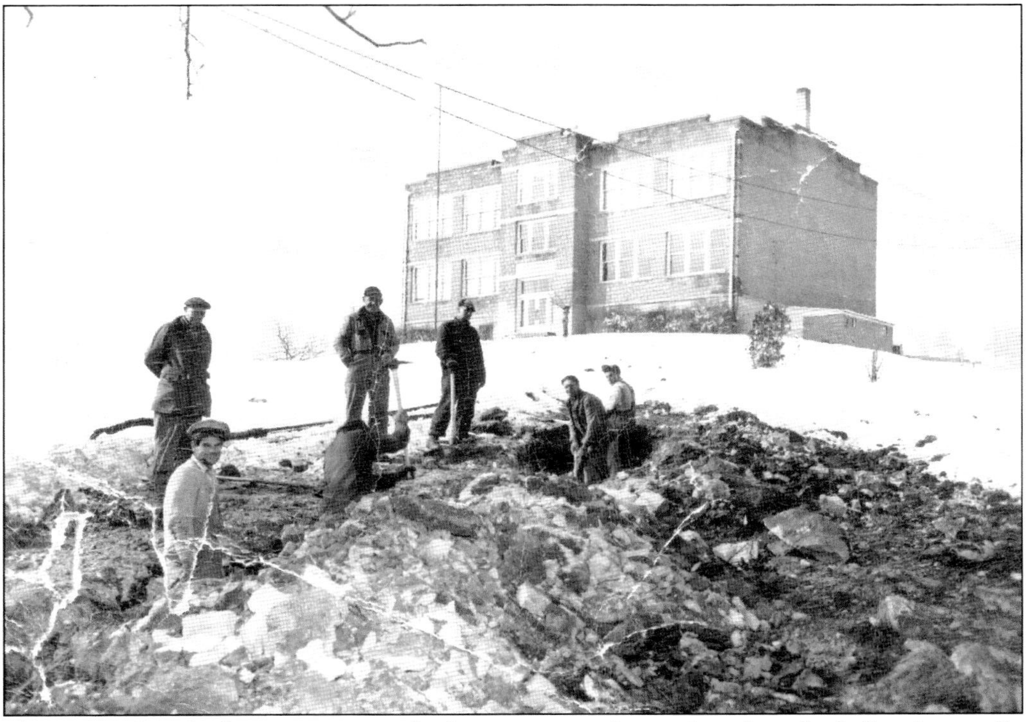

These men fix a broken water pipe, which went across the creek and up the hill to Lanesville High School, in 1940. The pipe apparently broke because of the cold; the only identified worker is Homer Schellenberger, third from the left, who owned the nearby house where the break occurred. The men are believed to be from Bachman's quarry. (Courtesy of Marvin Zabel.)

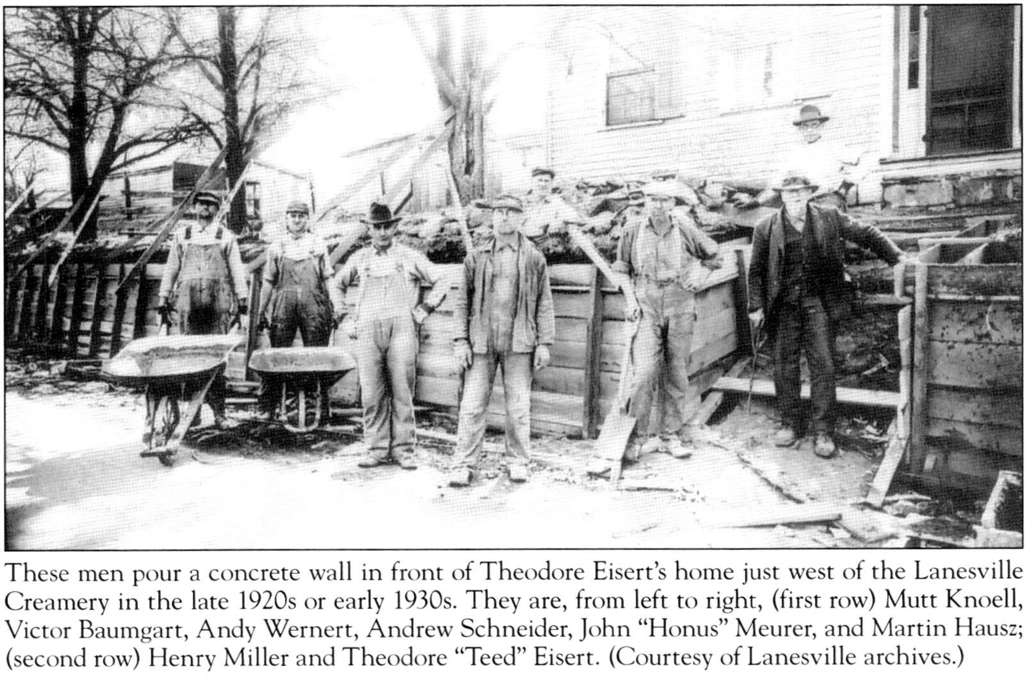

These men pour a concrete wall in front of Theodore Eisert's home just west of the Lanesville Creamery in the late 1920s or early 1930s. They are, from left to right, (first row) Mutt Knoell, Victor Baumgart, Andy Wernert, Andrew Schneider, John "Honus" Meurer, and Martin Hausz; (second row) Henry Miller and Theodore "Teed" Eisert. (Courtesy of Lanesville archives.)

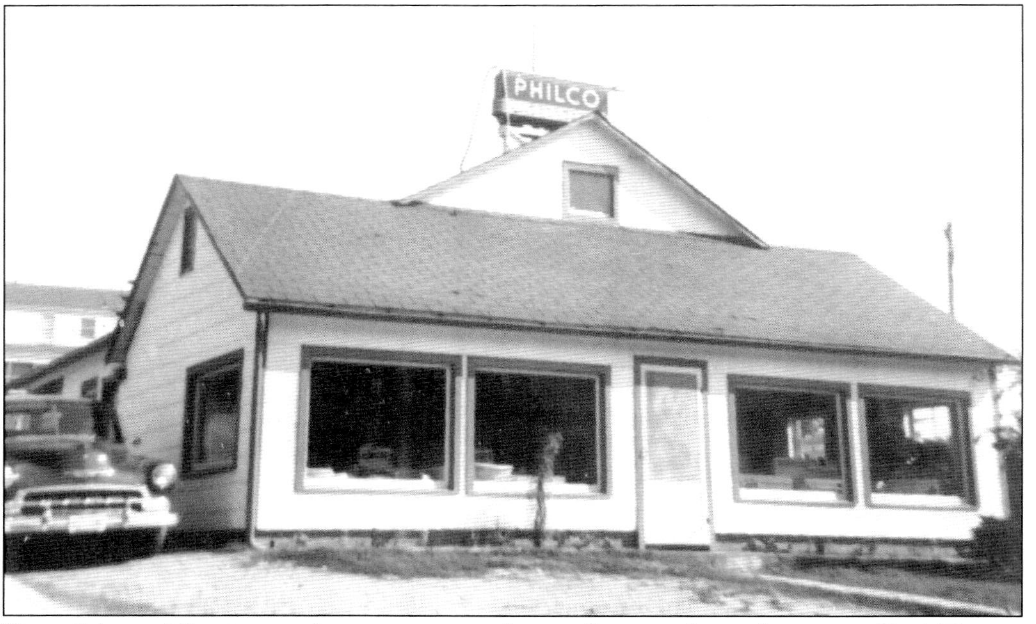

Eisert Sales and Service, on the main street in Lanesville across from what is now Hog's Tavern, is seen here in 1949. Eisert's served Lanesville until 1964, but the building still exists today. It became Ron Kochert's insurance office in 1969, staying there until 2001 when Kochert built a new office building west of town. (Courtesy of Ron Eisert.)

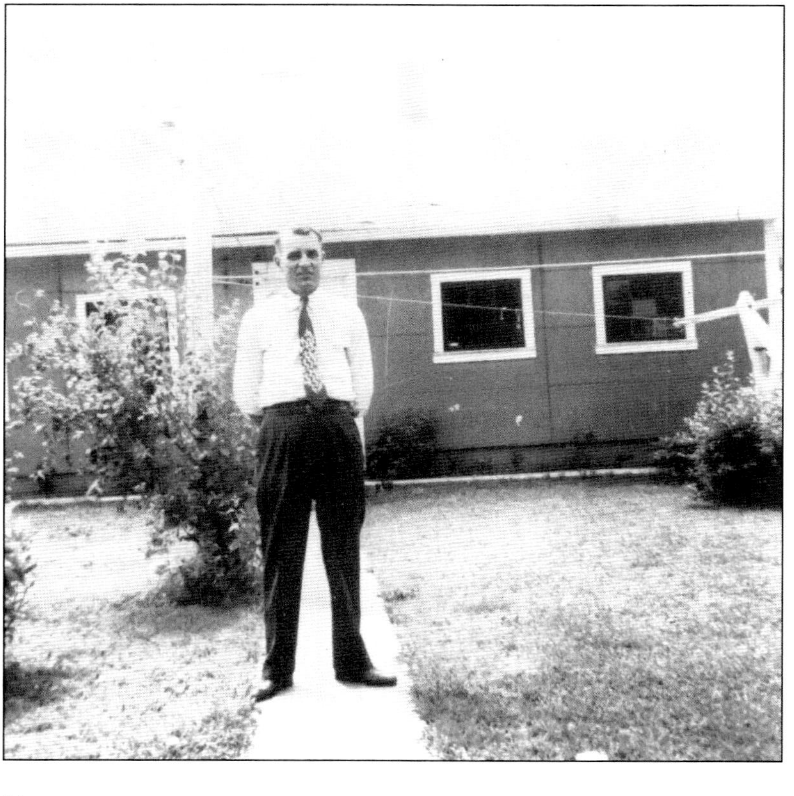

Alfred J. Eisert, the proprietor of Eisert's Sales and Service, stands behind the store. Alfred ran the appliance store from 1947 to 1964, selling many makes and models of appliances during the post–World War II boom. (Courtesy of Ron Eisert.)

This is a small sampling of the appliances Eisert Sales and Service carried. Mr. Eisert's store carried all makes of appliances, from General Electric to Maytag, and was the main supplier of Philco products. Refrigerators, freezers were big sellers and televisions were just becoming popular when the store opened. (Courtesy of Ron Eisert.)

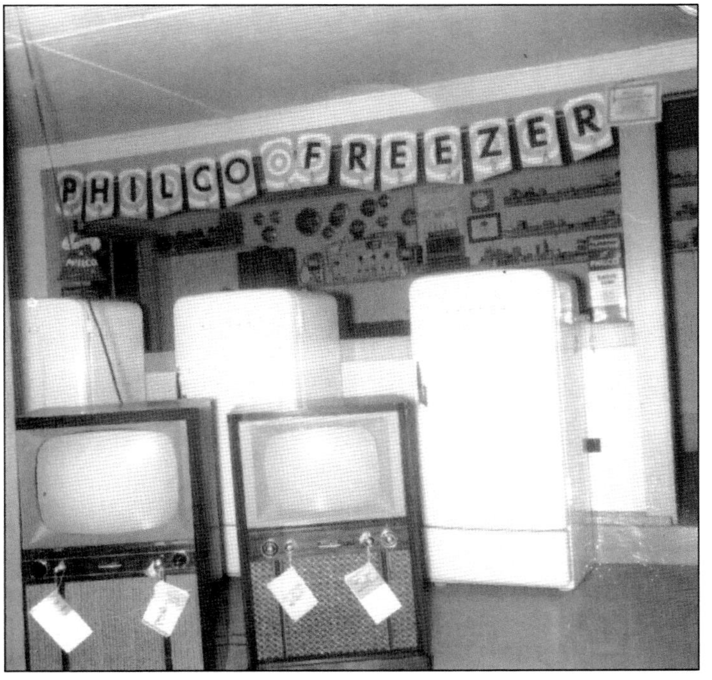

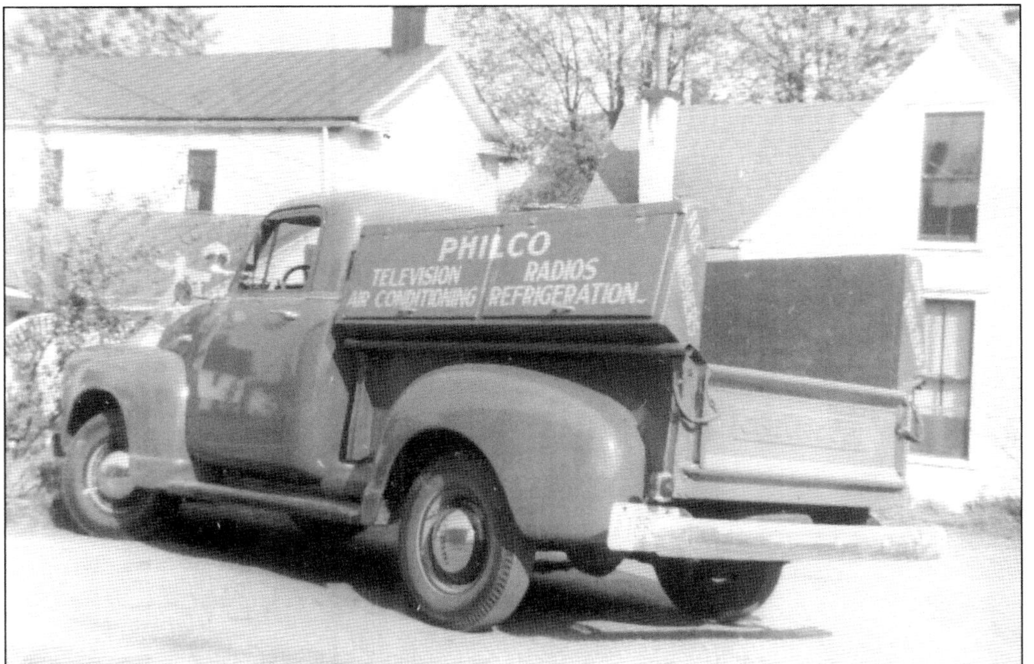

Eisert's 1948 blue Chevrolet service truck was a familiar sight around Lanesville in the late 1940s and 1950s. Alfred Eisert not only sold appliances, he also serviced them himself. He spent hours in his shop in the back of the store, repairing and preparing items for sale. If he sold it and it broke, he would fix it. The wooden toolboxes on the bed of the truck were custom made because nobody produced toolboxes for service trucks in the area at that time. (Courtesy of Ron Eisert.)

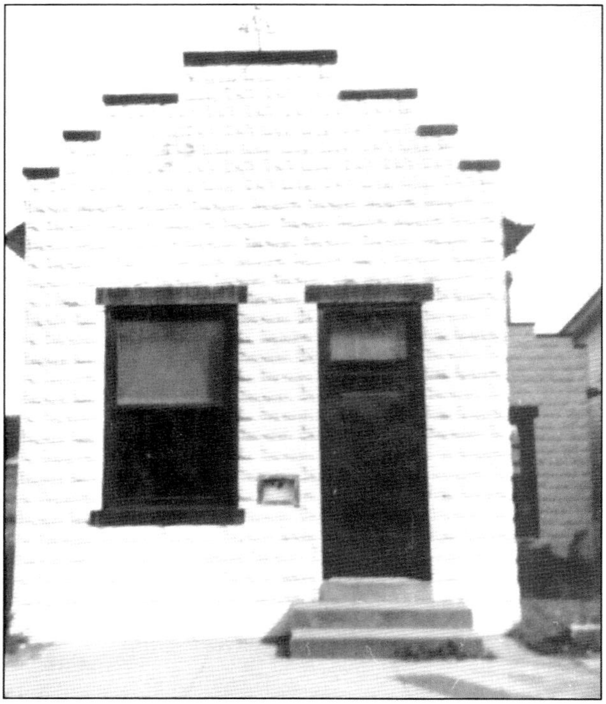

Farmer's State Bank is one of the older buildings in town; it is still standing and an important part of the town's history. This building was constructed in 1910 and served the people of Lanesville and Franklin Township for almost 100 years. The outward appearance was very recognizable for years, but with renovations and expansions, the little bank has grown over the years. In 2008, it became First Federal Savings Bank. Inside the building today, visitors are welcomed into the original part of the bank to see what it looked like many years ago. (Courtesy of Bill Baker and Farmer's State Bank.)

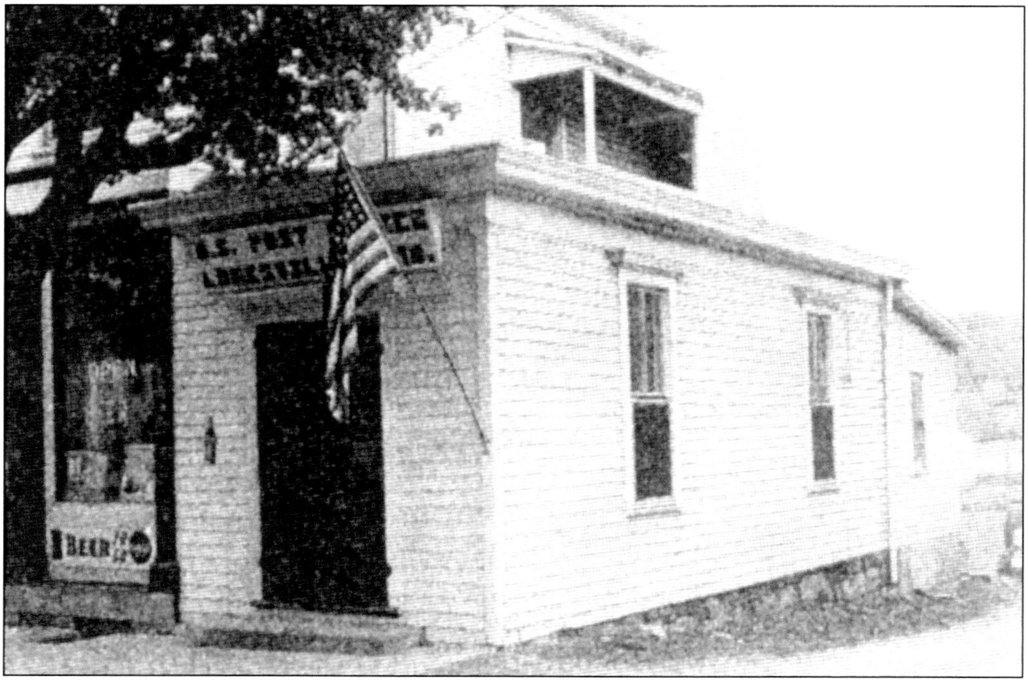

Seen here around 1950 is the second site of the Lanesville post office, just west across the alley from Baker's General Store. The post office was originally across the street from Baker's General Store and was later moved just west of the Farmer's State Bank in the 1960s. It is now housed in a more modern facility at the end of town. (Courtesy of Lanesville archives.)

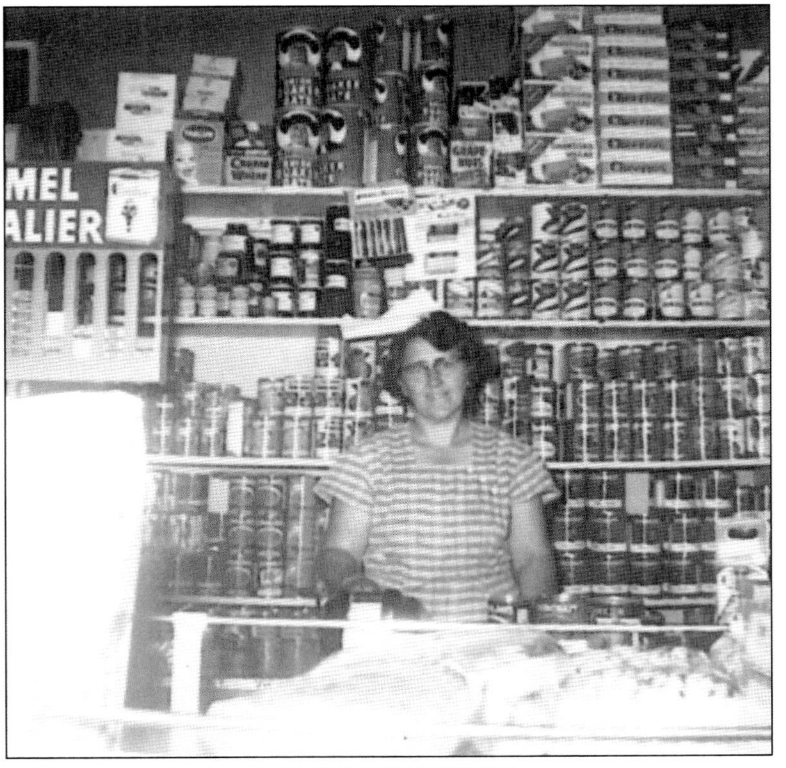

Theodora Lieber, pictured, owned and operated a small store carrying basic items that was located across from the Lanesville Mill on St. Mary's Drive. She ran the store with her husband, Orlin Lieber, in the 1940s and 1950s. Theodora would stay behind the counter and Orlin, who was also a bus driver for the Lanesville schools, used a converted bus to deliver groceries and other items to patrons in the area. (Courtesy of Marcella Bays.)

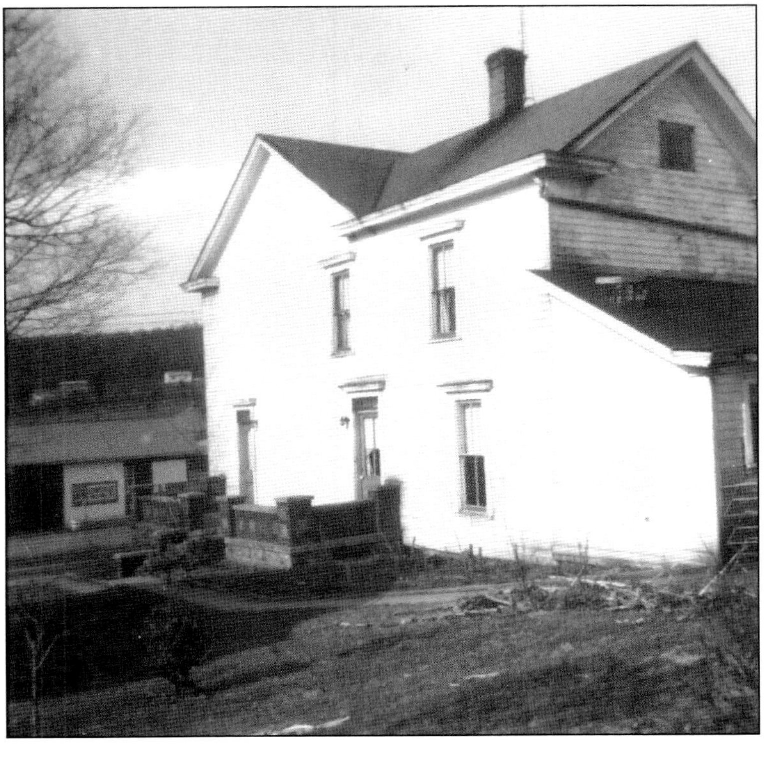

Orlin and Theodora Lieber's home and store was on St. Mary's Drive. In this image, the store is just out of sight to the far right. The Liebers stopped selling items in the early-to-mid-1950s, and the house was torn down in 1963. (Courtesy of Marcella Bays.)

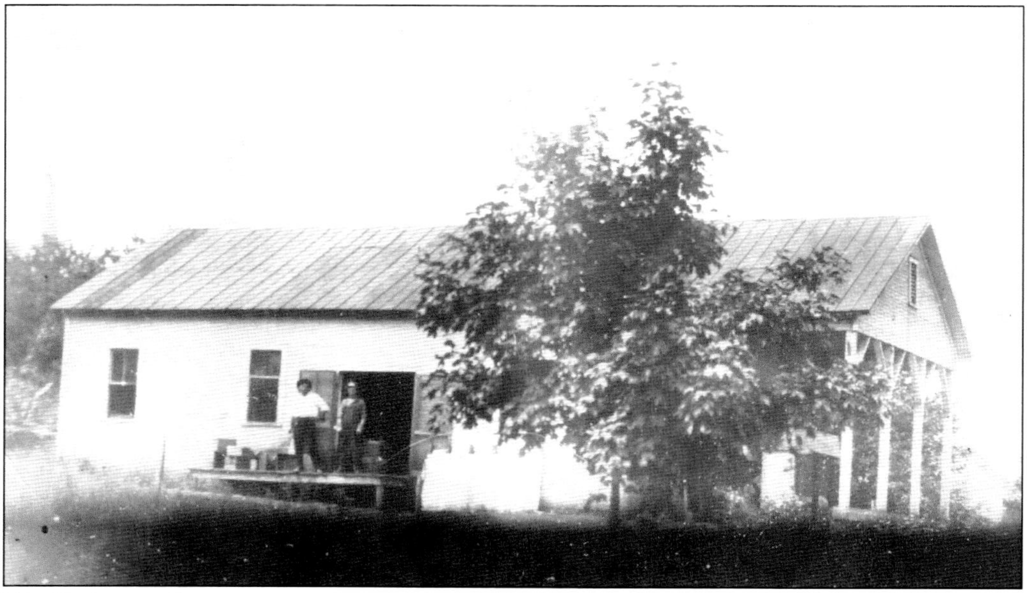

The Fachinger Creamery, seen here in the 1920s, was just east of town and produced butter from cream brought in by local farmers. The creamery, a very valuable business for local farmers and their families, produced Autumn Leaf butter, a staple in most households. It stayed in operation for about 30 years. (Courtesy of Evelyn Blum.)

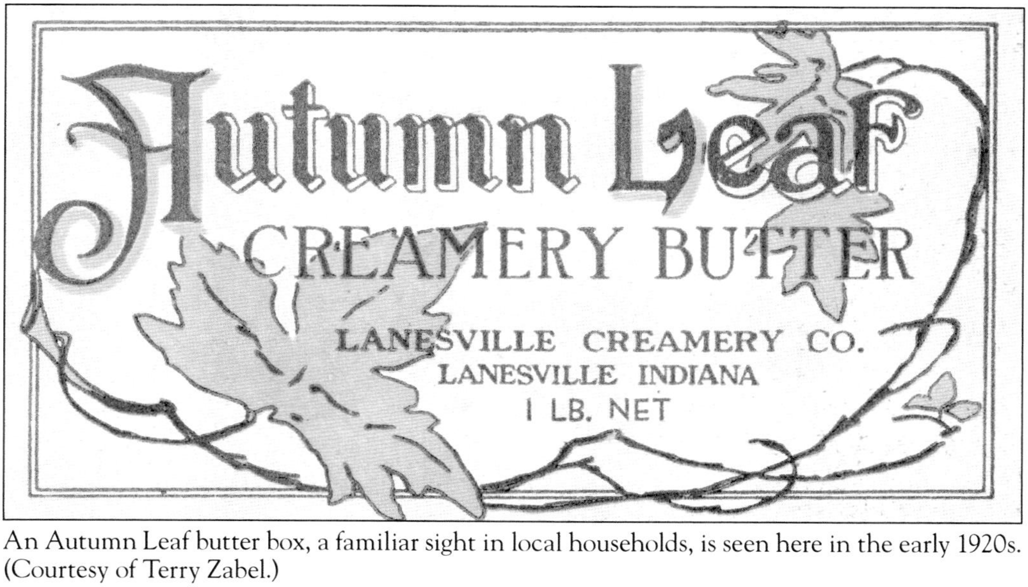

An Autumn Leaf butter box, a familiar sight in local households, is seen here in the early 1920s. (Courtesy of Terry Zabel.)

Two

The Schools

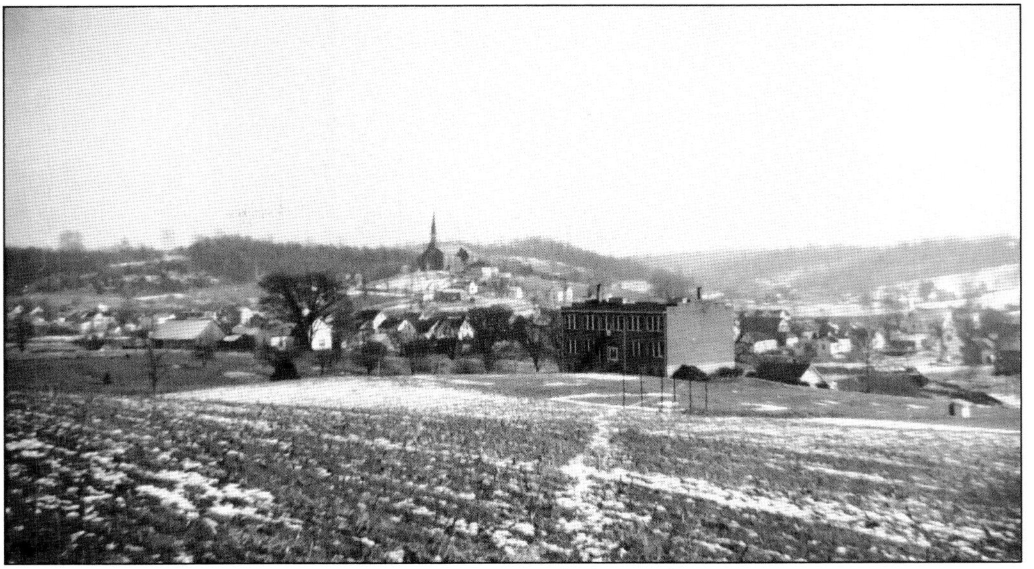

This great shot of Lanesville High School in 1941 looks south from Crestview Avenue. It is a familiar sight to most people who attend or have been to Lanesville Schools, because the schools built later sit on the same site. St. Mary's Catholic Church still sits in its same hillside location today. (Courtesy of Parvin Lambertus.)

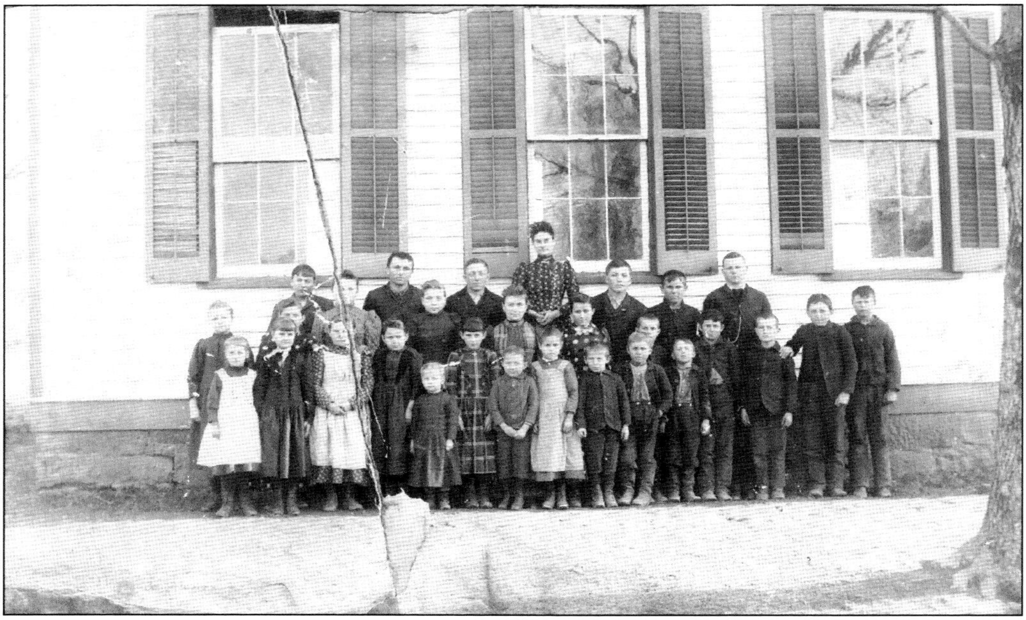

This is a late 1890s image of Franklin School No. 1, which was known as the Brock School. Lydia Turley was the last teacher at the school in the late 1930s. Bob Gehlbach bought the building in 1943 and lived in it until 1947 when it was torn down and its lumber was used to build a house across from the Harrison County Fairgrounds in Corydon. (Courtesy of Parvin Lambertus.)

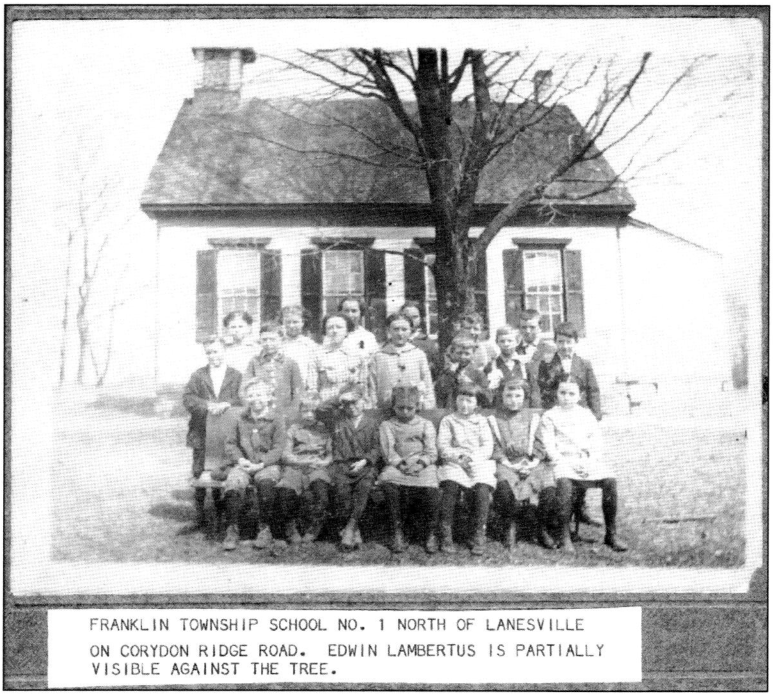

FRANKLIN TOWNSHIP SCHOOL NO. 1 NORTH OF LANESVILLE ON CORYDON RIDGE ROAD. EDWIN LAMBERTUS IS PARTIALLY VISIBLE AGAINST THE TREE.

Franklin School No. 1 was on the Old Corydon Ridge Road north of Lanesville. This 1910s class photograph included Leonard Lambertus and George Lambertus Jr. on the far left of the first row. Morris "Pop" Baker taught at this school around 1912 to 1914 when George "Buddy" Miller was the trustee. (Courtesy of Parvin Lambertus.)

Lanesville School No. 2 sat at the east end of town and was the biggest of the 10 schools in the township. Students from smaller schools in the county could attend to gain three more years of schooling before applying to Corydon to obtain their high school diploma. (Courtesy of Francis Zollman.)

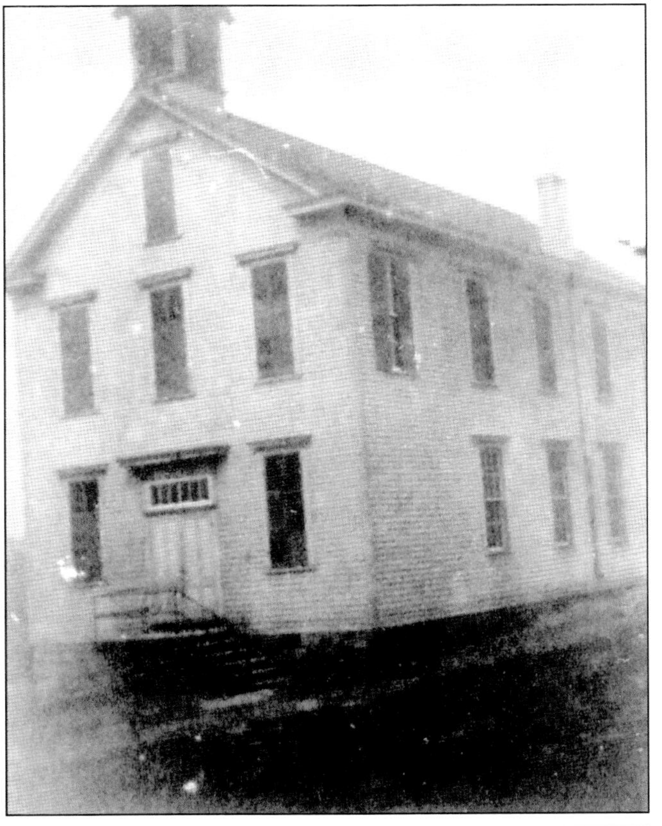

Students pose in front of Lanesville School No. 2 in 1904. This building served as the high school for the township until 1922 and a commencement ceremony was held for students who completed study beyond the eighth grade. Henry Miller tore down the building in the late 1920s and built a house using its lumber, which Oneda (Ott) Ringle lives in today. The railing and the front steps the kids are standing on still exist on that house today. (Courtesy of Lanesville archives.)

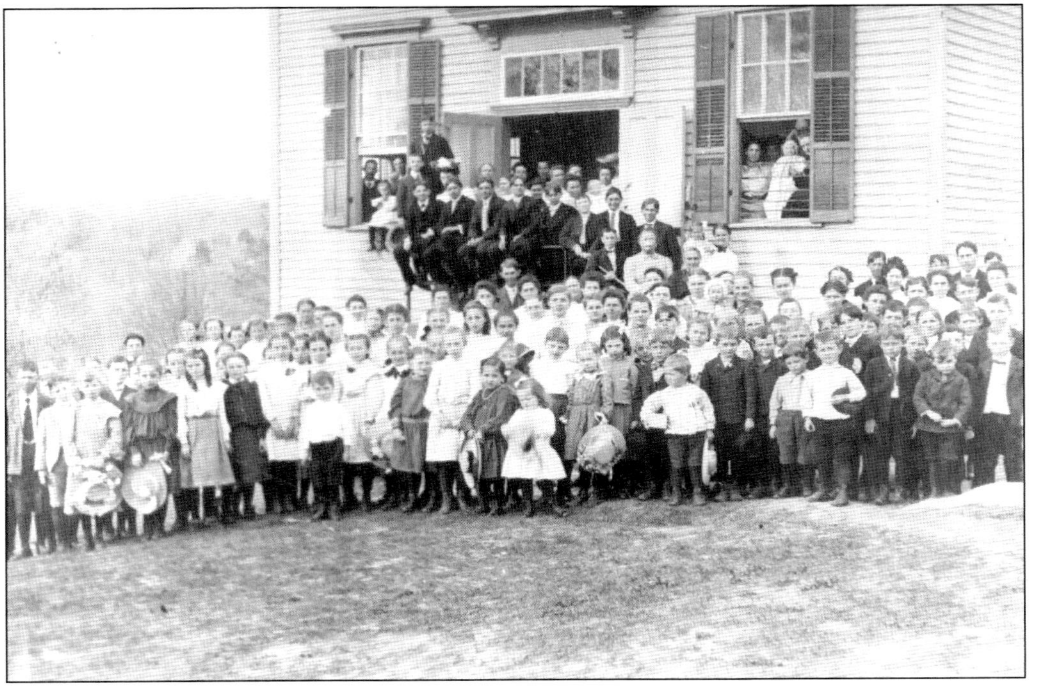

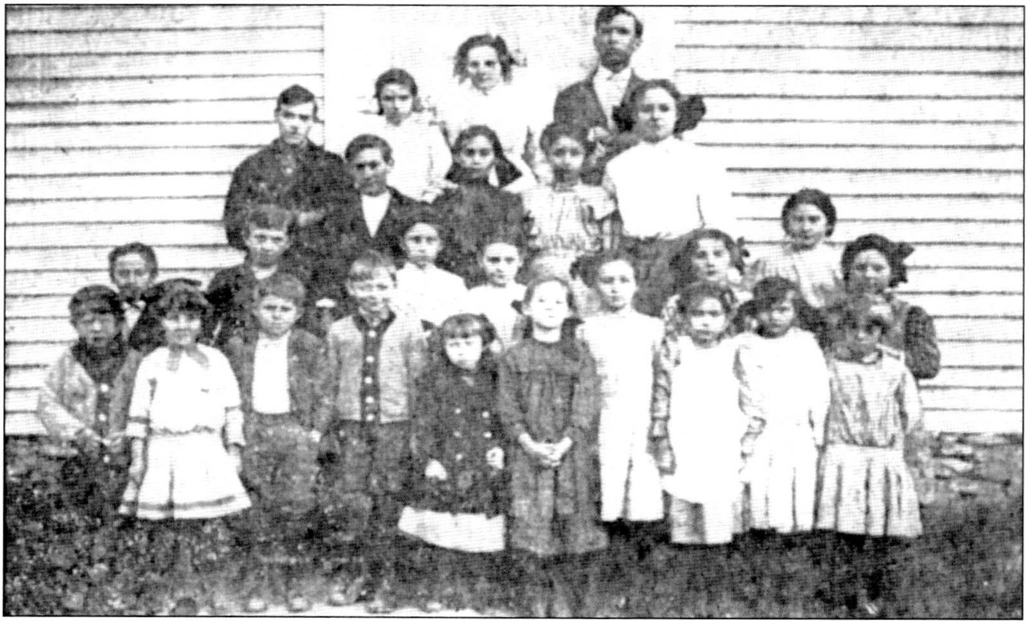

Franklin School No. 3 was known as the Washington School and was located on Crandall Lanesville Road at the corner of Emily Road. Bruce Markel was the teacher in this early-1900s image, and Blanche Yenowine Lotich, the girl standing in front of Markel, supplied the image for publication in the *Corydon Democrat* in 1961. (Courtesy of Blanche Lotich and the *Corydon Democrat* archives.)

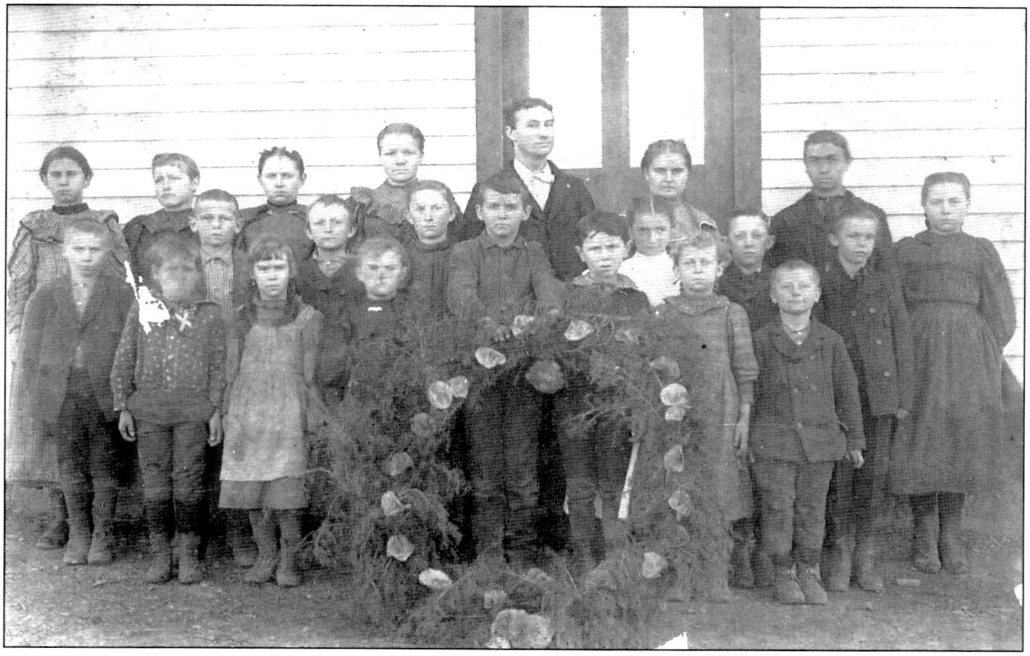

Teacher Sam Vost poses with his class at Franklin School No. 1 in the 1890s. Notice the wreath in the front center, perhaps made for a Christmas celebration. (Courtesy of Fredrick Porter Griffin Center.)

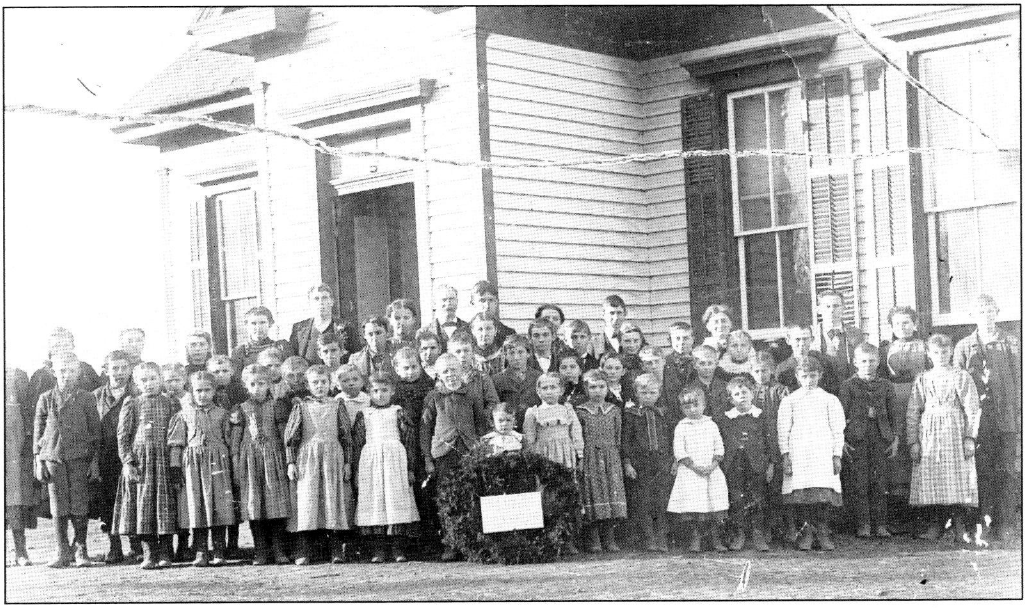

This photograph of Franklin School No. 6 was taken around 1892. The sign in front reads "No. 6 Franklin." The school was on Turley Road on the old Chester Mayfield farm and taught students until the late 1930s, when buses started taking township kids in the outlying areas to Lanesville Elementary School and Lanesville High School, which has housed elementary and high school students since 1922. (Courtesy of Marydee Meyer.)

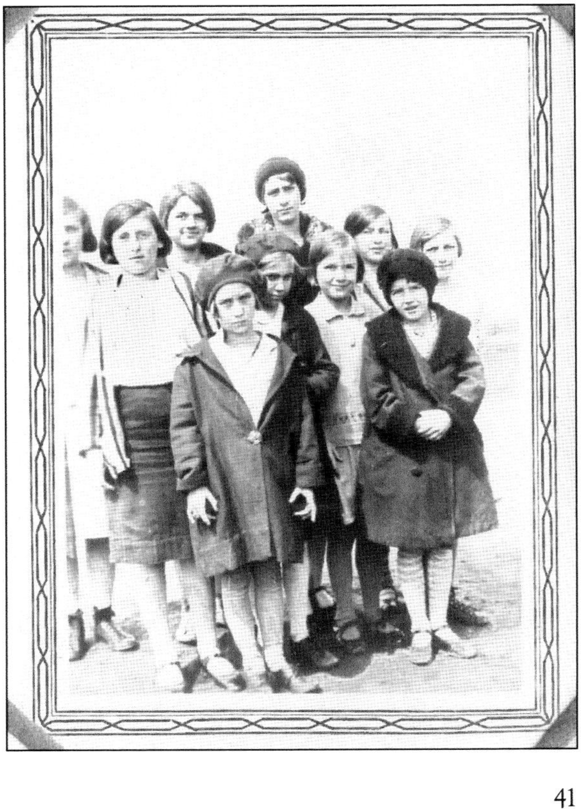

Students pictured at Franklin School No. 6 around 1928–1929 include, from left to right, (first row) Mary Bruce, Francis Bruce, Beulah Gehlbach and Mary Eckart; (second row) Marge Watson, Doris Bell, Lucielle Zurchmede, Margaret Bruce, Pauline Felker, and Mae Richert. School No. 6 taught students up to eighth grade and closed in about 1936–1937. (Courtesy of Jim Felker.)

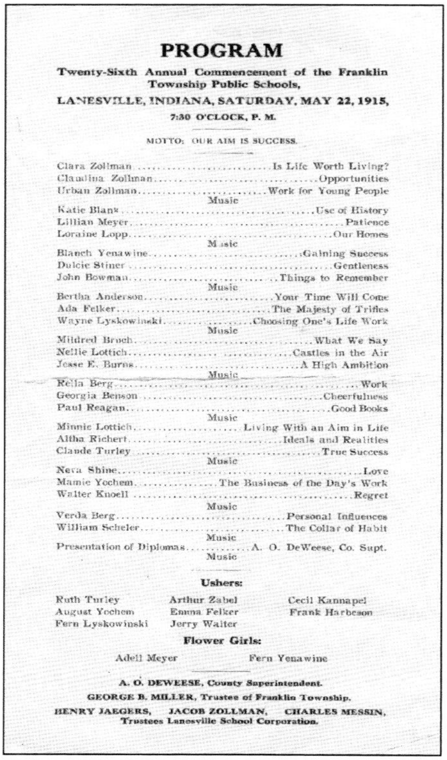

PROGRAM

Twenty-Sixth Annual Commencement of the Franklin Township Public Schools,

LANESVILLE, INDIANA, SATURDAY, MAY 22, 1915,

7:30 O'CLOCK, P. M.

MOTTO: OUR AIM IS SUCCESS.

Clara Zollman.......Is Life Worth Living?
Claudina Zollman.......Opportunities
Urban Zollman.......Work for Young People
Music
Katie Blank.......Use of History
Lillian Meyer.......Patience
Loraine Lopp.......Our Homes
Music
Blanch Yenawine.......Gaining Success
Dulcie Stiner.......Gentleness
John Bowman.......Things to Remember
Music
Bertha Anderson.......Your Time Will Come
Ada Felker.......The Majesty of Trifles
Wayne Lyskowinski.......Choosing One's Life Work
Music
Mildred Broch.......What We Say
Nellie Lottich.......Castles in the Air
Jesse E. Burns.......A High Ambition
Music
Rella Berg.......Work
Georgia Benson.......Cheerfulness
Paul Reagan.......Good Books
Music
Minnie Lottich.......Living With an Aim in Life
Altha Richert.......Ideals and Realities
Claude Turley.......True Success
Music
Neva Shine.......Love
Mamie Yochem.......The Business of the Day's Work
Walter Knoell.......Regret
Music
Verda Berg.......Personal Influences
William Scheler.......The Collar of Habit
Music
Presentation of Diplomas.......A. O. DeWeese, Co. Supt.
Music

Ushers:

Ruth Turley, Arthur Zabel, Cecil Kannapel
August Yochem, Emma Felker, Frank Harbeson
Fern Lyskowinski, Jerry Walter

Flower Girls:

Adell Meyer, Fern Yenawine

A. O. DEWEESE, County Superintendent.
GEORGE B. MILLER, Trustee of Franklin Township.
HENRY JAEGERS, JACOB ZOLLMAN, CHARLES MESSIN,
Trustees Lanesville School Corporation.

This program is from the 26th annual commencement of the then Franklin Township Public Schools in 1915, meaning the inaugural commencement was in 1889. It is believed that these commencement programs were held at Lanesville School No. 2 because it was the largest school in the township. This program was for students who had finished their eighth-grade education and were either finishing or continuing the extra three years at the Lanesville School to eventually apply to Corydon. For many, this was their last schooling opportunity before moving on to work. (Courtesy of Bill Lyskowinski.)

Some 30 pupils were enrolled at Franklin School No. 8 when this photograph was taken in 1912–1913. School No. 8 was called the West Central School and was located near the corner of Raccoon Creek Road and Corydon Ridge Road. Gertrude Zollman was the teacher when this image was taken. The school was also used by several churches in the area in the late 1880s and early 1890s, from the United Brethren to the Latter-Day Saints. (Courtesy of the *Corydon Democrat* archives.)

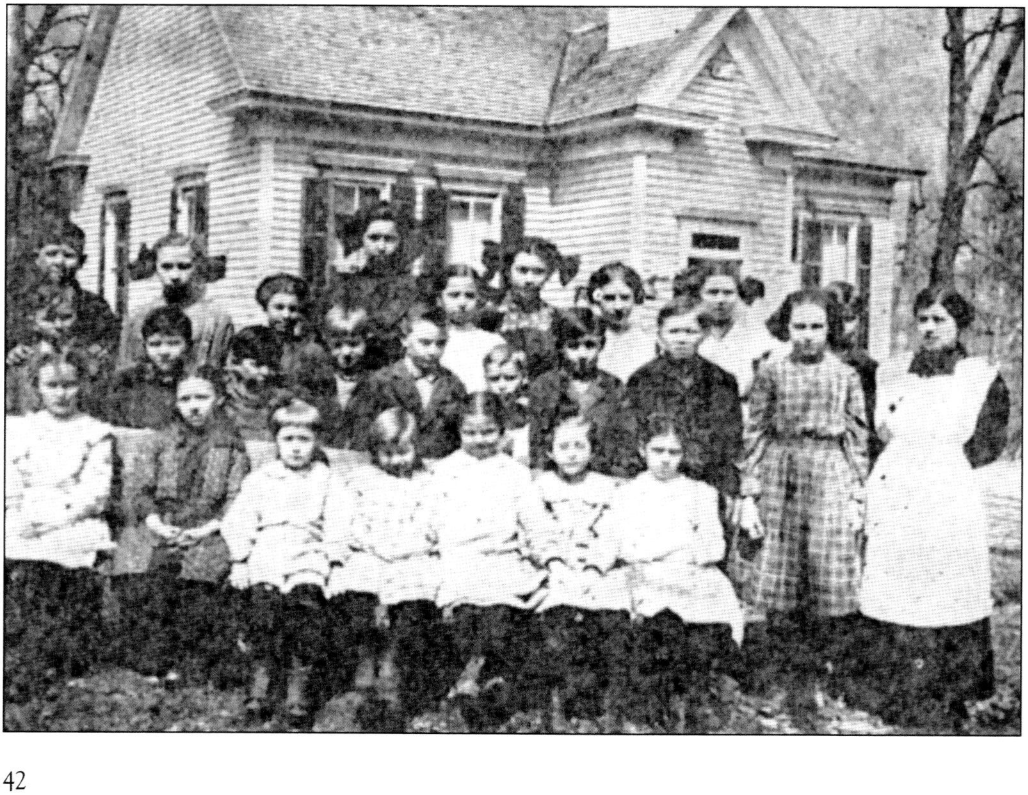

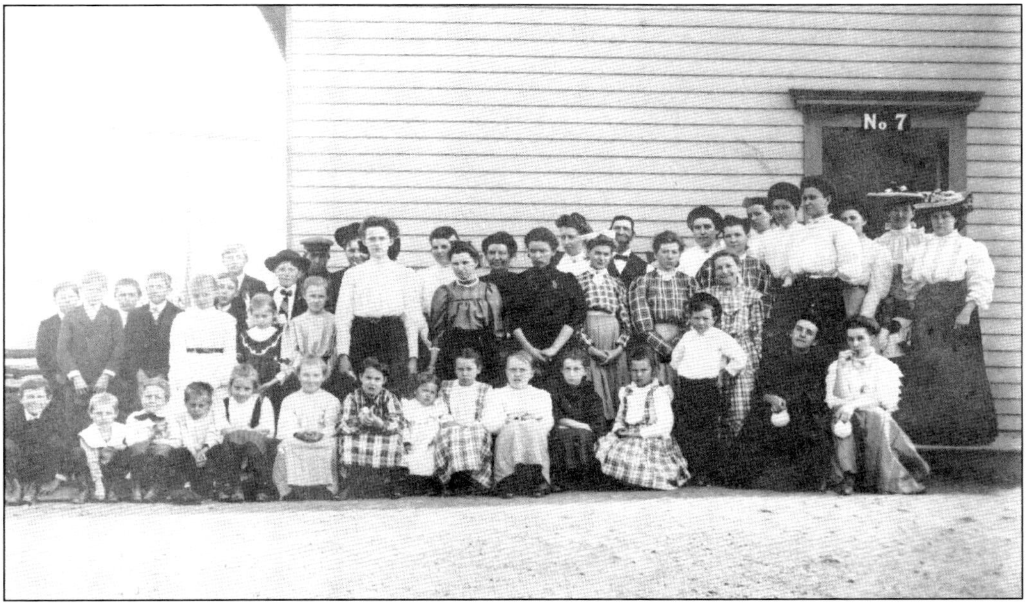

Students at Franklin School No. 7 pose for a school photograph in the early 1900s. This school was at the corner of Hess Jawtak Road and St. John's Church Road in southeast Franklin Township. Anna (Zollman) Voelker taught at the school during this period. Grades one through eight were accommodated at this school and at most schools at the time. The range of ages presented a challenge for teachers to make sure every student learned what was needed. (Courtesy of Carolyn Voelker.)

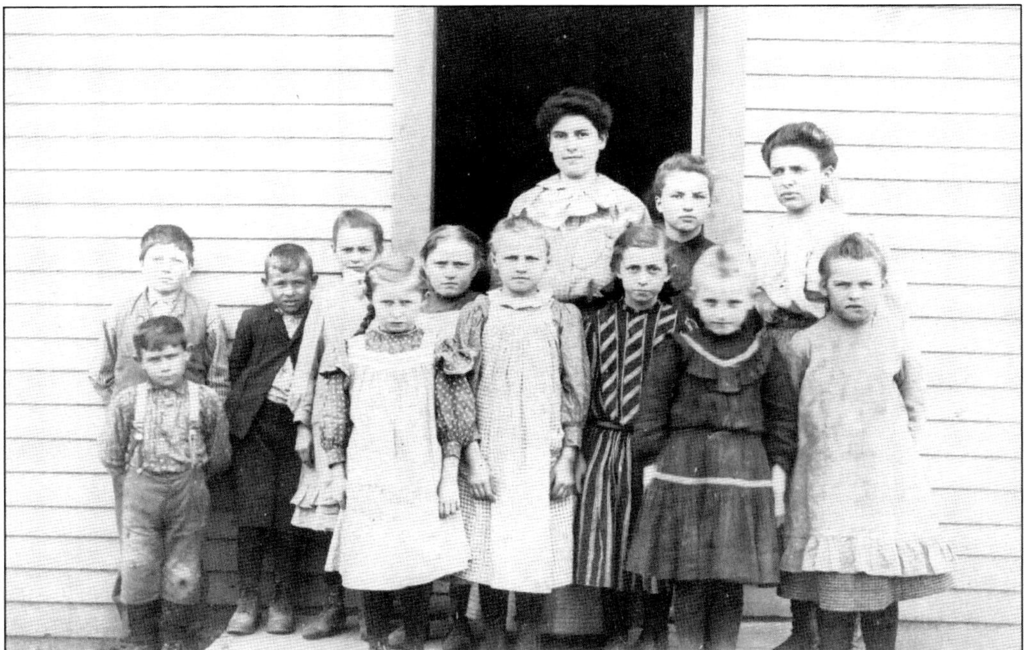

Anna (Zollman) Voelker stands in front of Franklin School No. 7 with a small group of her students, perhaps just one or two grades she was working with at the time. Fred and Anna Voelker lived on a farm just a few hundred feet west of the school. (Courtesy of Carolyn Voelker.)

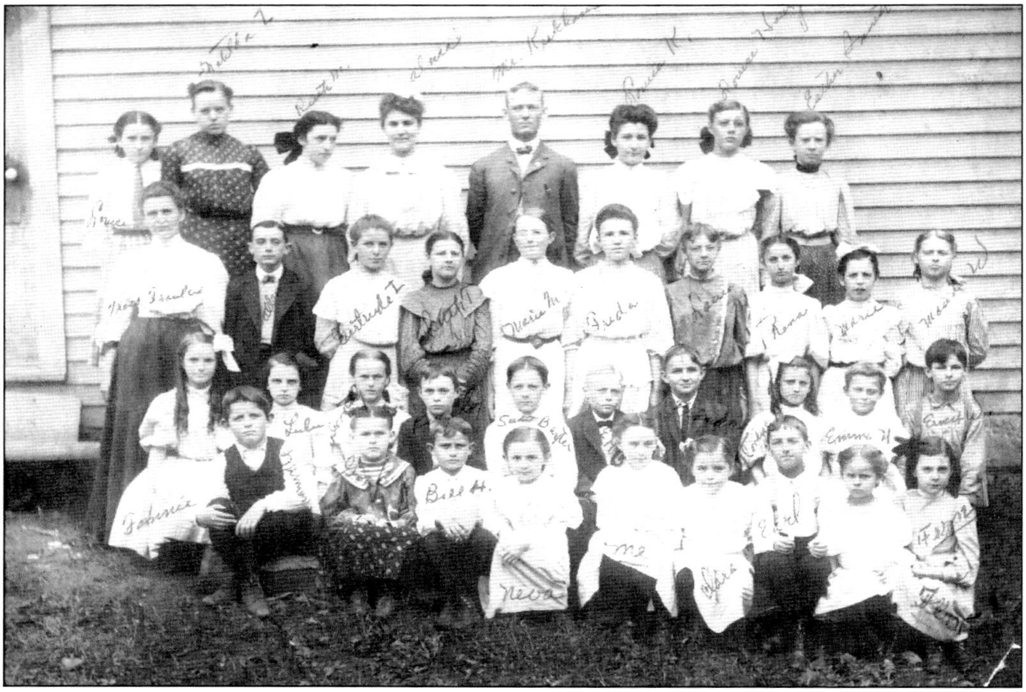

Both of these images are of unidentified Franklin schools. However, some record was passed along, as the names of some of the children and all of the teachers are identified. (Both, courtesy of Bill Lyskowinski.)

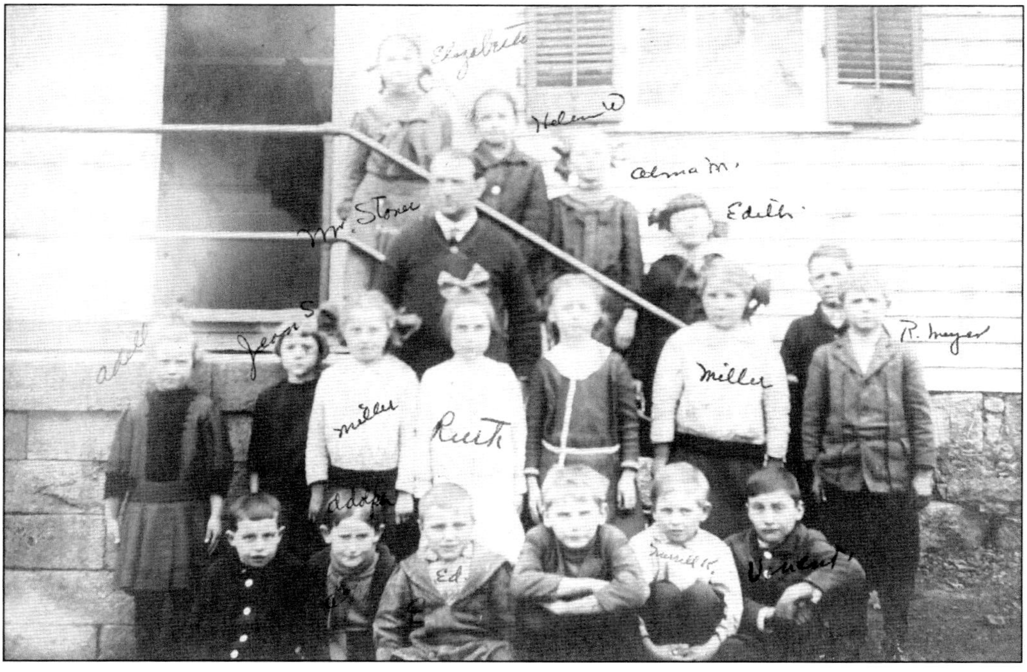

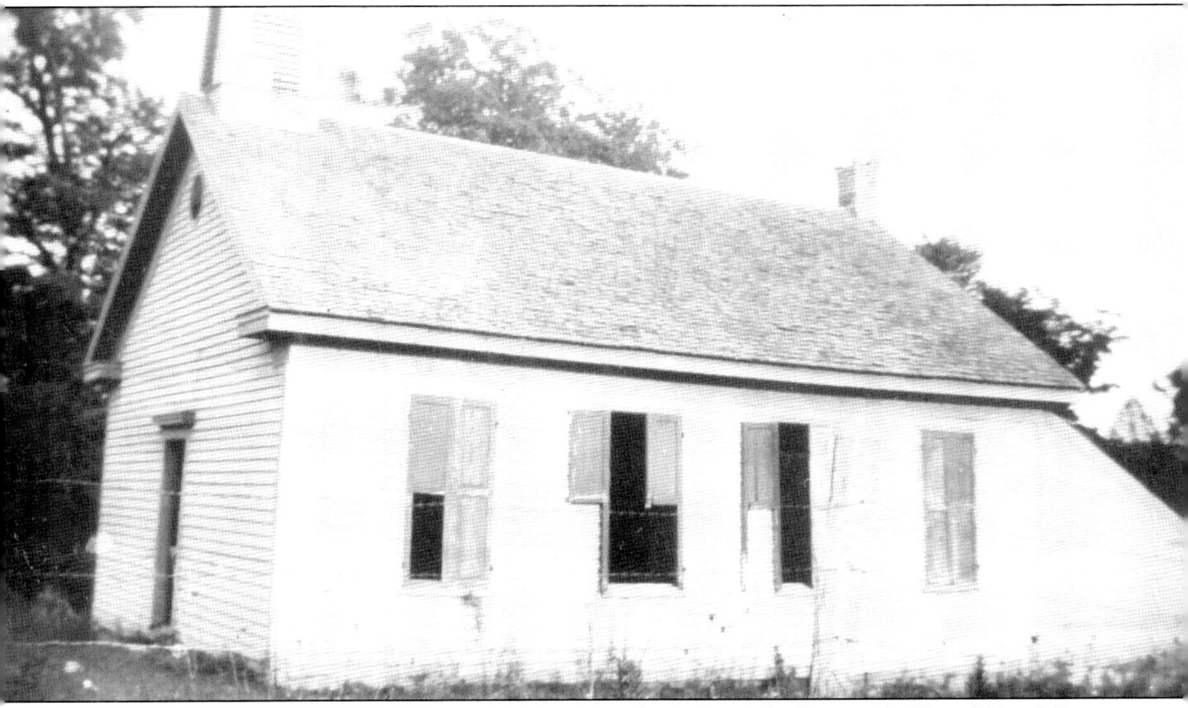

Franklin School No. 10 was at the corner of State Highway 62 and Pfrimmer's Chapel Road. It was built on the corner property of Stanley and Hilda Meyer and is seen here after the school had been closed for a few years. (Courtesy of Marydee Meyer.)

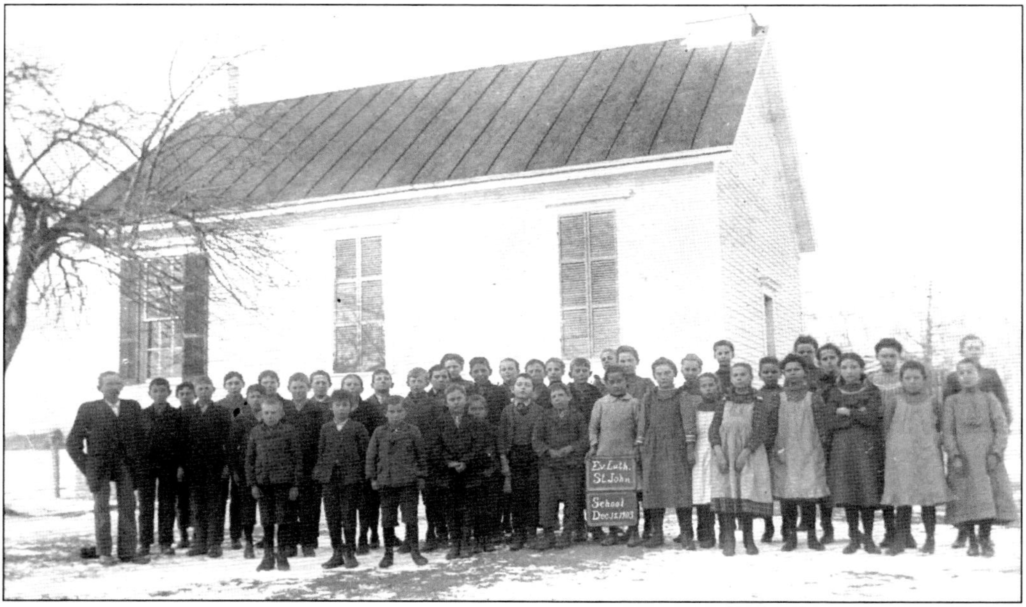

St. John's Lutheran School, one of two private religious schools in the township, is seen here on December 12, 1903. It was started in a log cabin in 1861, but this school was built in 1880 and taught grades one through eight. It remained the school building until a new structure was erected in 1938, at which time this building was dismantled and moved by Homer Schellenberger, who turned it into a residence in Lanesville. Today, Stan Courtney lives in the house built from this school. (Courtesy of Parvin Lambertus.)

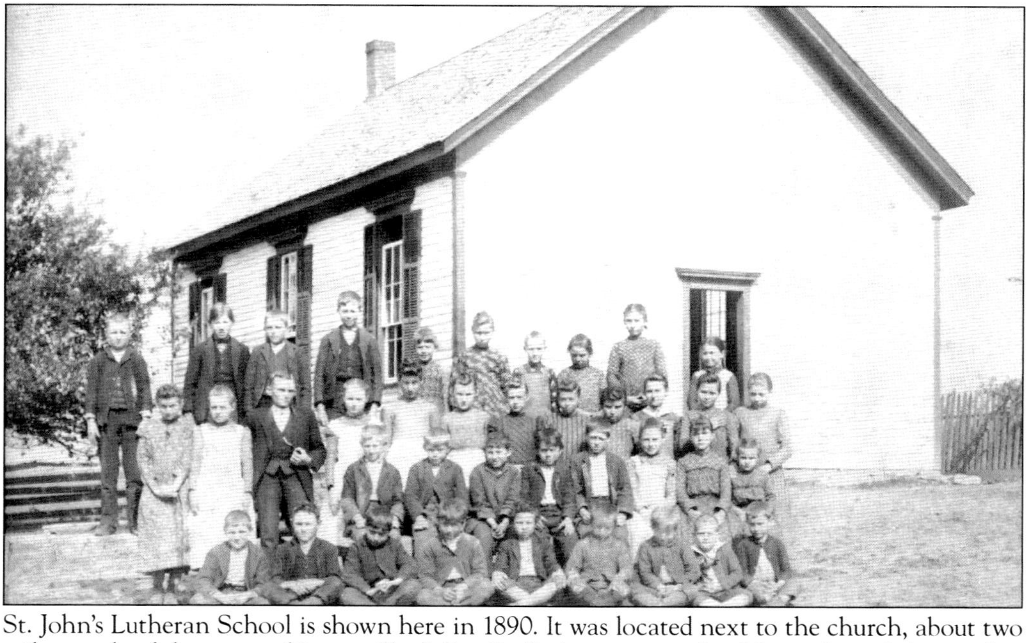

St. John's Lutheran School is shown here in 1890. It was located next to the church, about two miles south of the town of Lanesville. Julius Prelle (center row, third from the right) served as the teacher in this school for 28 years, dying of a stroke in the classroom in 1914. (Courtesy of Carolyn Voelker.)

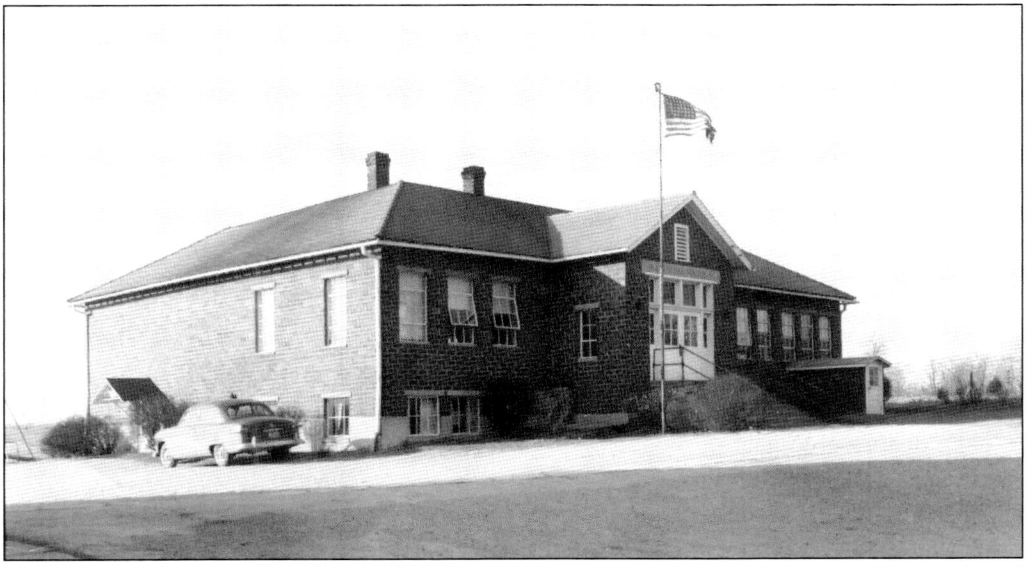

The new St. John's Lutheran School building is seen here around 1948. Built in 1938, it replaced the old wooden structure at a cost of $8,000. It contained two classrooms, a kitchen, a gym floor, and a stage. The building is still in use today. (Courtesy of Parvin Lambertus.)

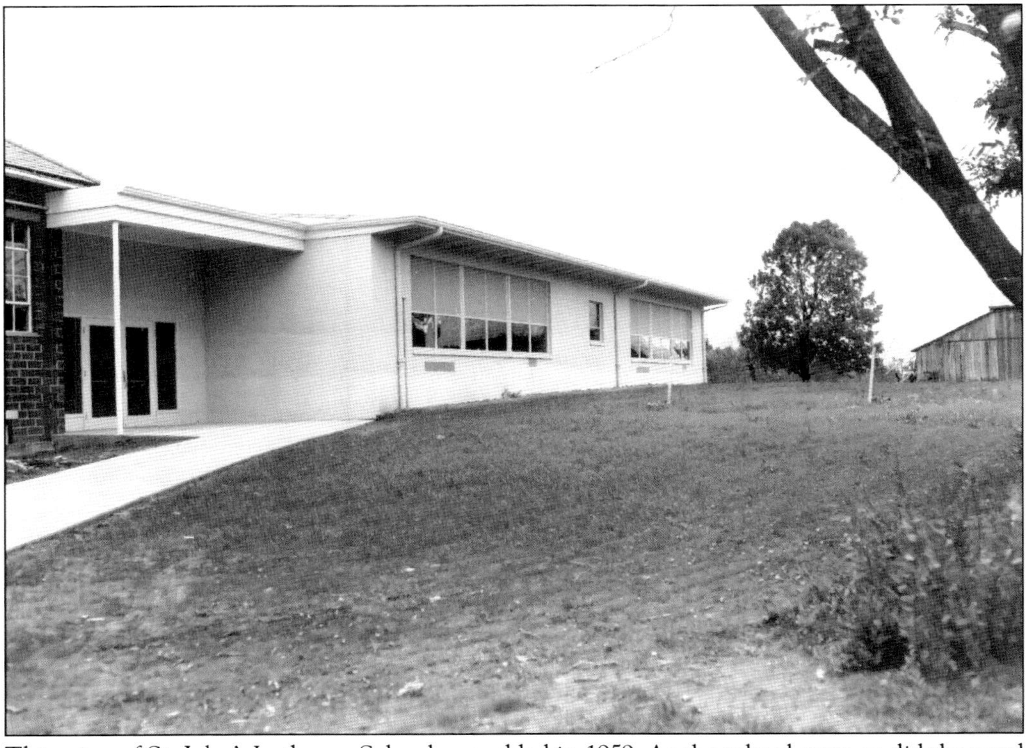

This wing of St. John's Lutheran School was added in 1959. As the school grew, so did the need for more classrooms; this addition added four classrooms. The school operated out of the two buildings until a 1997 renovation added a new cafeteria, more classrooms, and a new gymnasium. St. John's began in 1861 and still operates today. (Courtesy of Parvin Lambertus.)

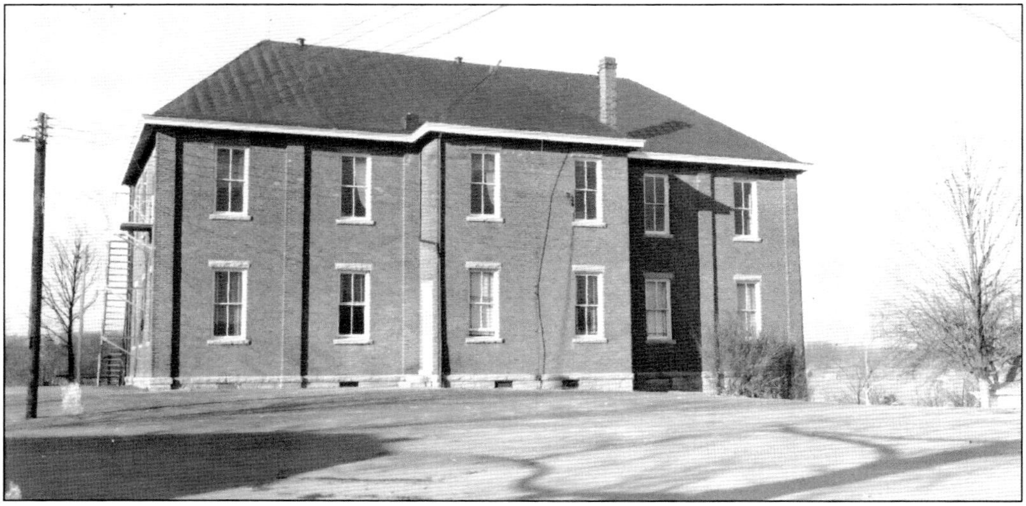

The back of St. Mary's Catholic School, just south of the church, is seen here around the late 1940s. Built in 1900, it housed grades one through eight until a new school was built in 1965. The bricks were made and prepared on the property when the school was built. Notice the fire escape on the left of the building. (Courtesy of Marvin Zabel.)

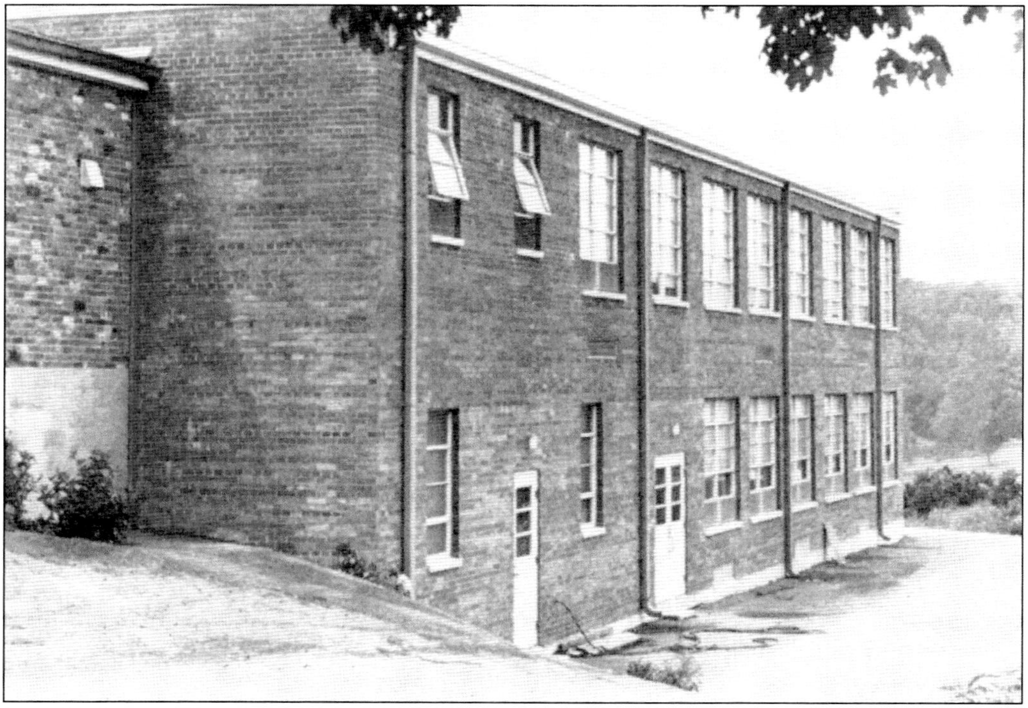

In 1965, this new St. Mary's Catholic School took the place of the one pictured above, also housing grades one through eight. Upon completion of the school, students could attend the neighboring Lanesville School or attend a Catholic high school to continue their education. In 1968, the seventh and eighth grades were sent to Lanesville Junior High School and the building became a grade school, educating students from kindergarten through sixth grade. The school closed in 1994. (Courtesy of St. Mary's Church, Lanesville.)

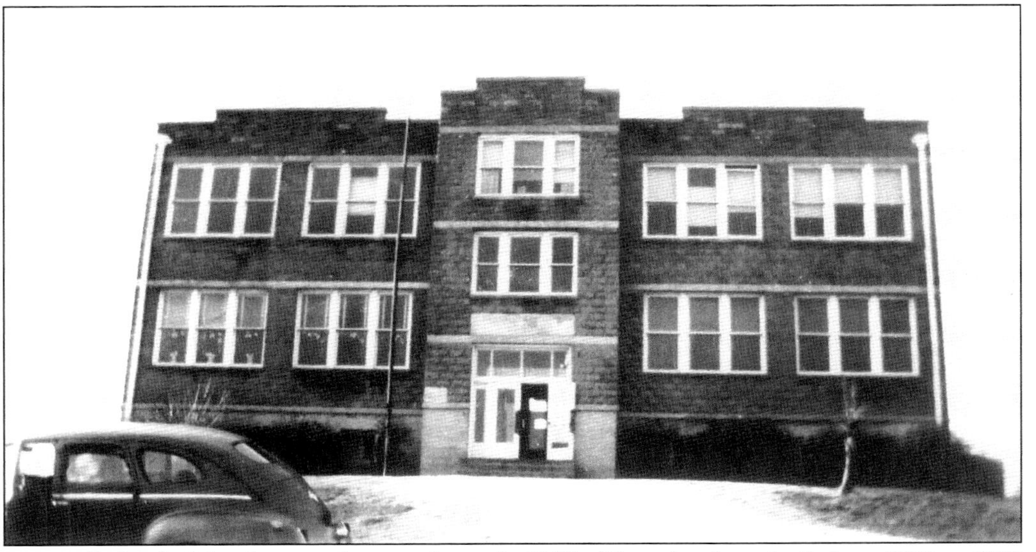

Lanesville High School is seen here in the early 1940s. The school was built from 1920 to 1922 and followed the typical design of schools from that period. All grades through high school were taught in the multistory building with a basement gymnasium. Molds were used to form the blocks and the nearby creek was used for water to mix the cement, gravel, and sand mixture to make the blocks. Once the blocks "cured," they were then laid and the structure was developed. John "Honus" Meurer, a stone worker for years in Lanesville, laid the blocks. This school's first graduating class, in 1923, had four students. The building was used until 1965, when a new high school was built. (Courtesy Bernice Barnickle.)

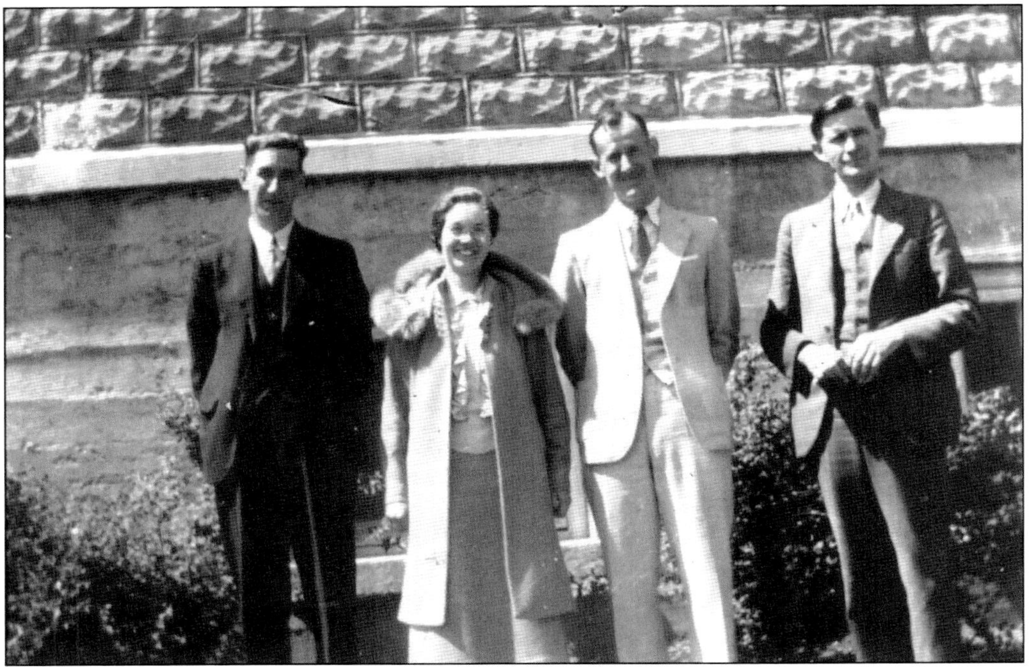

Pictured around the 1930s, this group of well-known Lanesville teachers included, from left to right, George Bickel, Zola Green, Adolph Zollman, and Herman Prage. (Courtesy of Jim Felker.)

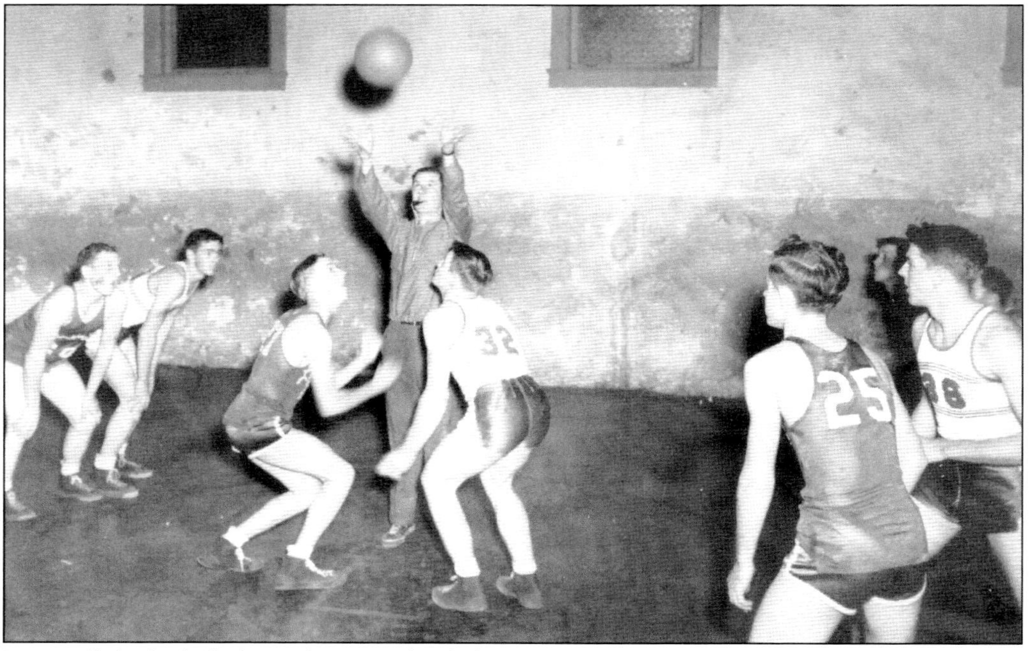

Lanesville basketball players (wearing the dark uniforms) enjoy a game in the basement gym of the old high school in the early 1940s. George Bickel, who coached at Lanesville for many years, is most likely the one tossing the ball at center court. Lanesville played many basketball games on the old concrete-floor gym with an *L* painted in the middle. There were no bleachers, and the ceiling was very low, so players had to shoot a little flat to get the ball into the basket. It was an advantage for the home team and quite a disadvantage for visiting teams. (Courtesy of Marvin Zabel.)

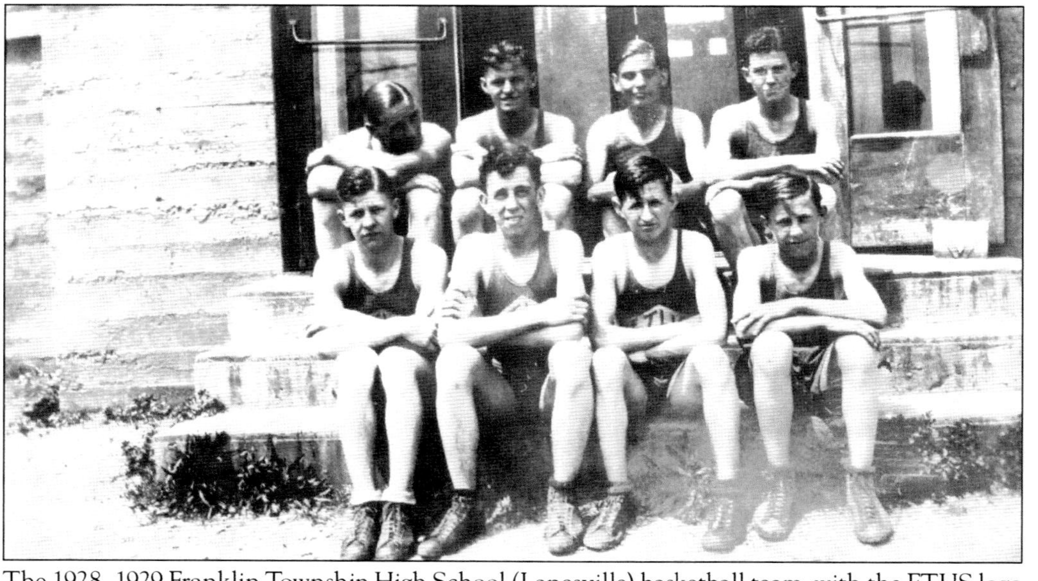

The 1928–1929 Franklin Township High School (Lanesville) basketball team, with the FTHS logo on their uniforms, included, from left to right, (first row) George Lambertus, Sonny Nance, William Richert, and John Reinhardt; (second row) John Baker, Clifford Walker, Ray Brown, and Francis Walther. They were coached by Claude Turley, not pictured. (Courtesy of Lennie Reinhardt.)

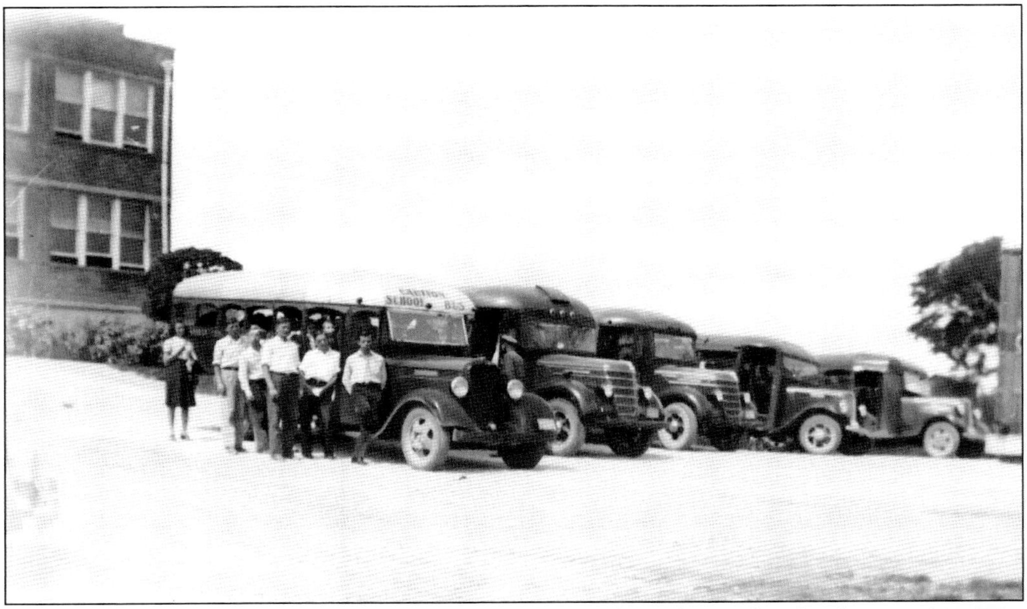

School buses were lined up and ready to take the students home for the day in 1941. The students are, from back to front, an unidentified young woman, Jim Harbeson, Bob Harbeson, Maurice Quebberman, and two unidentified. Sitting in their buses are drivers, from left to right, Orlin Lieber, Charles Schweitzer, Irwin Baumgart, Herman P. Zollman, and Asa Evans. (Courtesy of Eugene Gleitz.)

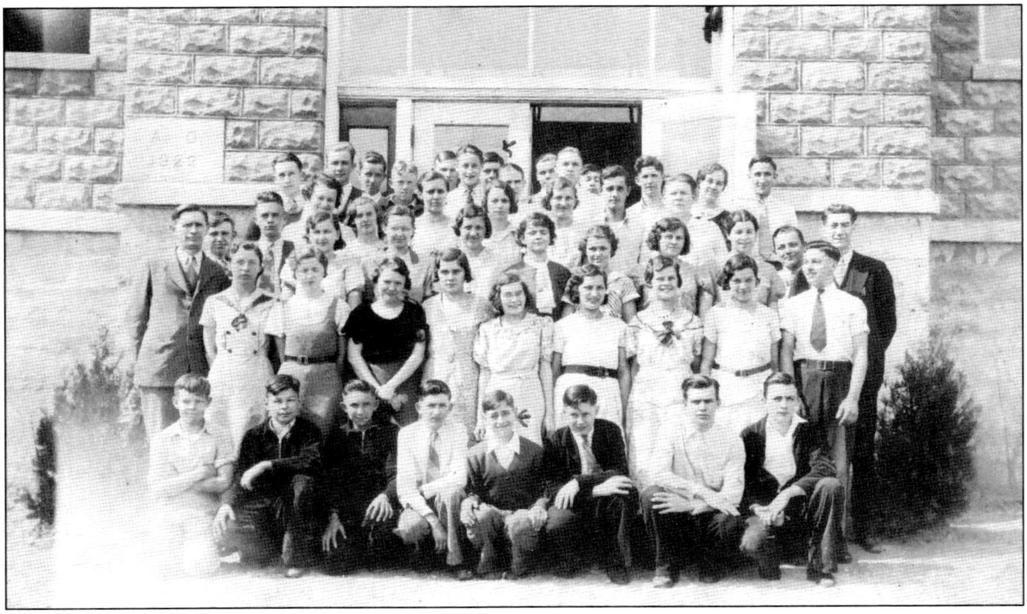

In this photograph from 1933–1934, Lanesville High School students pose with their teachers, Herman Prage (far left) and George Bickel (far right), who were both well-known figures in Lanesville schools. Prage was a teacher and principal for many years and George Bickel was a teacher and basketball coach. Notice the cornerstone with the inscription A.D. 1922 on the front of the school. Today, that stone sits at the present school site. (Courtesy of Carolyn Voelker.)

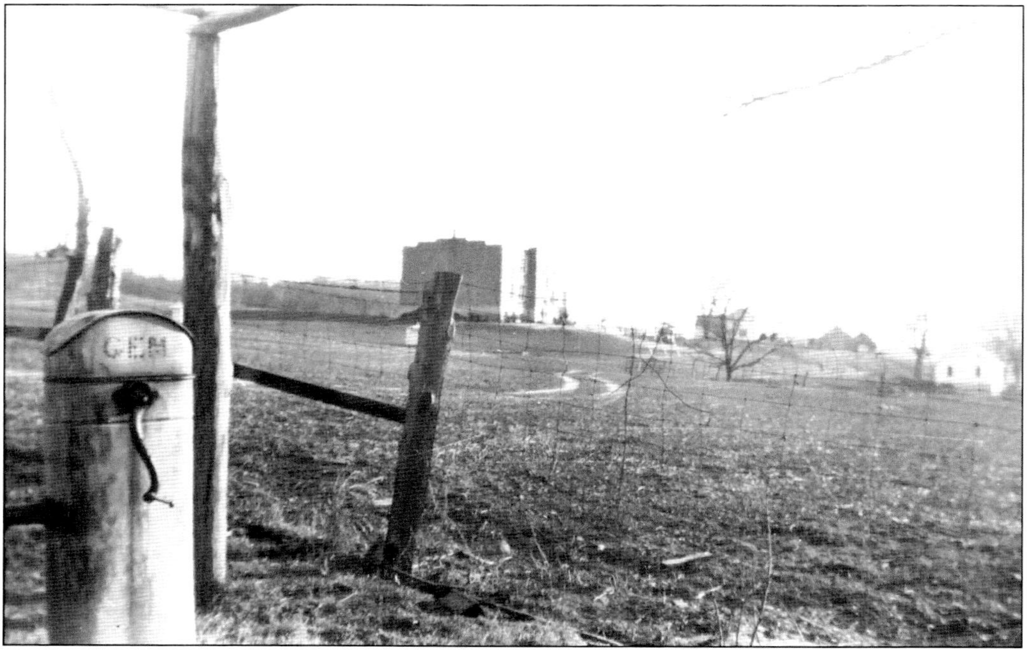

Lanesville School is perched on a hill overlooking the town in this 1941 photograph taken from the Herman Gleitz farm. From this angle, Auggie Blum's house, which now belongs to Steve Smith, is in the center, and Homer Schellenberger's house, now owned by Stan Courtney, is at the right. Eugene Gleitz owns the farm today and still has this view of Lanesville Schools. (Courtesy of Eugene Gleitz.)

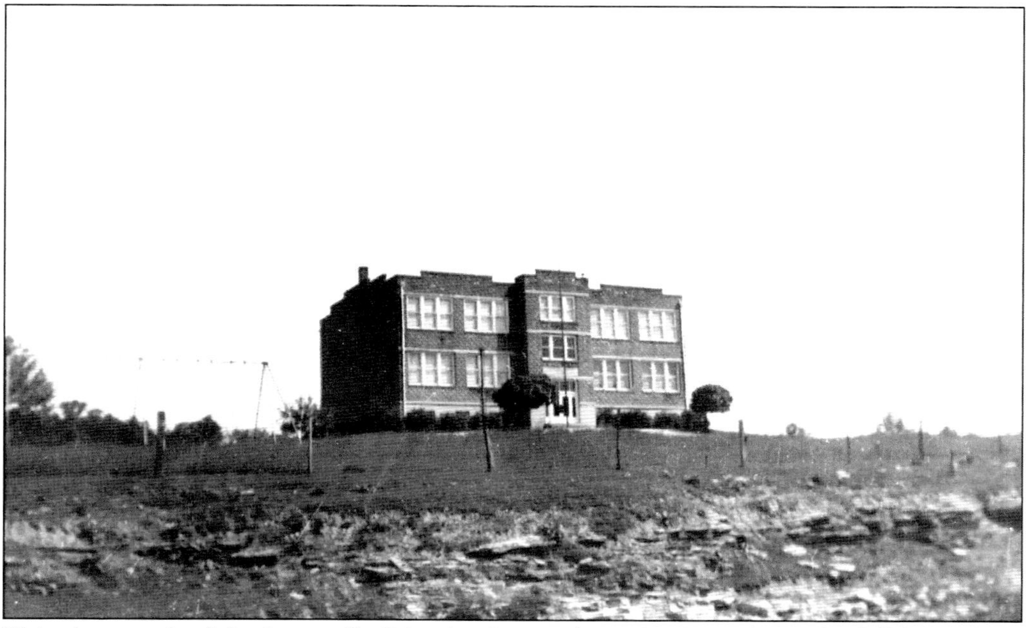

This photograph of the Lanesville School, taken in the early 1940s, shows the full front of the school facing south, overlooking Little Indian Creek and the town. New schools were eventually built in the same location. (Courtesy of Eugene Gleitz.)

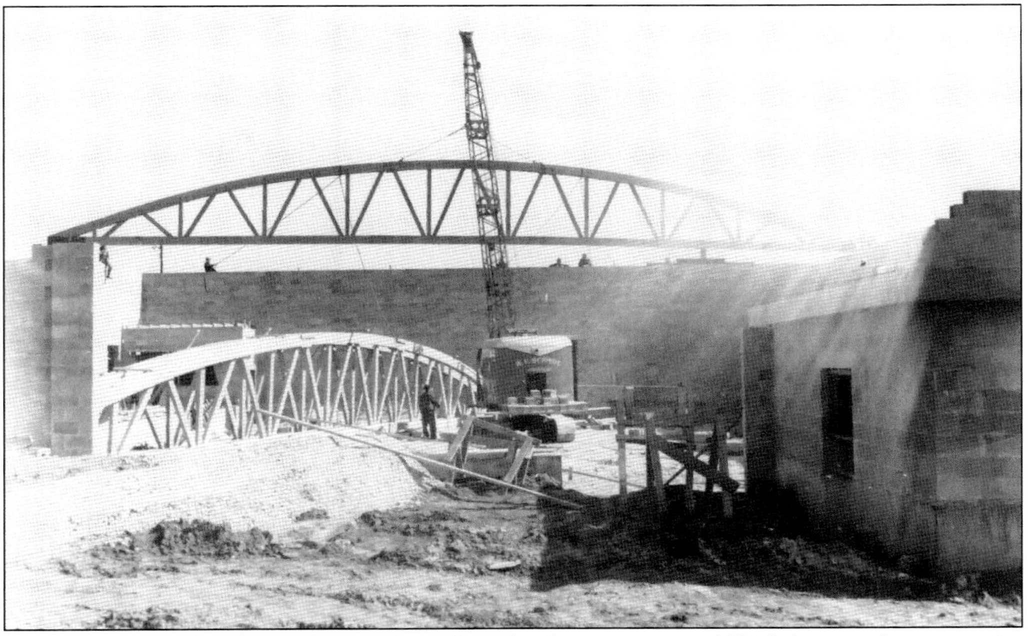

Construction workers hang the wooden rafters for the new gym in 1951. It became known as the Eagle Dome because of its shape. The gymnasium held about 900 spectators, compared to the old gym, which fit less than 200 people. Wooden beams were used because the town could not get steel beams at the time. The quirk made this gym different from those built at the same time, and it stood until 2004. (Courtesy of Marvin Zabel.)

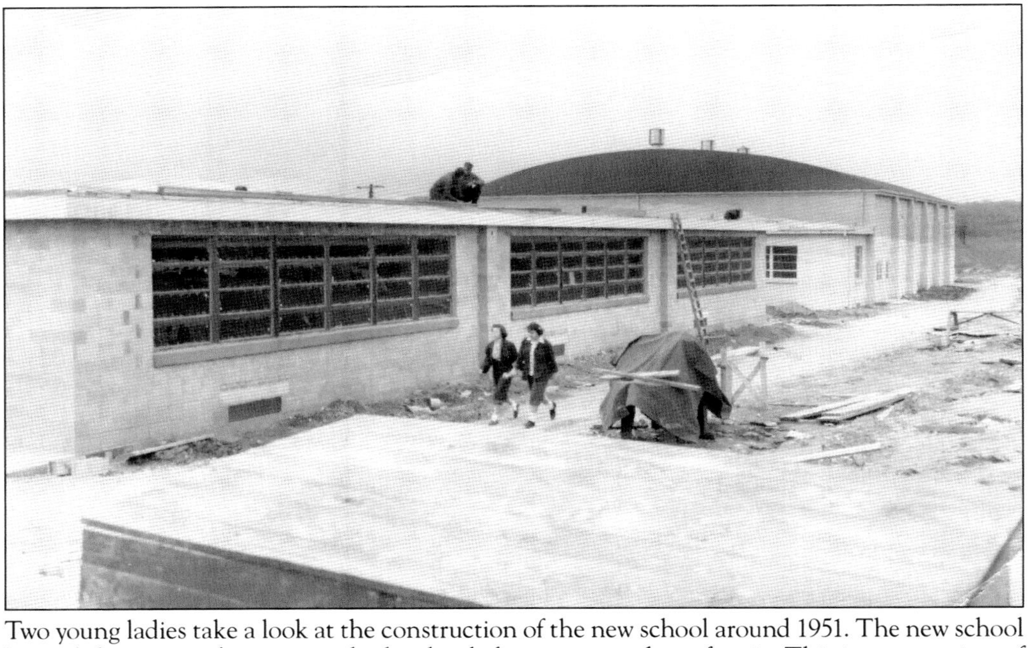

Two young ladies take a look at the construction of the new school around 1951. The new school housed the gym and stage, new high school classrooms, and a cafeteria. This is a great view of the finished Eagle Dome gym. After this building was completed in 1952, the old 1922 school became the elementary school. (Courtesy of Marvin Zabel.)

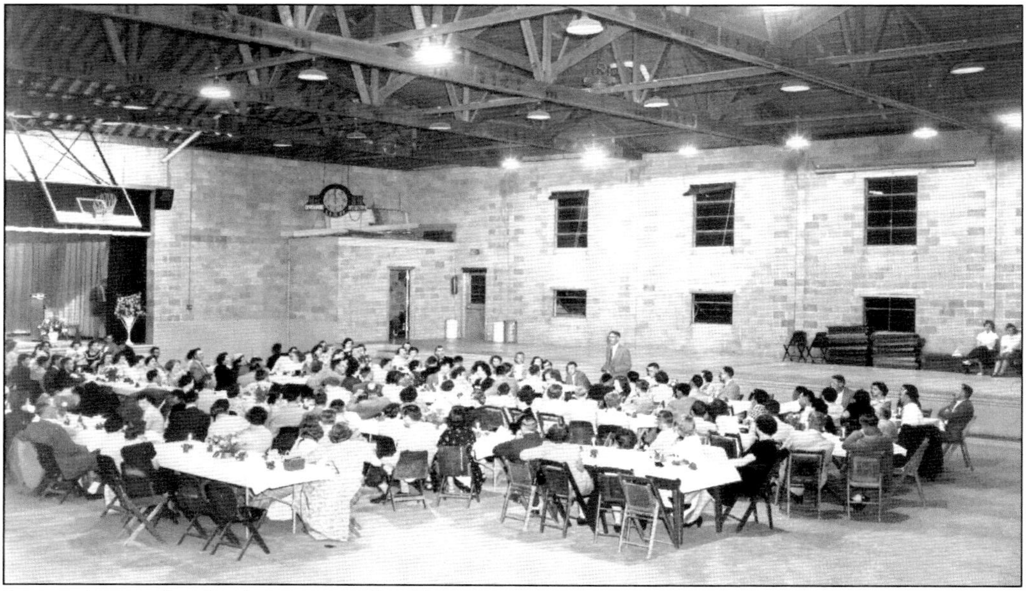

Pictured around 1953, the new gym held basketball games but also hosted banquets and graduation ceremonies. Herman Prage, standing in front of the concrete slab, leads the banquet festivities. The long concrete slab was also the first cafeteria—tables and chairs were set up and taken down each day so students could start eating lunch at school. The old score clock (top center) sits on the west end of the gym and was used before the school obtained a lighted clock a few years later. (Courtesy of Marvin Zabel.)

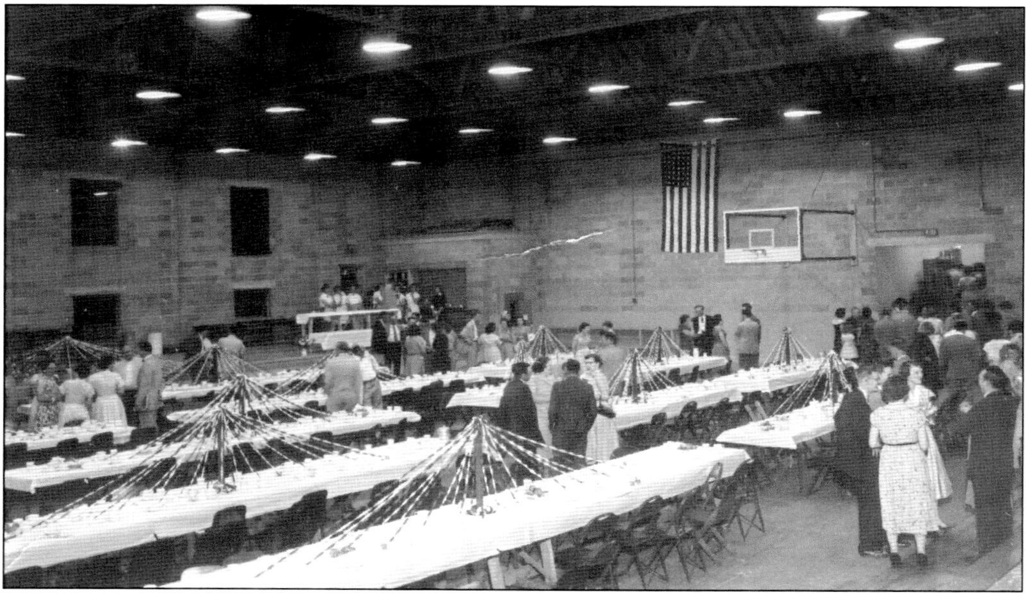

This view faces east looking toward the entrance to the gym around the mid-1950s. A set of steps went down to the gym floor on the far right. It appears that a dinner or banquet was taking place. School officials took great pains to make sure the gym floor was not scratched, covering the floor with heavy tarps before putting chairs or tables on the floor and forbidding shoes to be worn on the floor. (Courtesy of Marvin Zabel.)

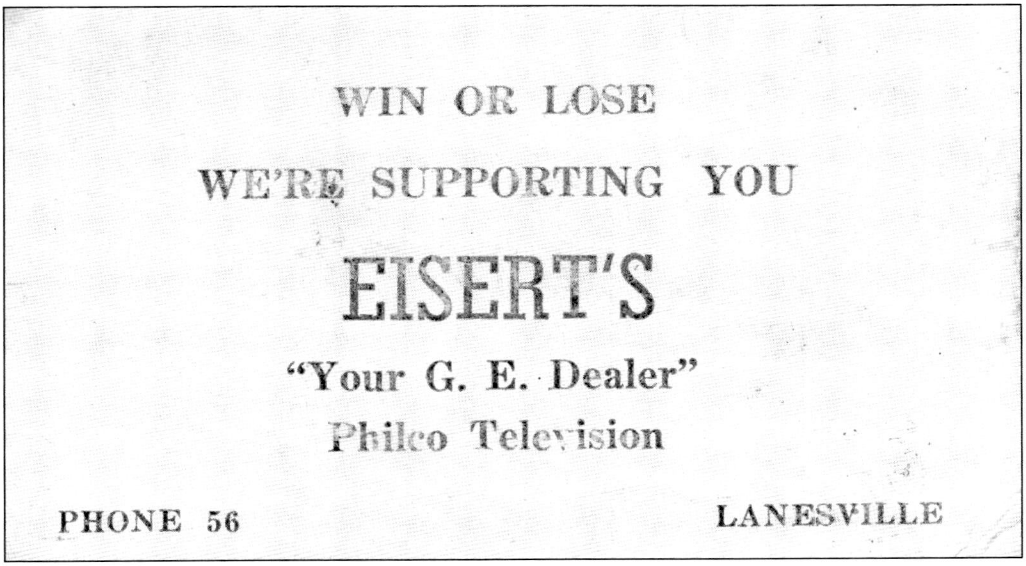

Local businesses were always supportive of the school. In 1958–1959, Alfred Eisert of Eisert's Sales and Service printed up this basketball schedule for the townspeople, letting folks know when games were as well as promoting his business. (Both, courtesy of Ron Eisert.)

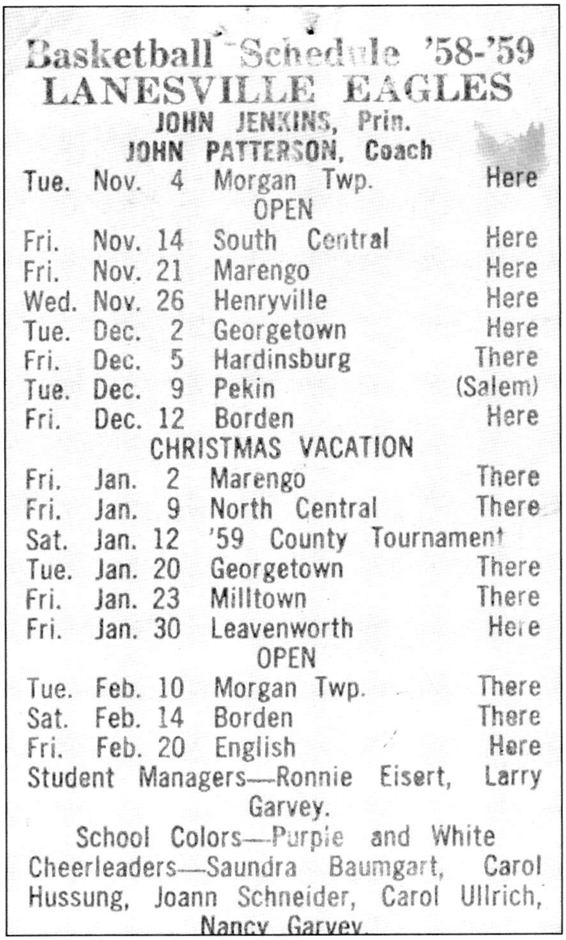
Basketball Schedule '58-'59
LANESVILLE EAGLES
JOHN JENKINS, Prin.
JOHN PATTERSON, Coach

Tue.	Nov.	4	Morgan Twp.	Here
			OPEN	
Fri.	Nov.	14	South Central	Here
Fri.	Nov.	21	Marengo	Here
Wed.	Nov.	26	Henryville	Here
Tue.	Dec.	2	Georgetown	Here
Fri.	Dec.	5	Hardinsburg	There
Tue.	Dec.	9	Pekin	(Salem)
Fri.	Dec.	12	Borden	Here
			CHRISTMAS VACATION	
Fri.	Jan.	2	Marengo	There
Fri.	Jan.	9	North Central	There
Sat.	Jan.	12	'59 County Tournament	
Tue.	Jan.	20	Georgetown	There
Fri.	Jan.	23	Milltown	There
Fri.	Jan.	30	Leavenworth	Here
			OPEN	
Tue.	Feb.	10	Morgan Twp.	There
Sat.	Feb.	14	Borden	There
Fri.	Feb.	20	English	Here

Student Managers—Ronnie Eisert, Larry Garvey.
School Colors—Purple and White
Cheerleaders—Saundra Baumgart, Carol Hussung, Joann Schneider, Carol Ullrich, Nancy Garvey.

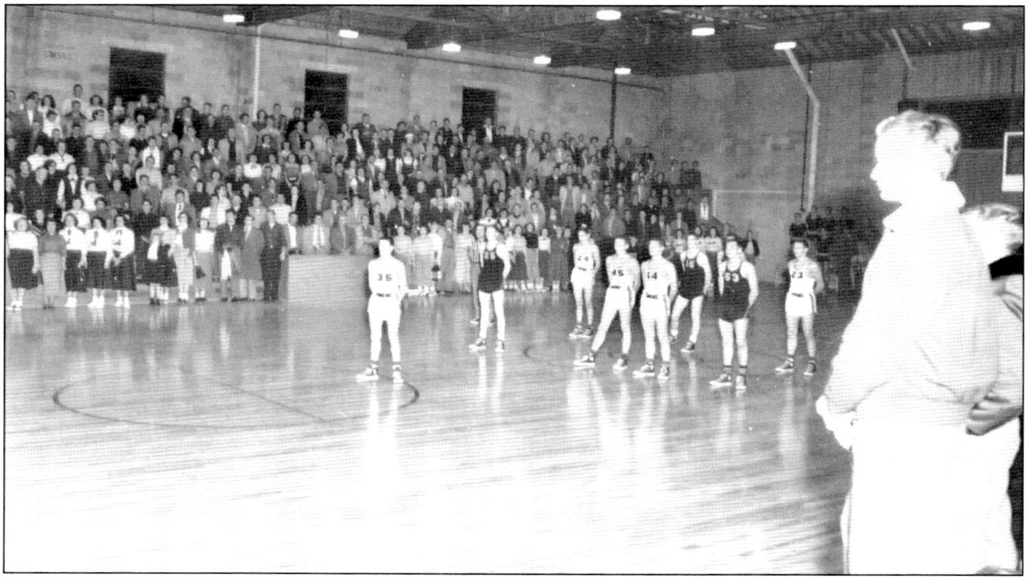

This scene is played out many Friday and Saturday nights in the Lanesville High School gym as fans and players pay respect to the flag and country. After these few minutes are over, the silence will be over until the final buzzer sounds to end the game. Here, teams are on the floor and ready to play, and the fans are ready for a great contest. (Courtesy of Marvin Zabel.)

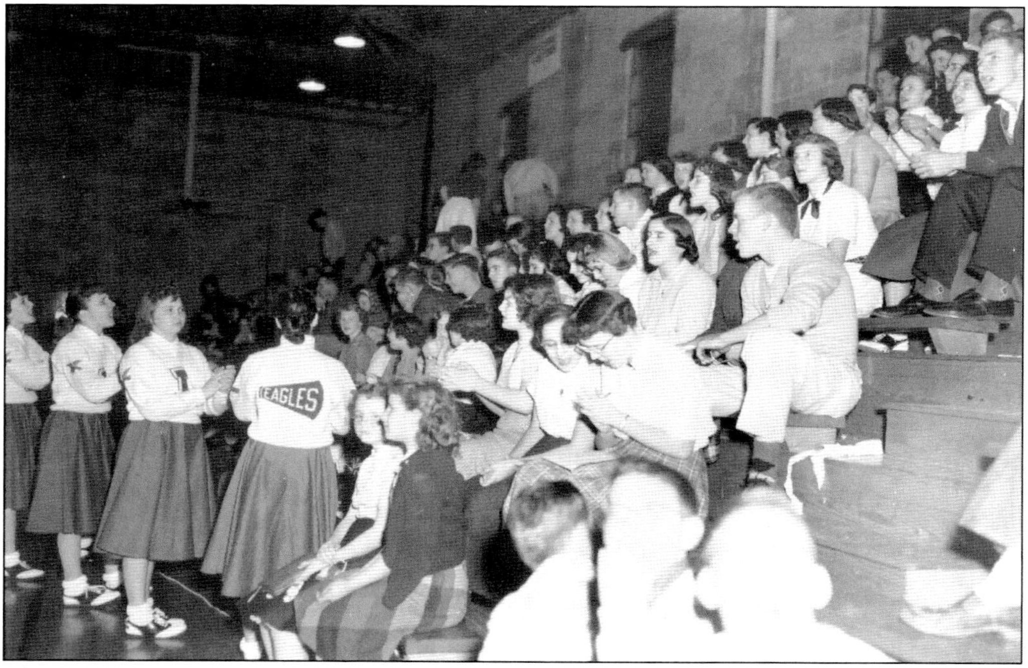

The Lanesville cheering section is ready to root the Eagles to victory. This photograph was taken during a big game in the mid-1950s. The cheerleaders are getting the crowd ready to lead Lanesville to victory, and the "sixth man"—the crowd—is responding. Teams did not want to play on the Lanesville court because the fans made it so loud it was hard for the other team to play their game. (Courtesy of Marvin Zabel.)

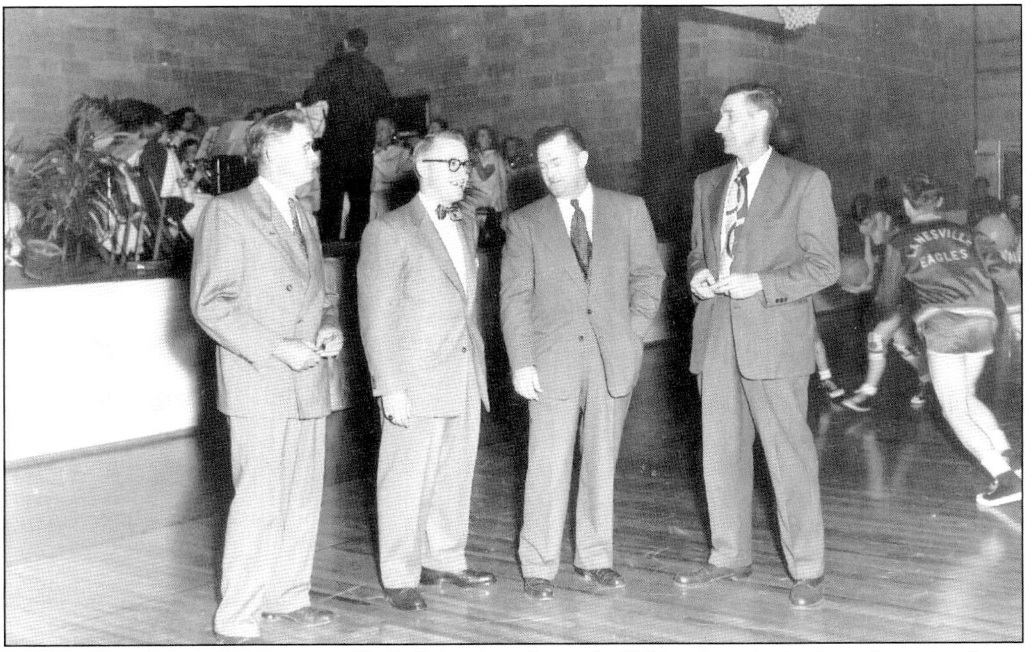

Before a big game at Georgetown High School in the early 1950s, the principals and coaches have a "meeting of the minds." From left to right are Lanesville principal Herman Prage, Georgetown coach Wilbur Richards, Georgetown principal Lawrence Moore, and Lanesville coach George Bickel. This meeting was a common thing before basketball games at the time. Though there were rivalries, many coaches and administrators from competing schools were also very good friends. (Courtesy of the Frederick Porter Griffin Center.)

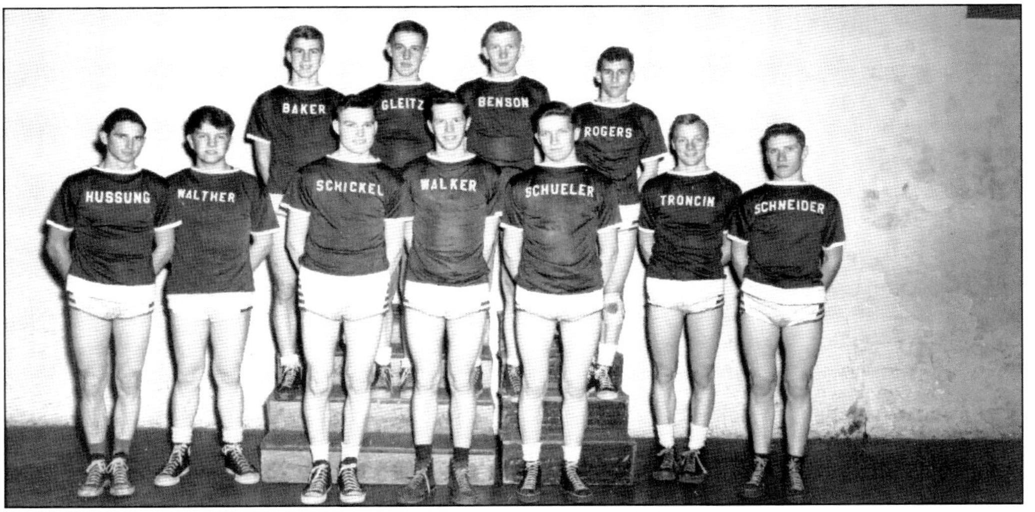

The 1950–1951 Lanesville basketball team won the coveted Harrison County Championship in 1951. Every January, all the high schools in Harrison County played a basketball tournament at Corydon High School. This Lanesville team was not favored to win the tournament, but for a few nights in January, the team put together three victories to win the championship. All the team members are shown here with their names proudly displayed on their warm-up uniforms. The men from that team still talk about being county champions to this day. (Courtesy of Bill Baker.)

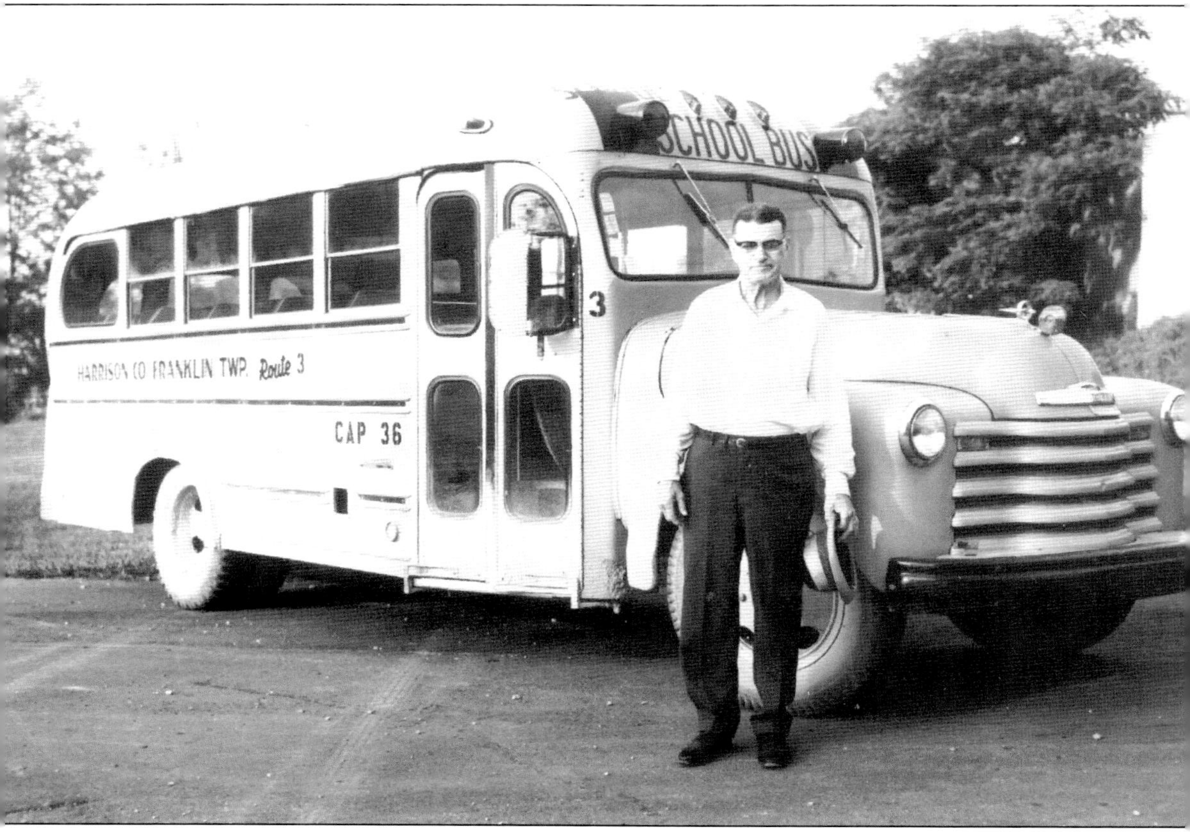

Asa Evans is seen here with his bus, Harrison County Franklin Township Bus No. 3, around the late 1950s. Evans drove school buses for many years for all the schools in Lanesville and Franklin Township. He owned a hardware and implement business in town and a garage at one time as well. He was well known around town and people have many great stories to tell about him. There were between eight and nine bus routes in the school system taking care of Lanesville students. Notice the capacity of 36 students is quite smaller than today's standard bus capacity of 66. (Courtesy of Carolyn Baker.)

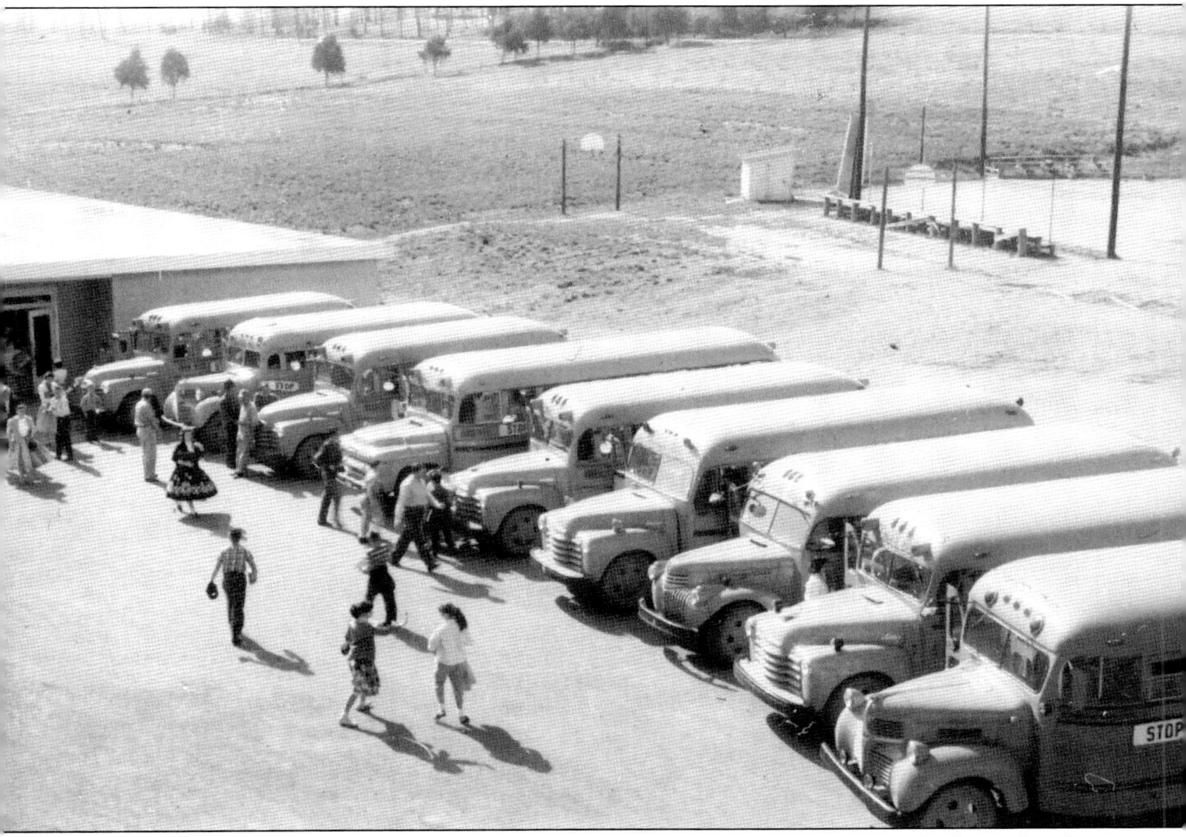

School has let out for the day at Lanesville in this typical 1958 scene showing the buses lined up and ready to take kids home from another grueling day in the classroom. Notice the different styles and makes of buses at that time. The bus drivers owned, maintained, and fueled their own buses and negotiated contracts with the school corporation for payment—also known as contract drivers. This method is still used today in Lanesville and in many Indiana schools. (Courtesy of Parvin Lambertus.)

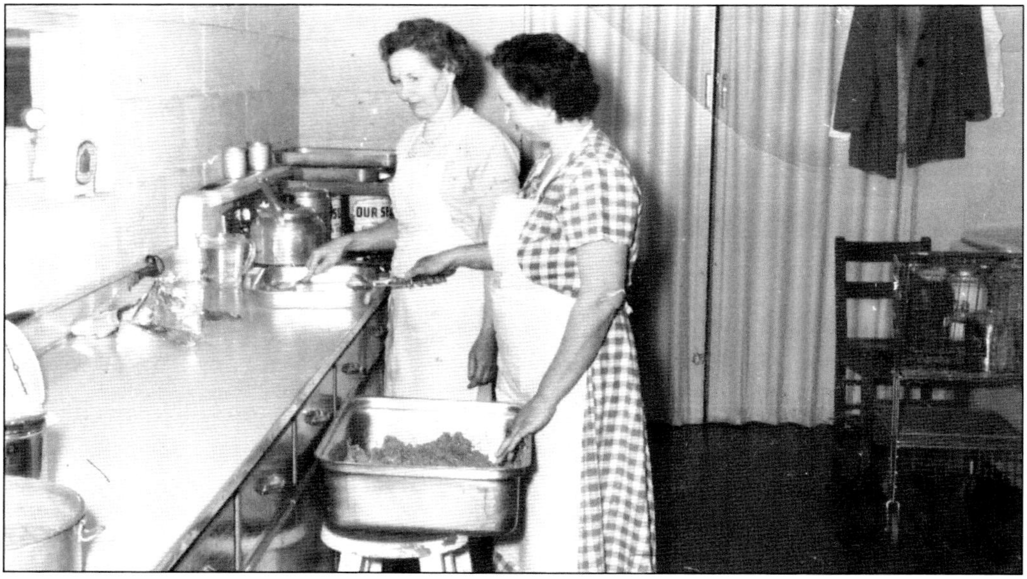

Pauline Cunningham (front) and Wanda Reinhardt (back) prepare meals for students in what was a familiar sight in Lanesville for many years. Before the early 1950s, children brought their lunches to school or walked home to eat lunch. After public schools started serving lunch, Cunningham was the school cafeteria head cook for about 40 years, starting the program in the early 1950s and retiring in the early 1990s. Cunningham and Reinhardt served many lunches over the years, and Cunningham had many other ladies help her as well. (Courtesy of Lennie Reinhardt.)

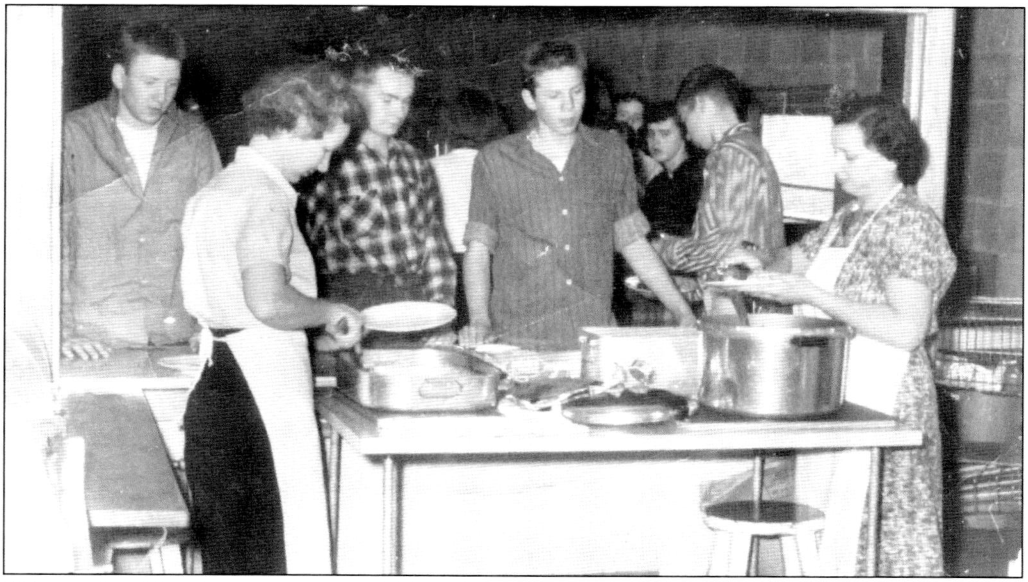

When school lunches became available at Lanesville Schools in the early 1950s, the new 1952 school building featured facilities for a cafeteria. Here, Pauline Cunningham (right) and Wanda Reinhardt (left) serve hungry students, who ate lunch on the "concrete slab" area in the high school gym. When the school was first built, tables and chairs were set on the slab for the dining area. Years later, the dining area was moved to a large room on the opposite side of the gym, a converted classroom, and served the students for many years. (Courtesy of Lennie Reinhardt.)

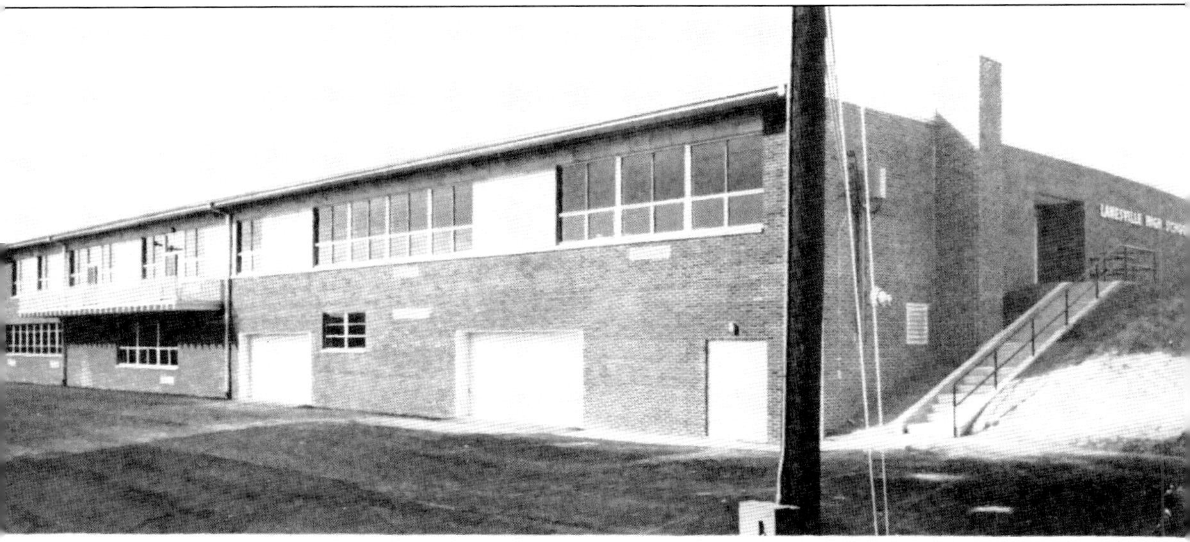

FRANKLIN TOWNSHIP HIGH SCHOOL

Dedication and Open House

Sunday, November 21, 1965 – 2:00 P.M.

This dedication pamphlet was distributed at the opening of the new Franklin Township High School (Lanesville High School) on Sunday, November 21, 1965 at 2:00 p.m. This school was a great improvement over the previous two schools, with the most modern equipment for schools at the time and a greatly expanded number of classrooms. It included an industrial arts room and an elevated band room. The old 1922 school was torn down to make room for the new school, and the old high school became the new elementary school. This school is still used today. In 1969, a junior high wing was added with extra classrooms on the west end of the school. In 1994, when Lanesville became incorporated and was not under the jurisdiction of the township trustee, it officially became Lanesville High School and a school board was elected, becoming the Lanesville Community School Corporation. (Courtesy of Lanesville High School.)

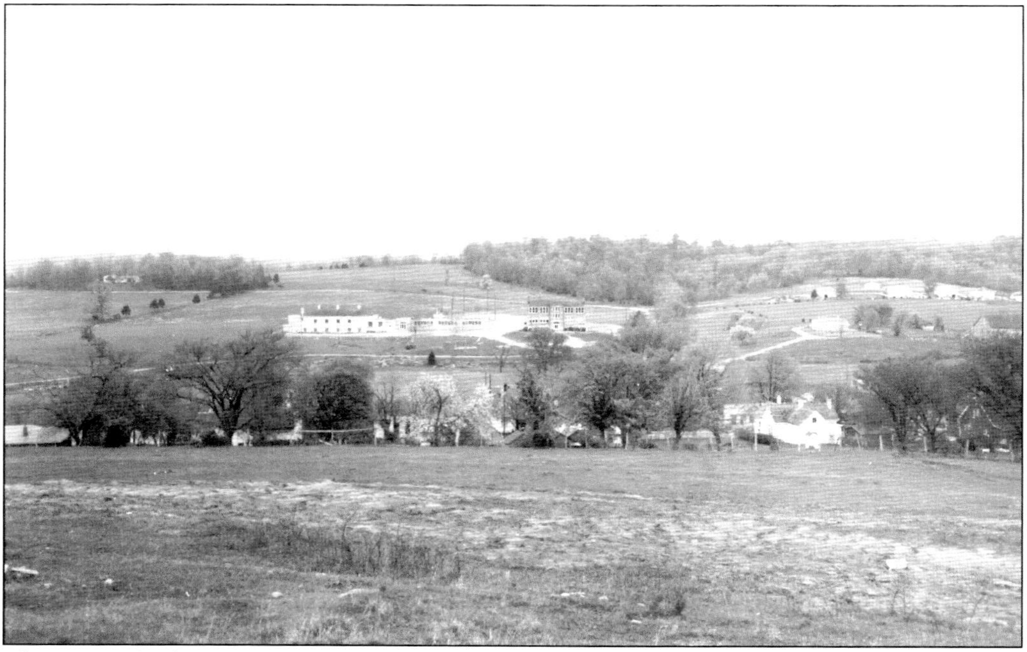

This image, looking north from town, shows the Franklin Township Schools in the mid-1950s. The old high school, which was made into a grade school, is visible, with the new high school just to the left. (Courtesy of Marvin Zabel.)

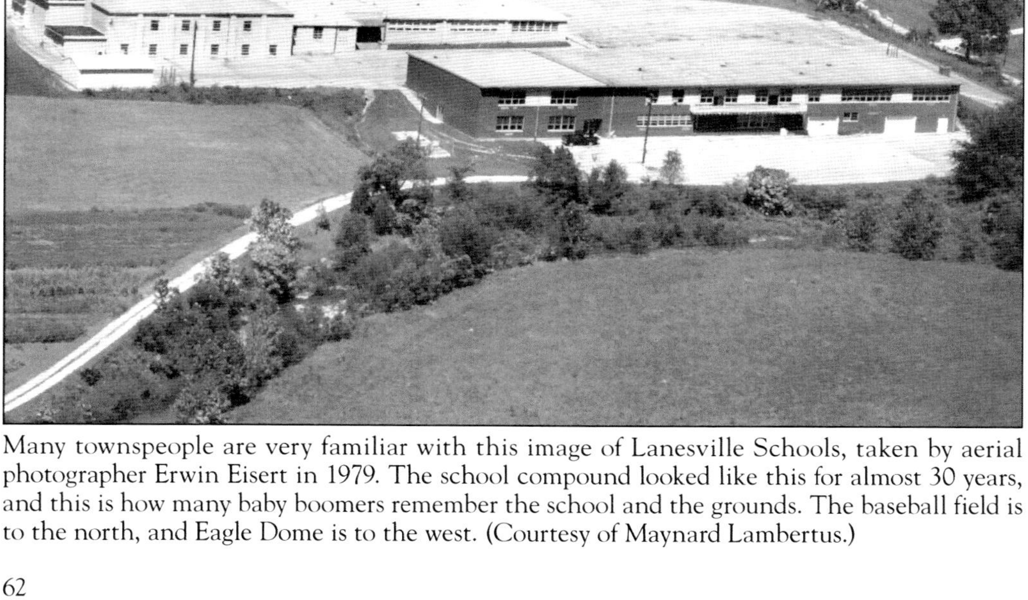

Many townspeople are very familiar with this image of Lanesville Schools, taken by aerial photographer Erwin Eisert in 1979. The school compound looked like this for almost 30 years, and this is how many baby boomers remember the school and the grounds. The baseball field is to the north, and Eagle Dome is to the west. (Courtesy of Maynard Lambertus.)

Three

THE CHURCHES

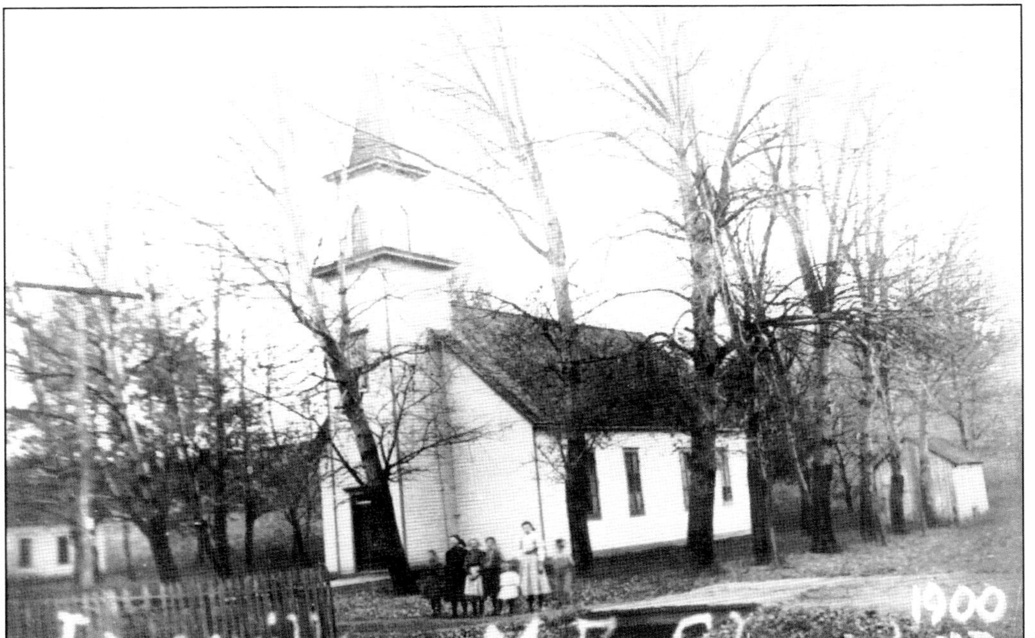

The Lanesville United Methodist Church is pictured in 1900. It was built in 1860 on land deeded to the church trustees by Ed Pennington, one of the founding fathers of the town, in 1859. James Armstrong and Peter Cartwright were two Methodist "circuit riders" who served as the church's first ministers. The small building on the left was the fellowship hall, which was originally St. Paul's Methodist Church near Breckinridge Road, which was abandoned in 1887. It was then purchased by the Franklin Township Grange and moved to the site. The Grange members used the building until 1935, when the church purchased it. The building is still being used today as a fellowship hall. (Courtesy of Carolyn Baker.)

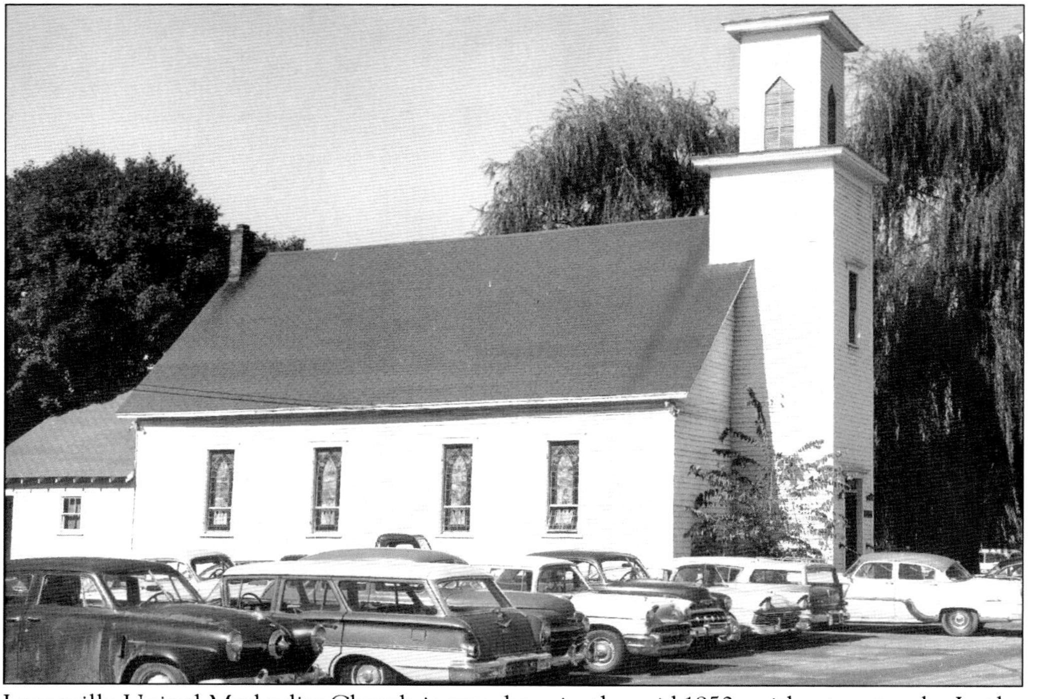

Lanesville United Methodist Church is seen here in the mid-1950s without a steeple. In the 1940s, the bell in the belfry stopped working. Workmen went up to the belfry and found a large amount of rotting and decaying wood in the structure, and it was unsafe to keep the bell or the steeple so both were removed and the belfry was closed off. The church received a new steeple in 2001. (Courtesy of Evelyn McPherson.)

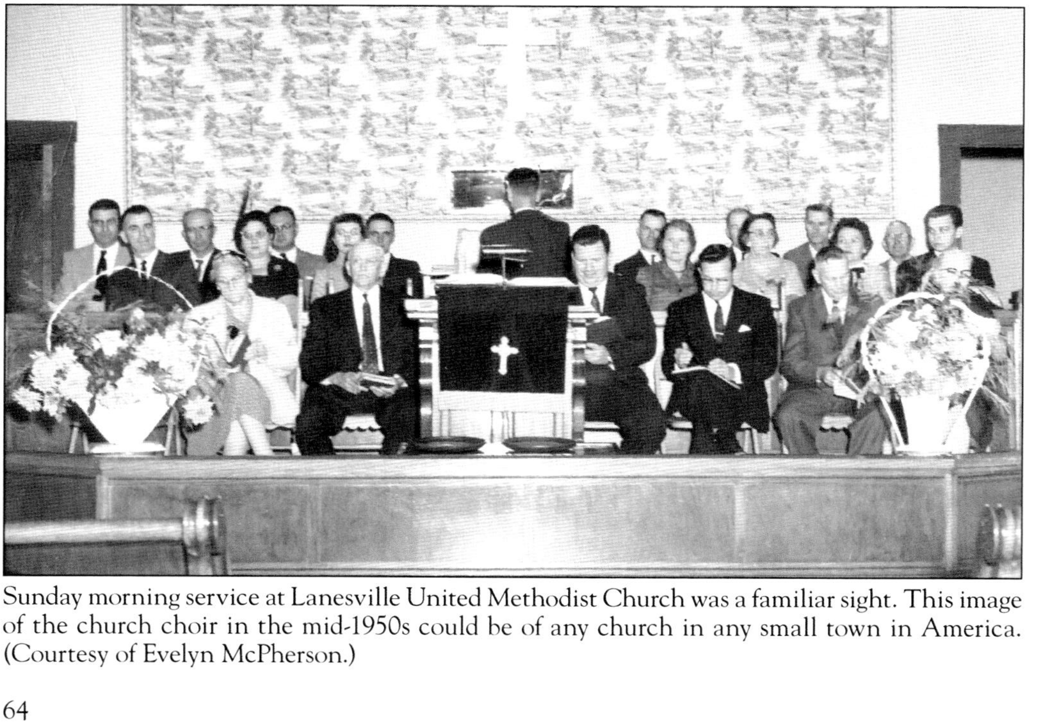

Sunday morning service at Lanesville United Methodist Church was a familiar sight. This image of the church choir in the mid-1950s could be of any church in any small town in America. (Courtesy of Evelyn McPherson.)

St. Peter's Church was founded by a group of six or seven families in south Franklin Township in 1852. This photograph of the congregation was taken in the late 1890s. The "Brick Church," as it was called early on, was built in 1880 and dedicated on May 26, 1881. Rev. Charles Raymond spearheaded the building of the church, which still holds services every Sunday. (Courtesy of St. Peter's Church.)

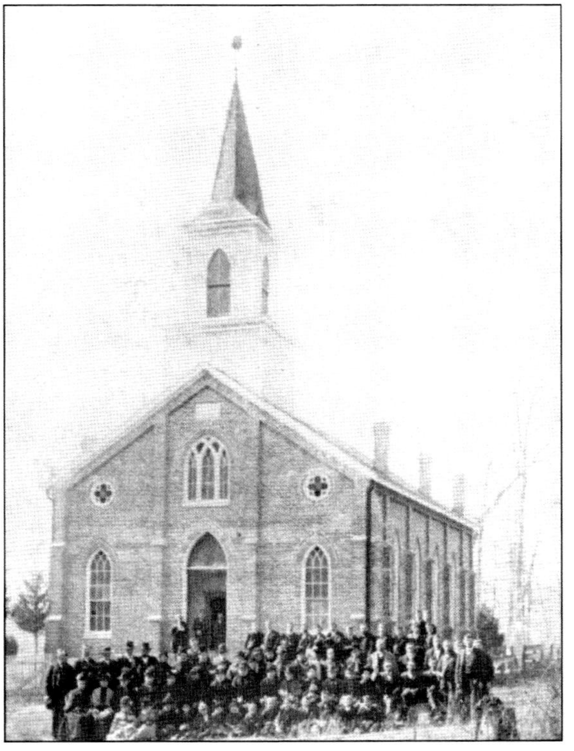

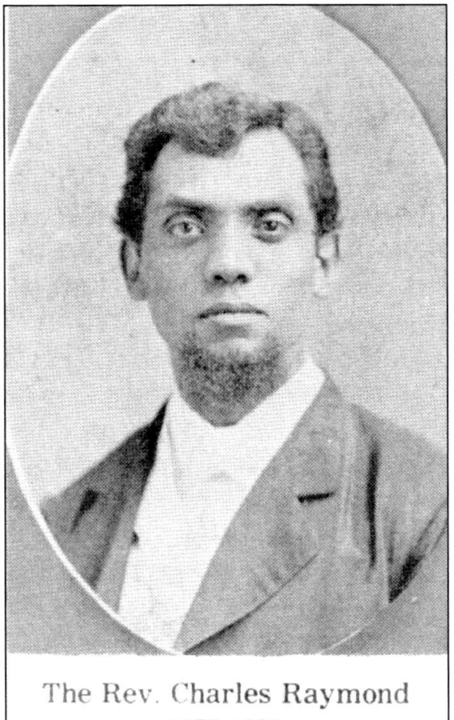

The Rev. Charles Raymond
1877-1881

Rev. Charles Raymond, the minister of St. Peter's Church from 1877 to 1881, is credited with getting the "Brick Church" built. He was remembered as a very good leader and an energetic worker—just the leader the early church needed to build a sanctuary. (Courtesy of St. Peter's Church.)

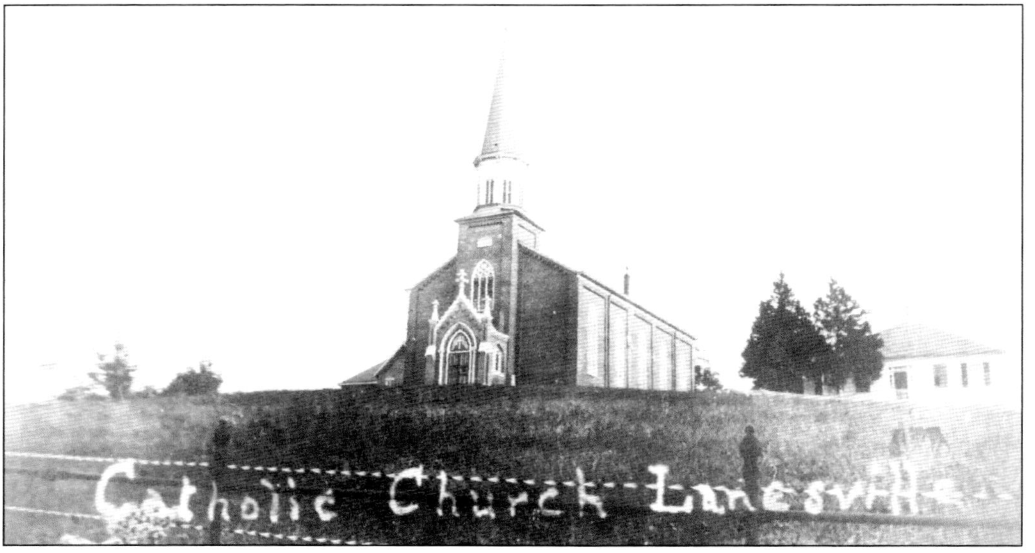

St. Mary's Catholic Church is seen here in the early 1900s during the ministry of Rev. Augustine Peckskamp, who led the church from 1893 to 1921. The church was built high on a hill just south of town in 1860 and stood until 1948. The Sisters' Convent is just to the right, and the school is peaking out of sight directly to the left of the church. Notice the fence going around the property, allowing horses to graze on the hillside. (Courtesy of Marvin Zabel.)

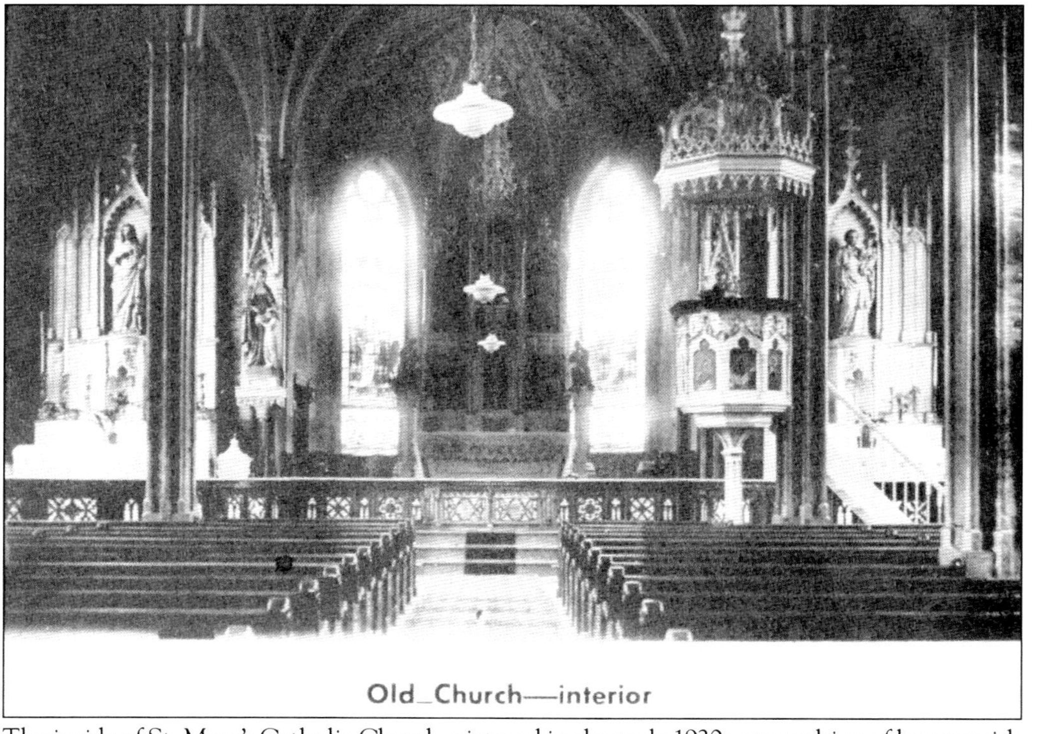

Old_Church—interior

The inside of St. Mary's Catholic Church, pictured in the early 1920s, was a thing of beauty with its hand-carved statues and stained-glass windows. The St. Mary's Parish had much to be proud of in this building. (Courtesy of St. Mary's Church, Lanesville.)

Rev. Clement E. Hunger was pastor at St. Mary's Catholic Church from 1930 to 1962 and is one of the best-known pastors in the church's history. He was the priest at the time of the "Great Fire" on July 30, 1948, which completely gutted the inside of the iconic sanctuary. He is well known for his dedication to his church community and to the church building and its sacred items. While the fire was burning the church, he rescued the Blessed Sacrament from the altar. As he was reentering the church to save the holy vessels, he was restrained by fireman Leonard Jaegers just as the steeple crashed through the roof and to the floor just a few feet from them. No one was hurt, but this act of love and bravery is well remembered in the church community to this day. (Courtesy of St. Mary's Church, Lanesville.)

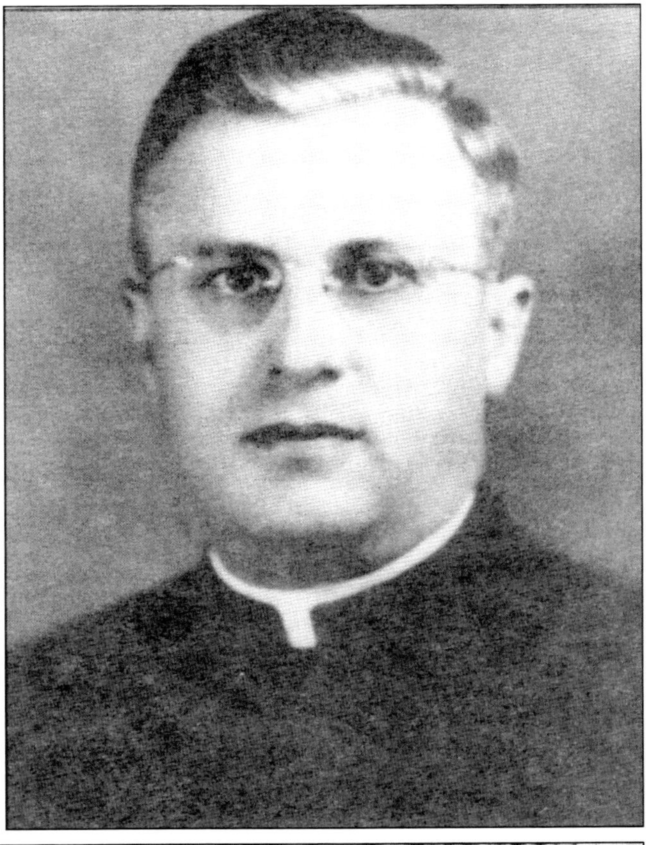

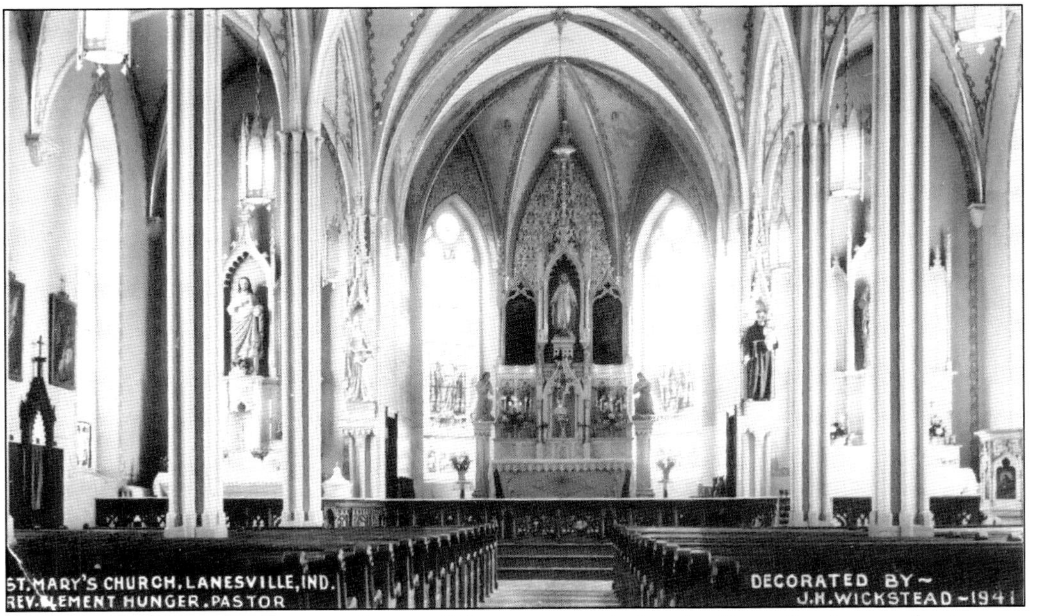

St. Mary's Catholic Church is seen here in 1941, seven years before the Great Fire destroyed it. It was a beautiful sanctuary, and the fire saddened the whole community. (Courtesy of Marvin Zabel.)

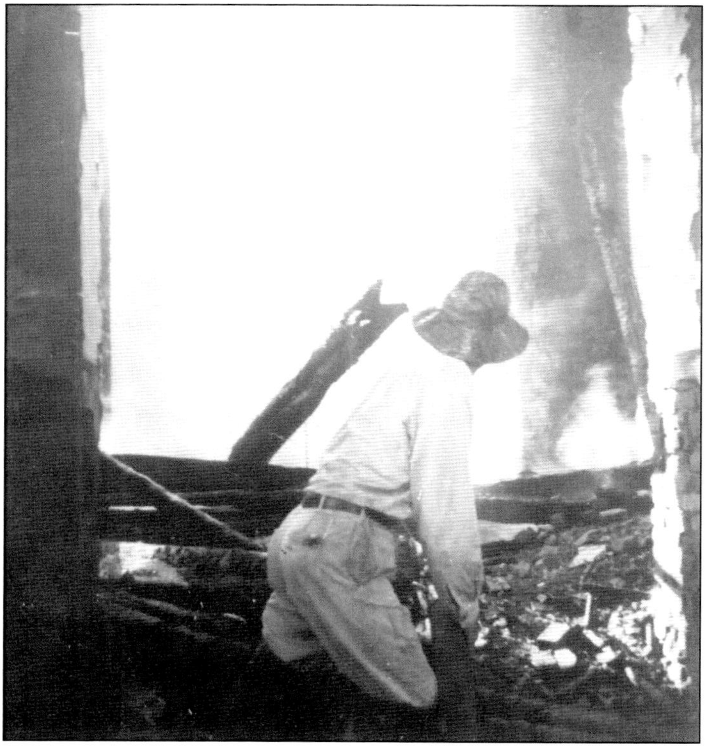

This photograph was taken inside of St. Mary's Catholic Church as fire chief Maurice Kochert went through the smoldering rubble putting out what was left of the fire. All that remained of the church were the four outside walls. (Courtesy of Dolores Dotson.)

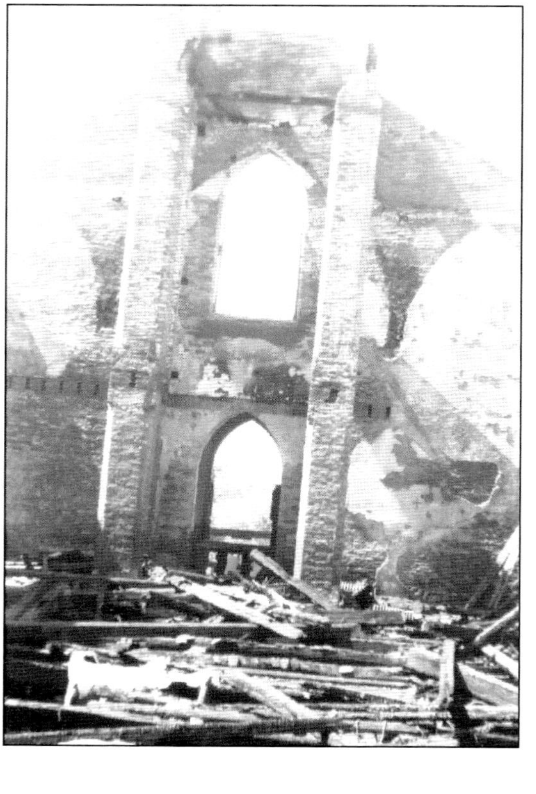

This view shows the inside of the church after the 1948 fire was put out. It was very sad not only for the St. Mary's parishioners but for the Lanesville community as a whole. The people in town who are old enough to remember can recall what they were doing on the day St. Mary's church burned. (Courtesy of Russell Bachman.)

This 1948 aerial view of the burned-out St. Mary's Catholic Church shows the utter destruction of the fire, which started in the steeple tower after lightning struck it during a summer storm. The fire went undetected for several hours. By the time firemen saw the fire, it was too late—the entire interior of the church was engulfed and nothing could be done to stop it. (Courtesy of Marvin Zabel.)

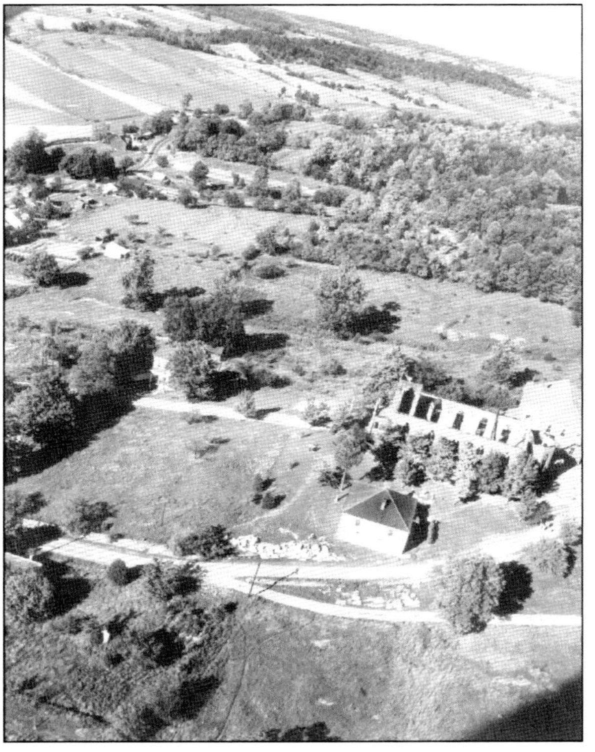

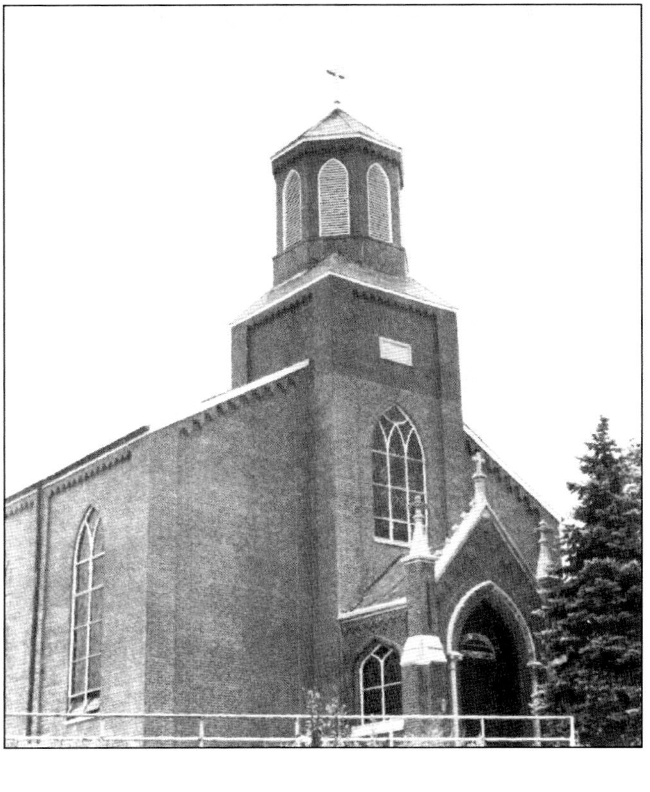

It took 20 months and $200,000 to build a new St. Mary's Catholic Church, seen here in 1950. This building is still standing and is a viable part of the Lanesville community today. (Courtesy of St. Mary's Church, Lanesville.)

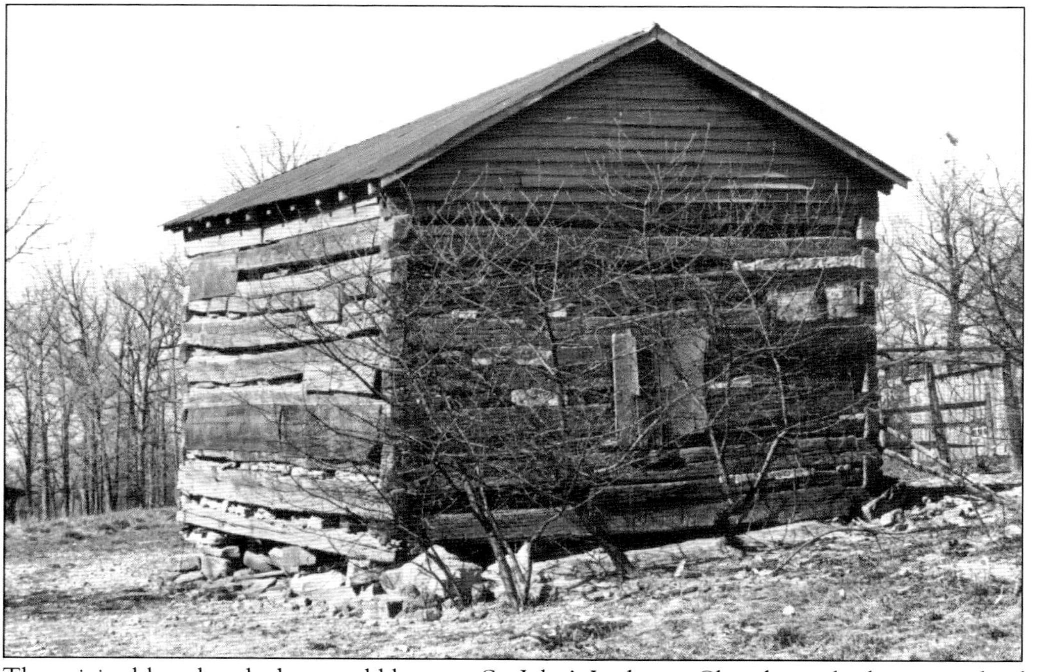

The original log church that would become St. John's Lutheran Church was built just south of Lanesville in 1846 to house the worshippers who settled in the area in the 1830s and 1840s. Many familiar local names, including Zollman, Blank, Voelker, Reinhardt, and Woertz, came from Mensfelden, Germany, and this original church was on the Lloyd Biel farm. The parishioners remained in this building until 1870, when they built a larger, beautifully ornate structure a few miles to the east. In 1984–1985, church preservationists dismantled and moved the log church across the road from St. John's. (Courtesy of Parvin Lambertus.)

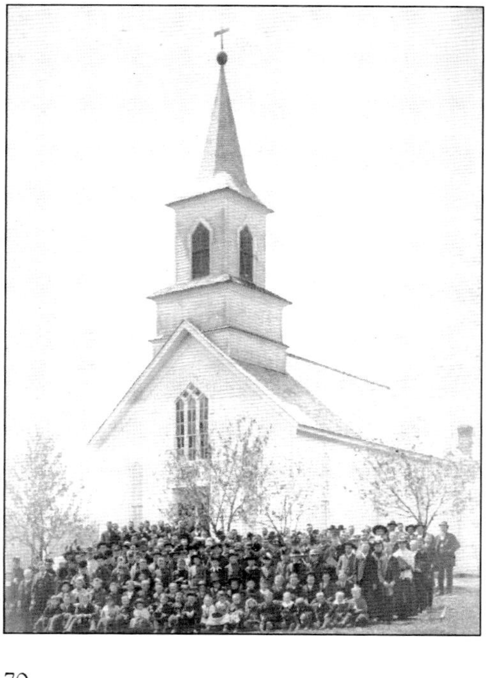

St. John's Lutheran Church is pictured in 1897. As evident by the number of people in front of the church, the congregation once housed in the small confines of the log church grew to be very large. Today, the church still looks very much like it does in this image, although an addition in back was constructed in 1903. The congregation has always played an active role in the Lanesville community and will for years to come. (Courtesy of Parvin Lambertus.)

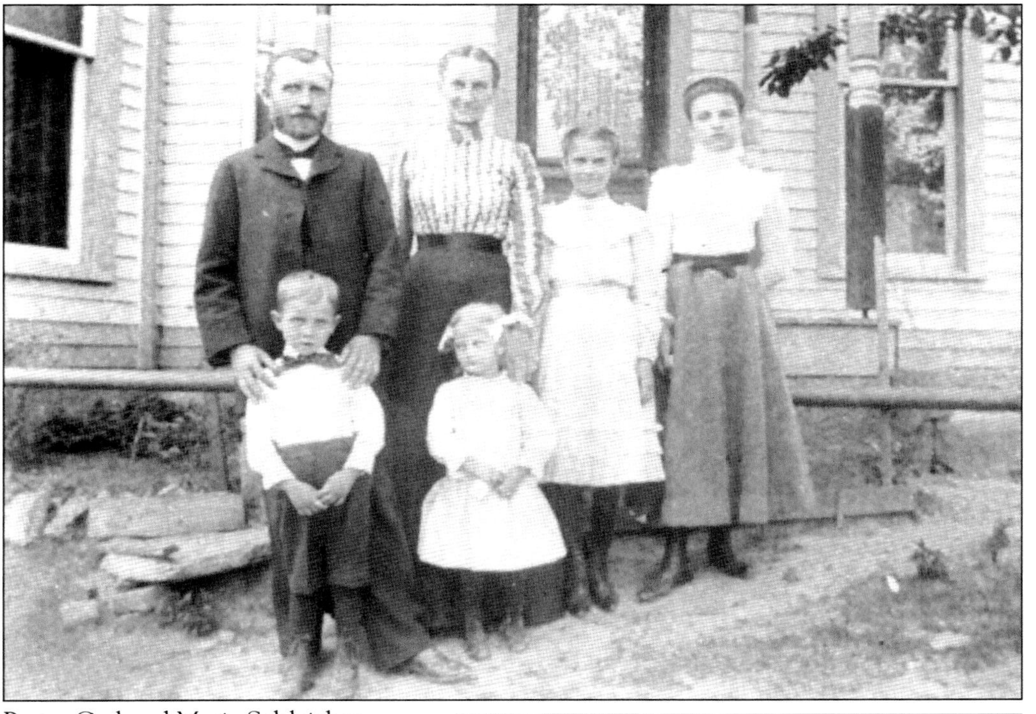

Pastor Carl and Maria Schleicher and their family pose in front of the parsonage in 1907. Son Edwin and daughter Hilda are in the front, and daughters Olga and Clara are in the rear. Edwin died at the age of 13 and is buried in the St. John's Lutheran Church cemetery. Reverend Schleicher served the St. John's congregation longer than any other pastor—from 1893 to 1919. (Courtesy of Parvin Lambertus.)

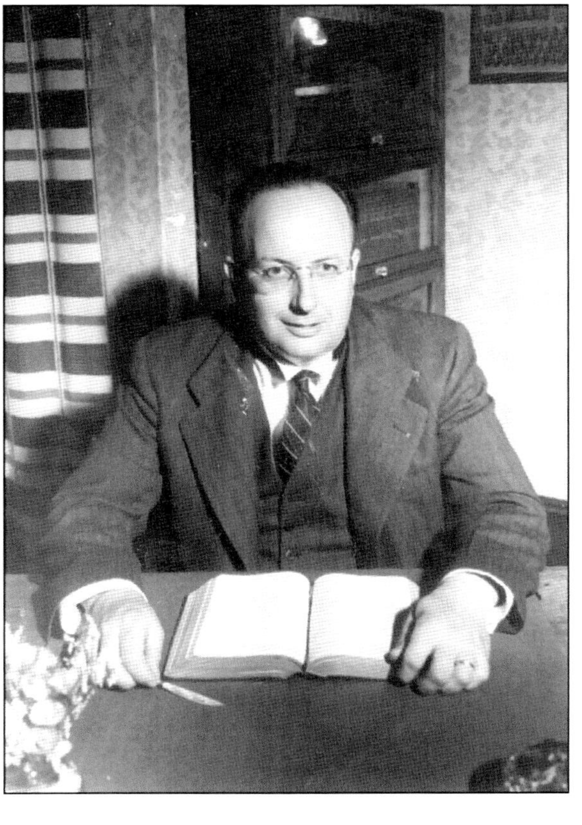

Rev. Omar Rau, seen here, was pastor at St. John's Lutheran Church from 1942 to 1955. He was a well-known figure in the Lanesville community and served a long stint as pastor at the church. In addition to being a minister, Reverend Rau was a gardener, woodworker, and groundskeeper. He was very active in the church community and will always be remembered with great love and respect. (Courtesy of Carolyn Walther.)

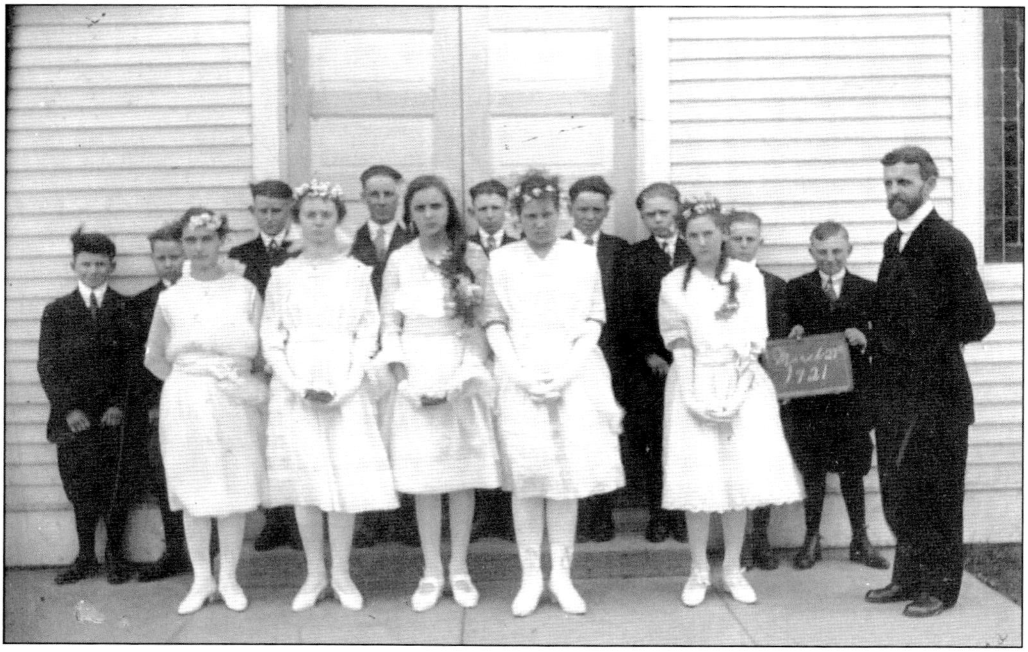

The Confirmation class at St. John's Lutheran is seen here in 1921. At the age of 13, children go through a training and study of the Lutheran church. When they complete the course of study, they are confirmed to be members of the Lutheran church. Pastor Otto Schumm, seen here, was pastor from 1919 to 1923. He conducted the training and confirmed these young folks into the Lutheran faith. (Courtesy of Carolyn Voelker.)

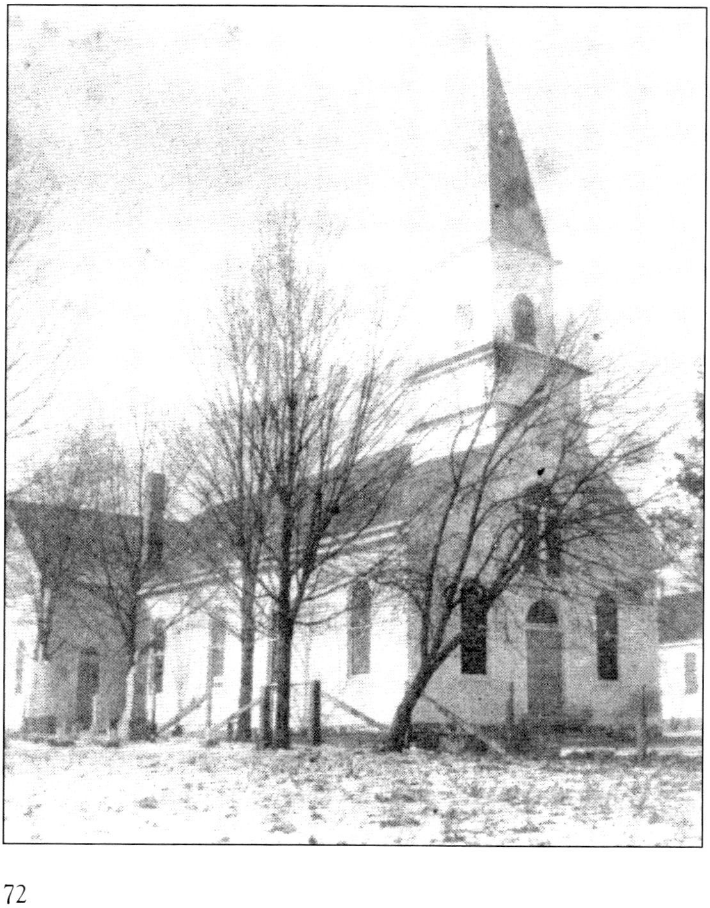

St. John's Lutheran Church stands majestically against a cold winter day in 1922. The 1903 rear addition is seen here. (Courtesy of Parvin Lambertus.)

Pfrimmer's Chapel United Methodist Church, seen here around the 1950s or 1960s, was first started by John George Pfrimmer in 1812, making it the oldest United Brethren church in Indiana. In 1820, it organized the first Sunday school west of the Allegheny Mountains. The church used today was built in 1866 and remodeled in 1927. It started from a small log structure like many of the other churches in the township and still stands as a vibrant part of the spiritual community. (Courtesy of Pfrimmer's Chapel.)

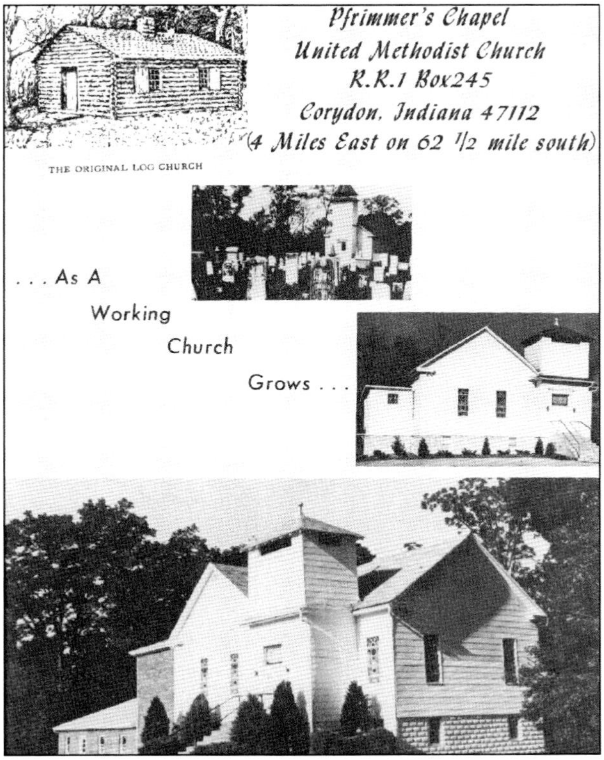

The large congregation of Pfrimmer's Chapel poses in front of the church in the early 1900s. (Courtesy of Pfrimmer's Chapel.)

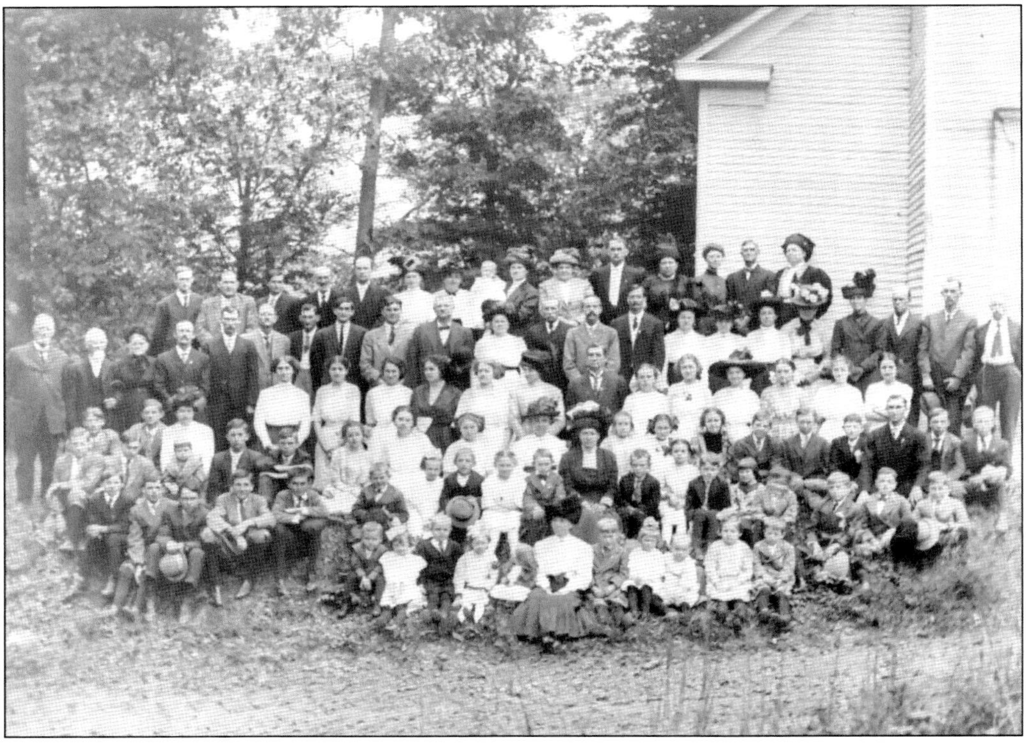

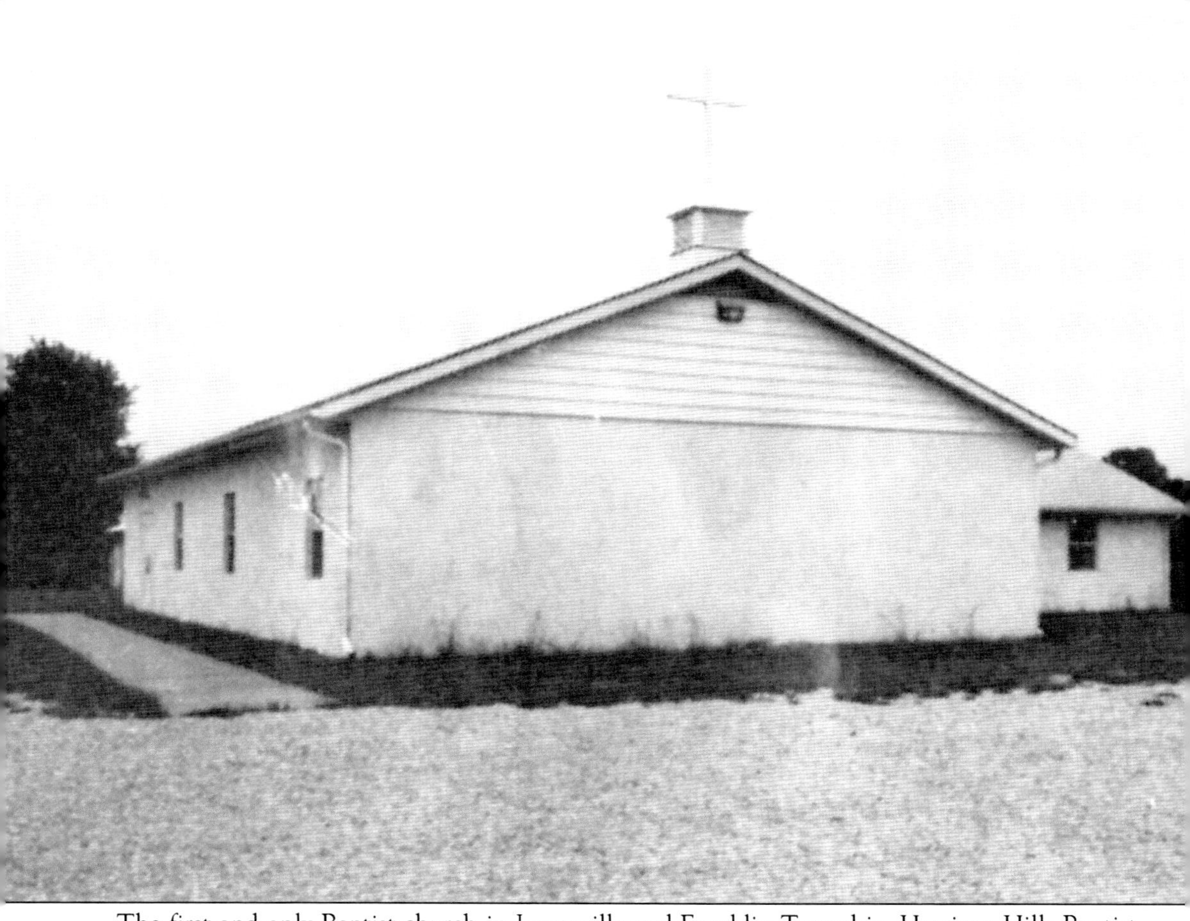

The first and only Baptist church in Lanesville and Franklin Township, Harrison Hills Baptist Church, about two miles north of Lanesville, is seen here in 1975, the year it was dedicated by a small group coming from Highland Baptist Church in Edwardsville. Church members began meeting in the basements of members' homes until they could purchase land and build a church. Harrison Hills is still going strong today, nearly 40 years after its inception. (Courtesy of Gayle Hack.)

Four

The Farms and the Farmers

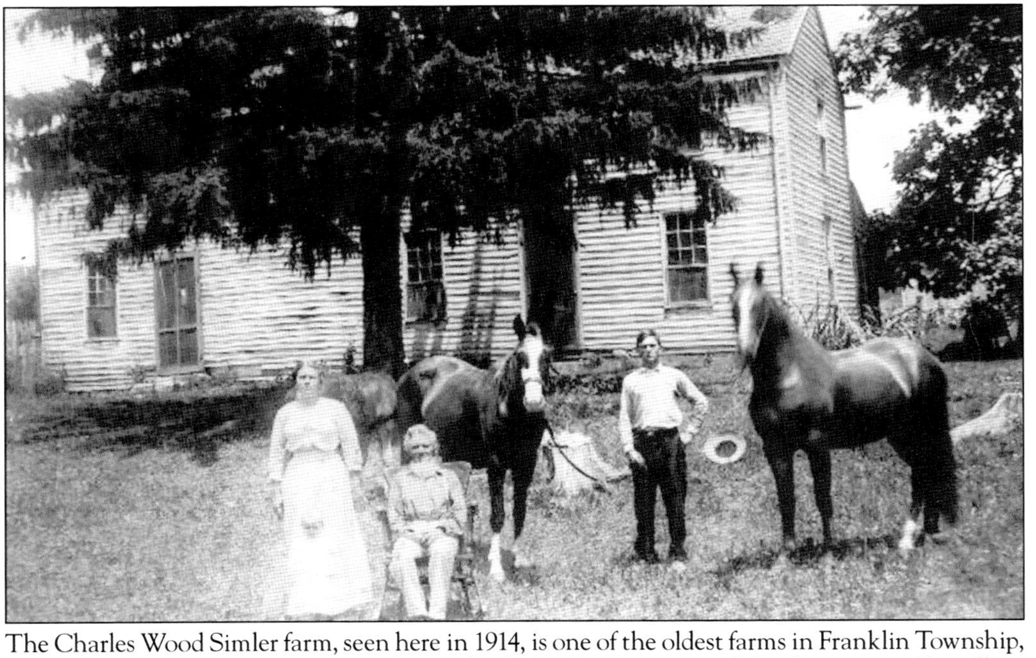

The Charles Wood Simler farm, seen here in 1914, is one of the oldest farms in Franklin Township, on the corner of Old Salem and Tandy Roads. Philip Gresham owned the farm originally, selling it to David Wood Gresham in 1851. Mary Elizabeth Gresham married John "Jasper" Simler, a schoolteacher and farmer, in 1881. Their son Charles Wood Simler was born in 1889. From left to right, the family included Eldora Evans Simler, young Wilma Simler Miller, John "Jasper" Simler, and Charles Wood Simler. The horses were named Queen (left) and Tom (right). The farm was in the Simler family for seven generations. (Courtesy of Jeanette Nolan.)

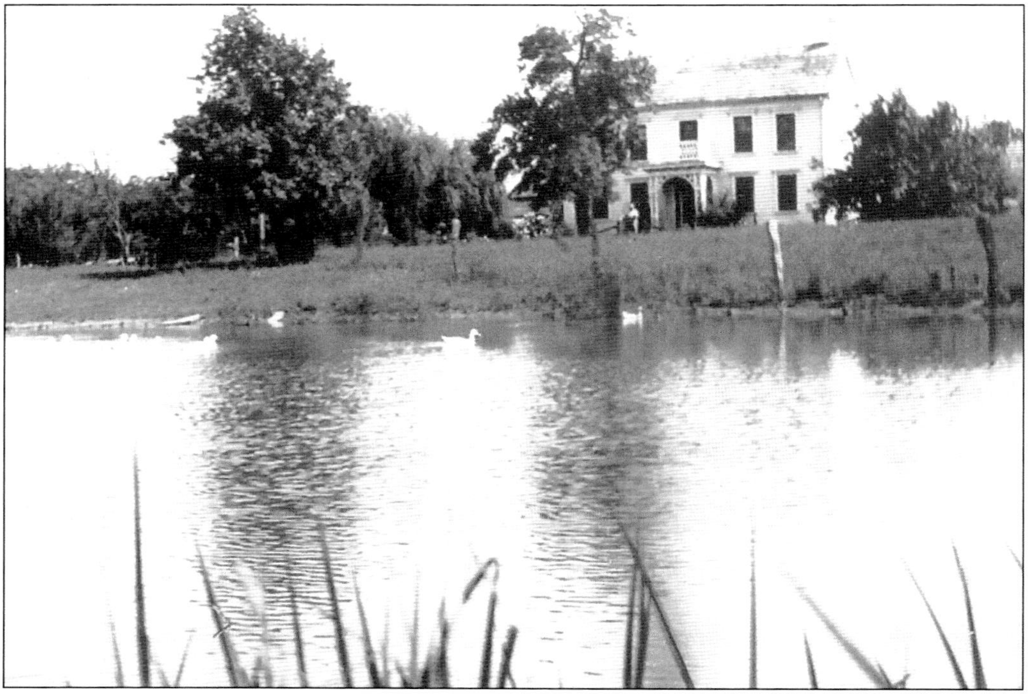

The Ed Richert farm, seen here in 1920, sits next to the Ben Cunningham farm in south Franklin Township on St. Peter's Church Road. Edgar Richert, Ed's father, died in a sawmill accident on the farm. This farmhouse is gone today but is now the site of the Turtle Run Winery. (Courtesy of Virgil Leffler.)

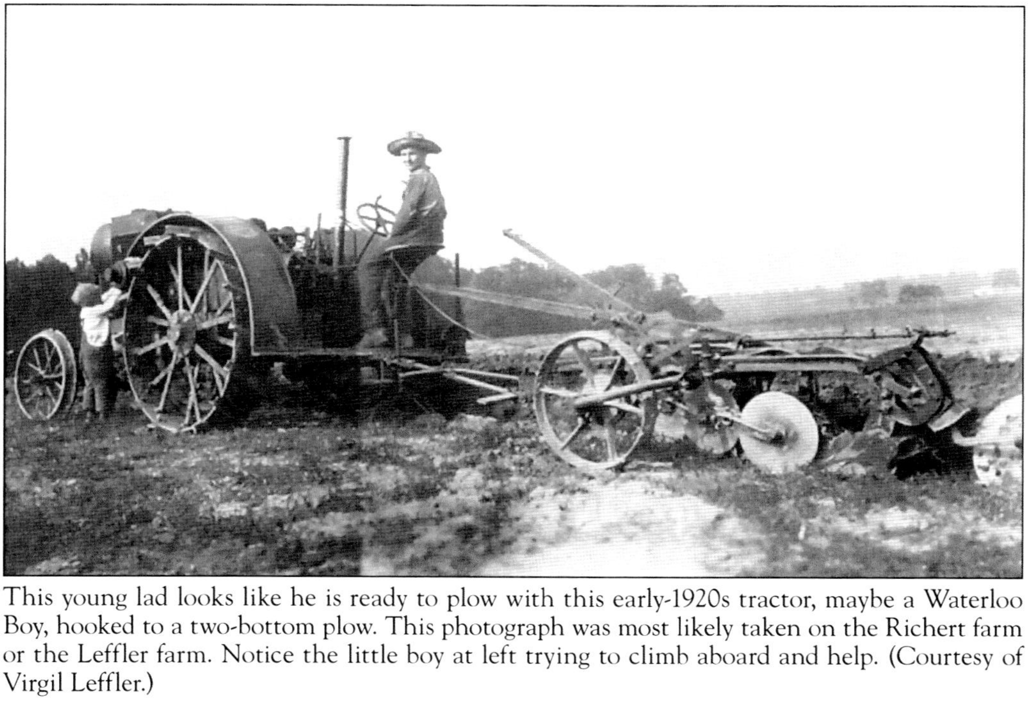

This young lad looks like he is ready to plow with this early-1920s tractor, maybe a Waterloo Boy, hooked to a two-bottom plow. This photograph was most likely taken on the Richert farm or the Leffler farm. Notice the little boy at left trying to climb aboard and help. (Courtesy of Virgil Leffler.)

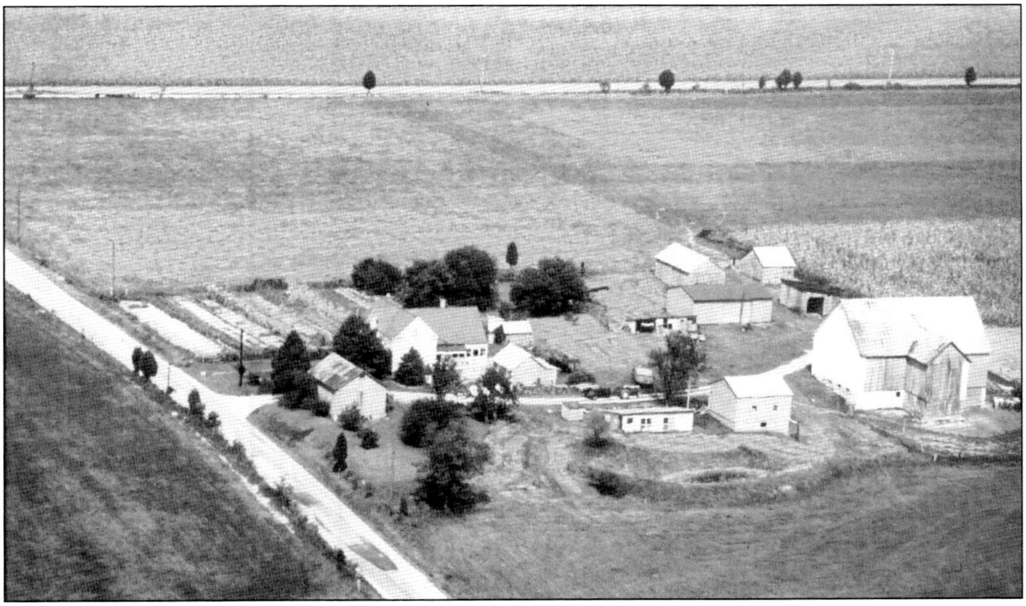

The Virgil Leffler farm, shown here in 1978, has not changed very much since William and Zelma Leffler owned the farm. William Leffler bought the farm from Ed Richert when he married Zelma Richert, Ed's daughter. It is still farmed by the Leffler family today. The white building next to the road was a store and post office for the small entity of Utan, Indiana, around 1896. The building still stands today with a "Utan 1896" sign hanging on the side. (Courtesy of Erwin Eisert Aerial Photographs.)

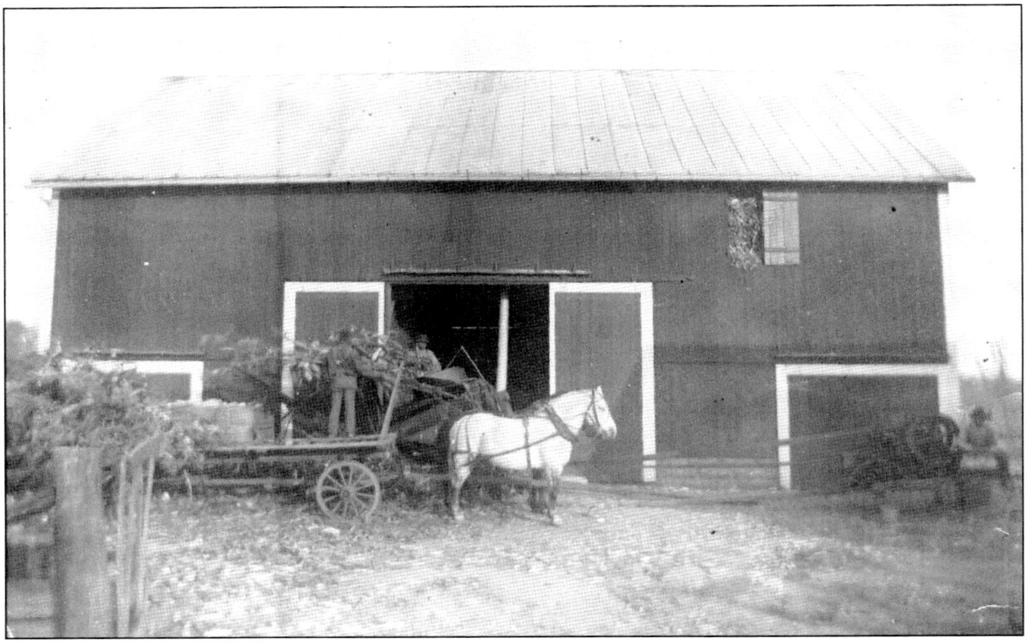

Farmers shred corn on the Edwin Lieber farm—now the Sherry Ott Turner farm—in 1929. This machine was the predecessor to the corn picker. Notice how calmly the big white horse stands while this very loud machine runs the corn shredder. (Courtesy of Carolyn Voelker.)

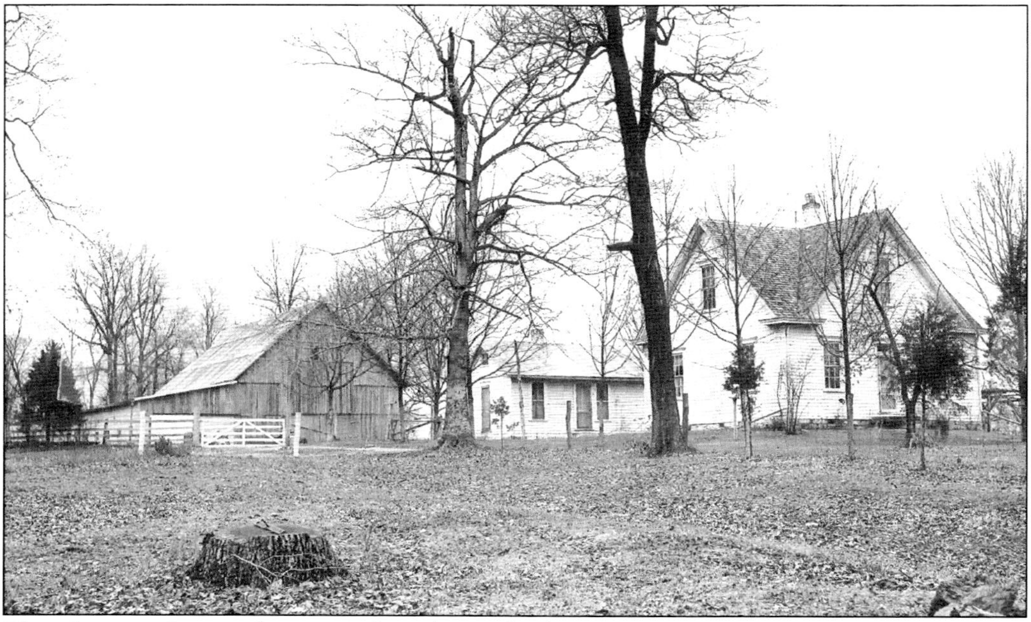

This photograph was taken in 1945 on the Paul Schneider farm in south Franklin, once owned by Conrad "Coonie" Richert. The farm was passed down to Conrad's son Robert who sold it to Oscar Schneider in 1937. Oscar then sold the 126 acres, farm buildings, and house to Paul Schneider in 1944 for $5,500. Paul Schneider still lives there today, and the land is still being farmed. (Courtesy of Joann Rakestraw.)

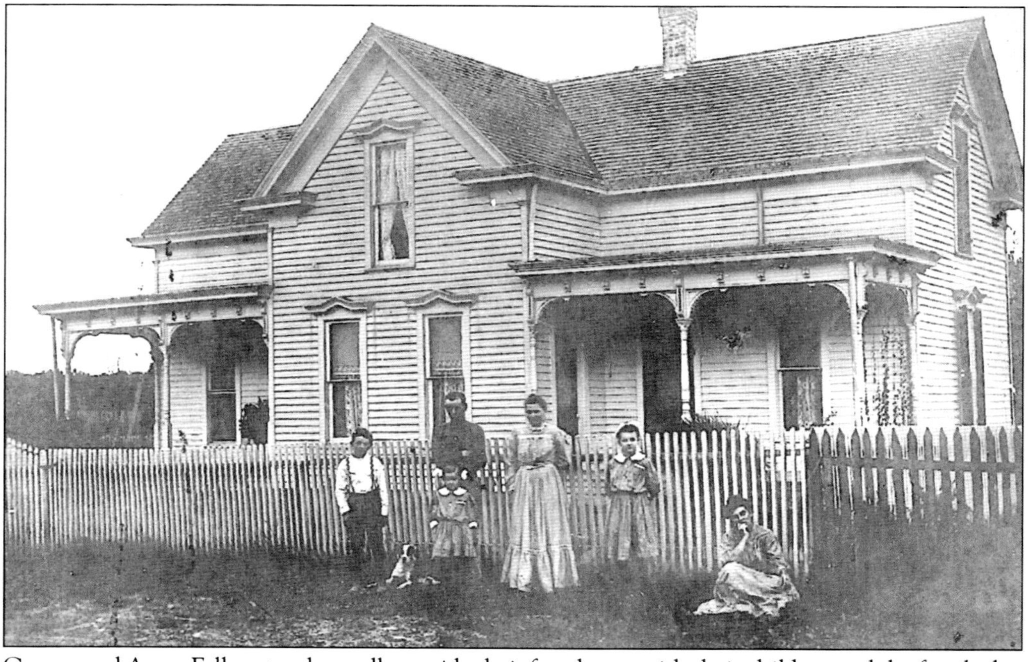

George and Anna Felker stand proudly outside their farmhouse with their children and the family dog in the late 1890s or early 1900s. The farm was later the Ben and Pauline (Felker) Cunningham farm. The house still stands today and has not changed very much. (Courtesy of Blake Cromwell.)

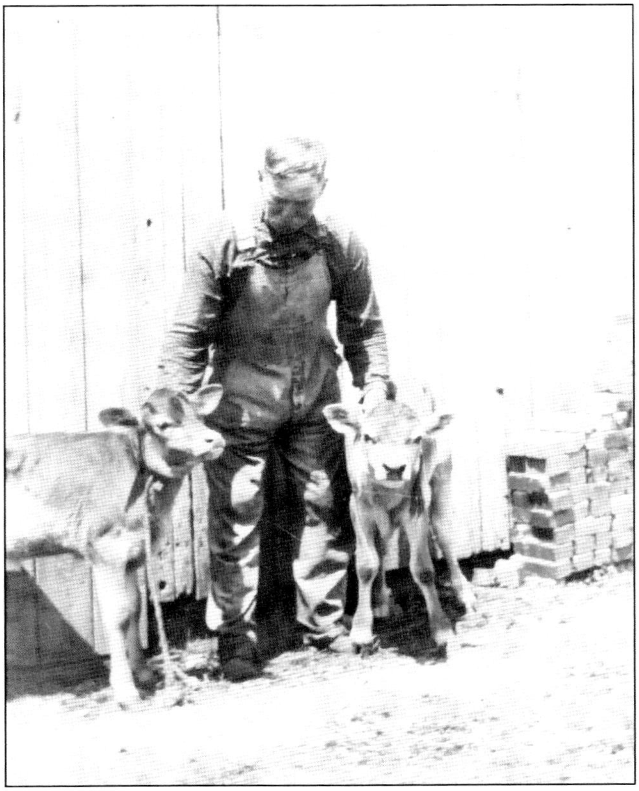

This prize set of Jersey calves was a big deal on the George Felker farm in 1904. The twin calves were worth showing off. (Courtesy of Blake Cromwell.)

This snowy scene was photographed on the Edward P. Walther farm in the mid-1900s. The farm is on St. John's Road south of the intersection with Hess Jawtak Road and across from the Maurice Lieber farm. Notice the split-rail fence down the lane, a common style at the time. (Courtesy of Sharon Gleitz.)

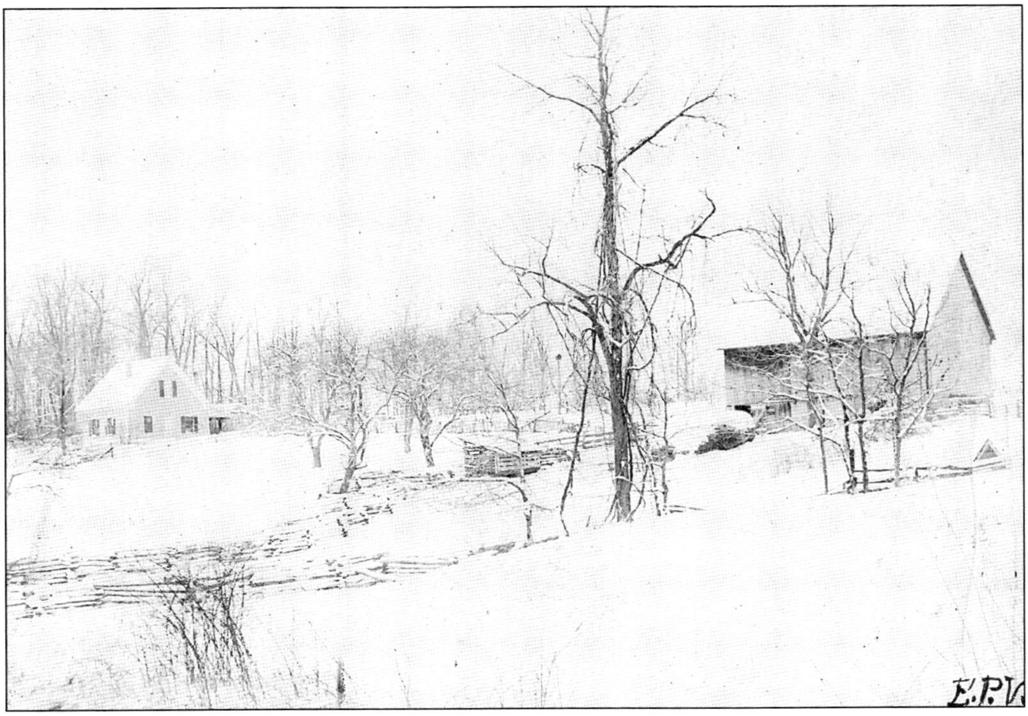

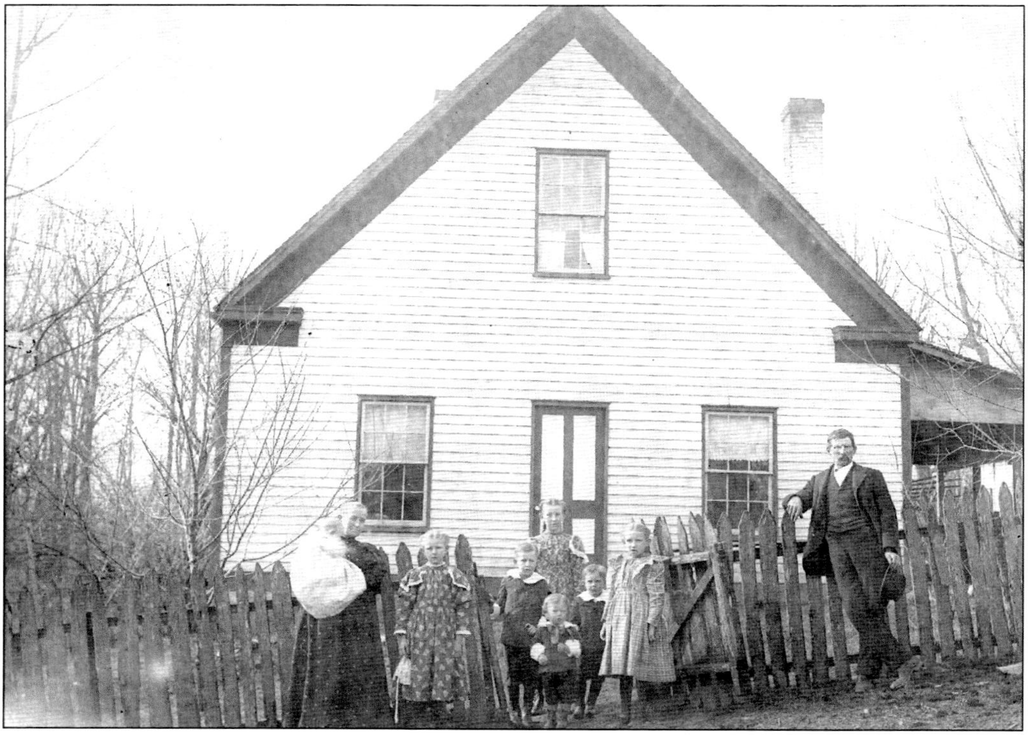

This up-close image of the Edward P. Walther farmhouse was taken in 1902. The family included, from left to right, Katherine (Green) Walther holding baby Edmund, Amelia, Loreena, Emile, Robert, Louie, Gussie, and Edward P. Walther, who died not long after this photograph was taken. (Courtesy of Carolyn Voelker.)

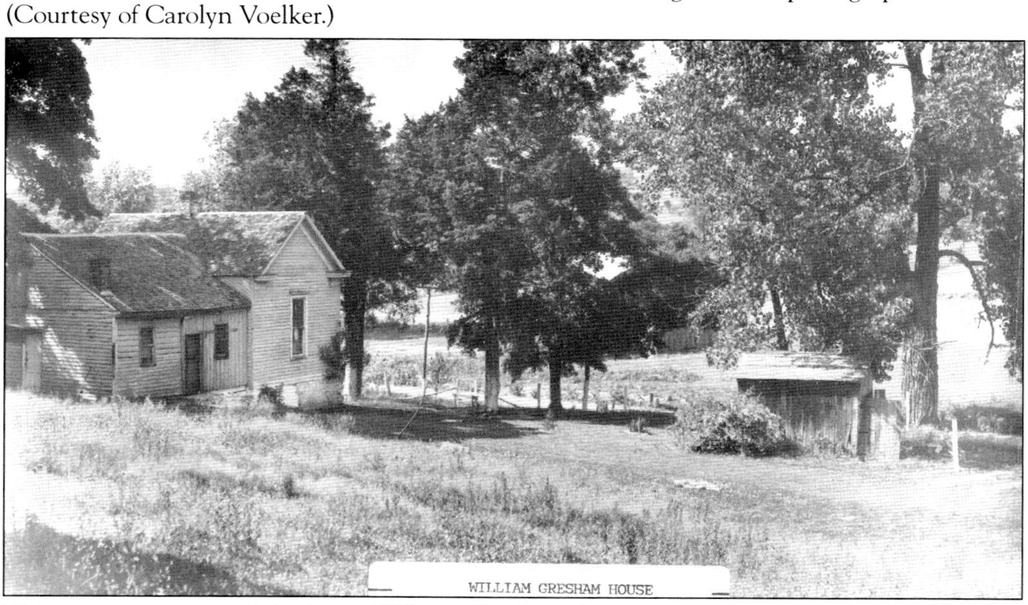

This house was part of the large William Gresham farm just a mile south of Lanesville that William Gresham bought in 1825. The homestead sat across the road from this house on what is now the Cletus Zollman farm. (Courtesy of Porter Griffin Library.)

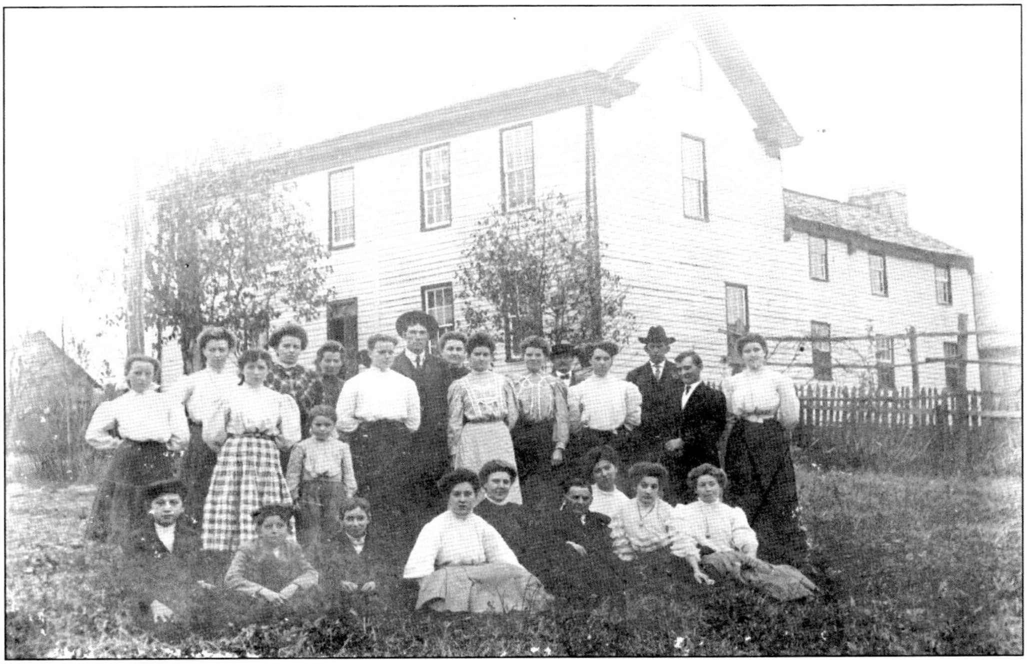

Several members of the Voelker family pose for a group photograph in front of the Albert Bauer farm in the early 1900s. Notice the impressive size of the house, which sat just south of St. John's Lutheran Church. Annetta and Frank Price live on the property today. (Courtesy of Carolyn Voelker.)

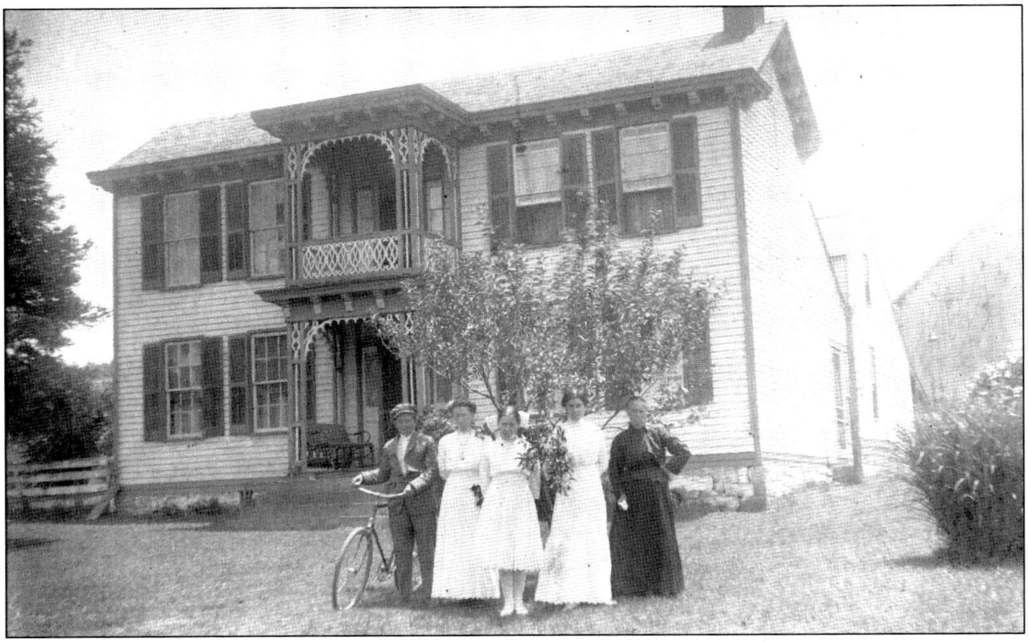

The John Philip Zollman home, seen here in the early 1900s, was the original structure on what would become the Oscar Voelker farm, just west of Lanesville. Longtime resident Francis Zollman was born in this house in 1923. His father, Herman Zollman, was also born in the house. (Courtesy of Carolyn Voelker.)

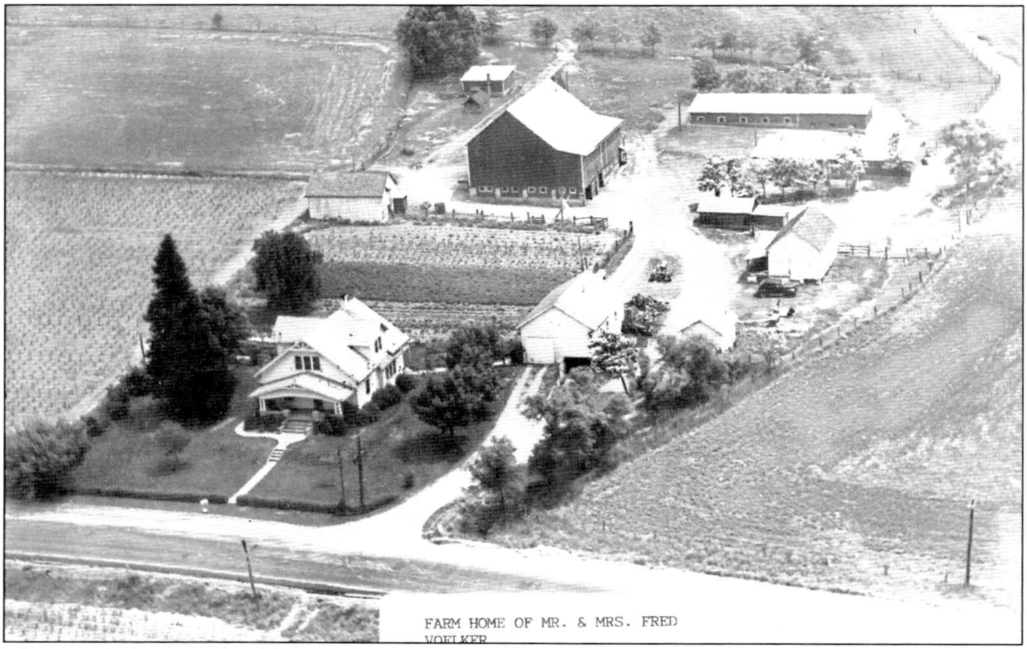

This aerial photograph of the Voelker farm was taken in the early 1940s. The house design came from a Sears and Roebuck catalog and was slightly modified. Fred (Fried) and Anna (Zollman) Voelker moved onto the Zollman place in the early 1930s and had this house built in 1934. Their son, Oscar Voelker purchased the farm in 1951, and it is still lived in today by Oscar's daughter, Carolyn. The barn and many of the buildings look very much the same. (Courtesy of Carolyn Voelker.)

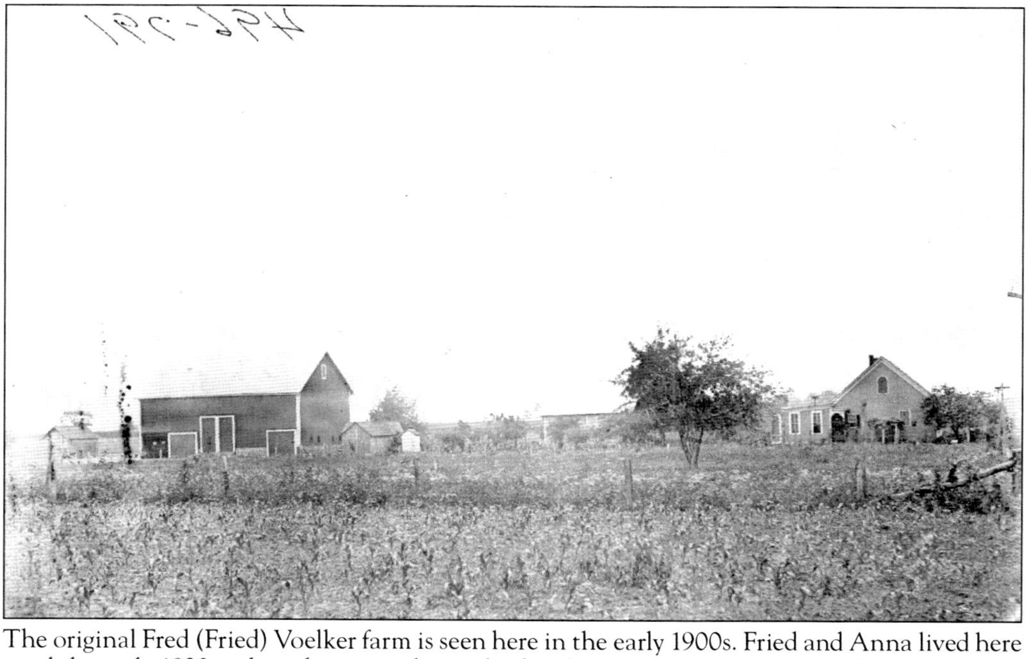

The original Fred (Fried) Voelker farm is seen here in the early 1900s. Fried and Anna lived here until the early 1930s, when they moved into the farmhouse pictured at the top of this page. This is now Virgil Jawtak's farm, just south of Lanesville. (Courtesy of Carolyn Voelker.)

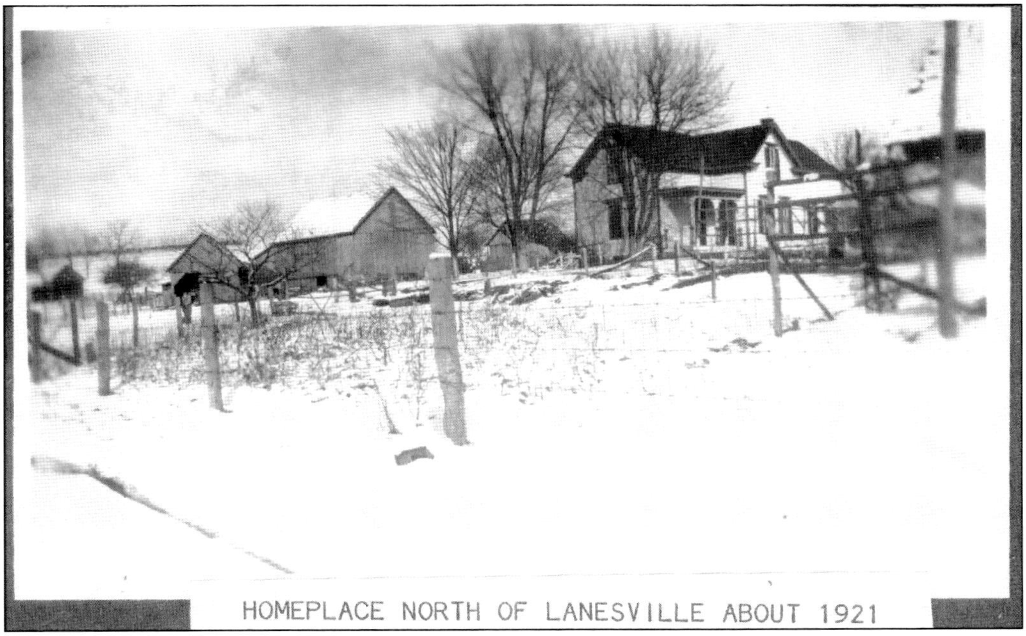

George and Anna (Gehlbach) Lambertus married in 1898 and lived on this farm, seen here in 1921, on Lazy Creek Road just north of Lanesville. It is farmed by Larry Eisert, whose father, Willard Eisert, and mother, Margaret (Lambertus) Eisert, took over the farm in 1946. (Courtesy of Parvin Lambertus.)

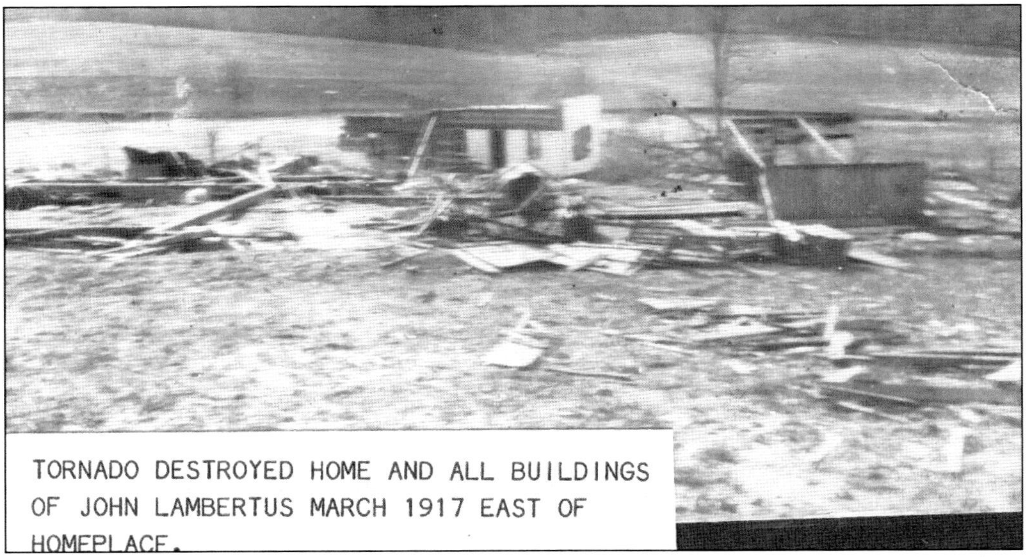

John Lambertus owned this farm just east of his brother George's farm on Lazy Creek Road. In March 1917, while attending his mother's funeral at St. John's Lutheran Church about five miles away, a tornado hit just north of Lanesville, ripping through the valley and destroying John Lambertus's home, barn, and outbuildings. A cake was left sitting on a cake stand on the kitchen table by a neighbor for after the funeral. When John returned home, he found his house and farm completely destroyed but the untouched cake still sitting on the cake stand on the kitchen table. (Courtesy of Parvin Lambertus.)

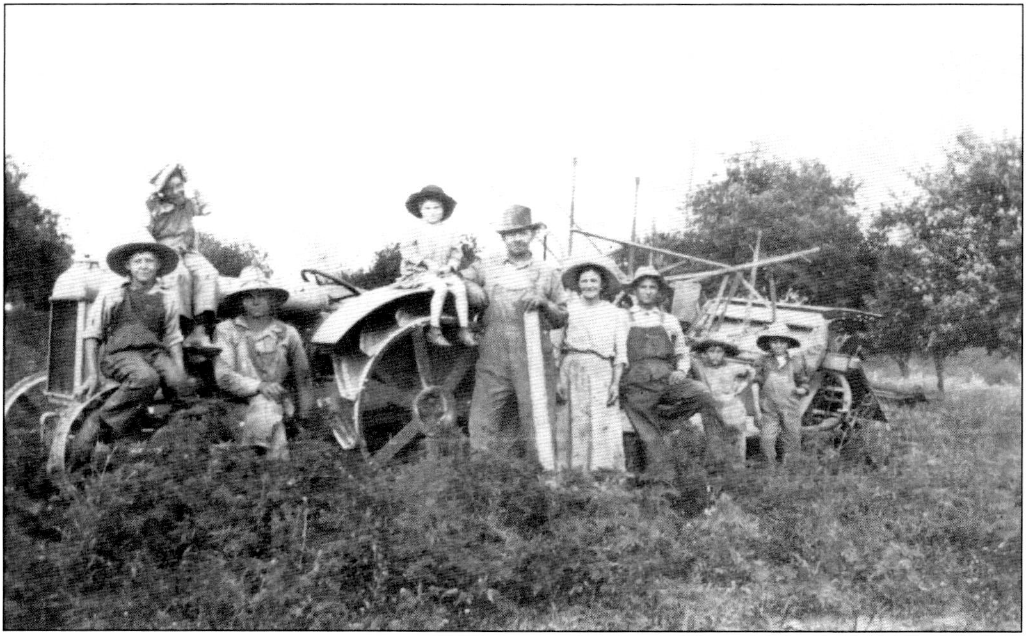

The Lambertus family cuts wheat on their farm in 1923. They are, from left to right, George, Louis, Edwin, Margaret, Grandpa George, Grandma Anna, Leonard Gehlbach, son Louis, and unidentified. They are standing in front of a binder that was pulled by their old Fordson tractor. (Courtesy of Parvin Lambertus.)

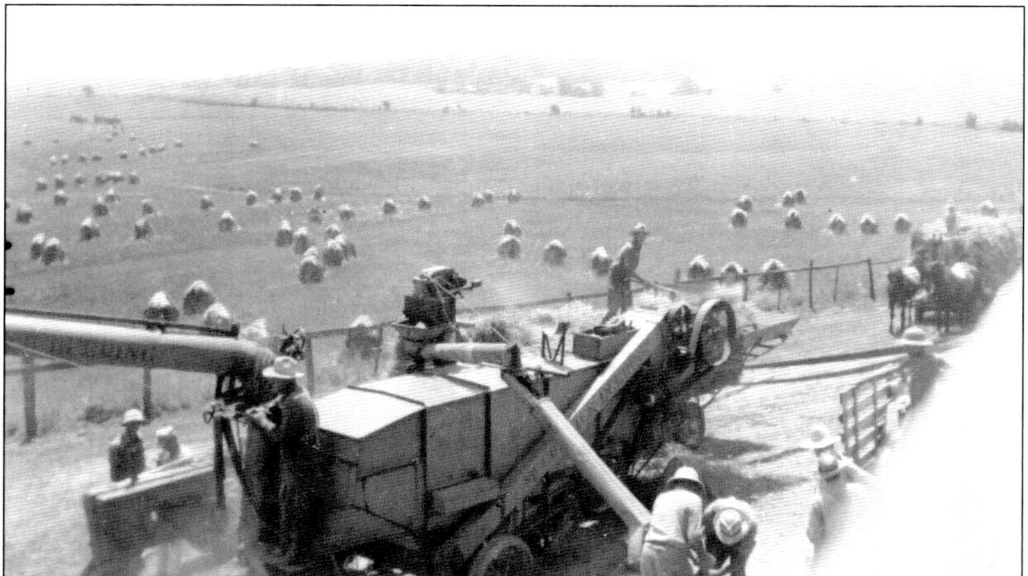

Not every farmer had a threshing machine like this one, so men throughout the farming community came together to help their neighbors bring in the wheat and thresh it by separating the kernels of wheat from the stalks. This photograph was taken on Edwin Lambertus's farm around 1952. Owen McPhillips, from New Middletown, was the owner of the threshing machine. Today, Maynard Lambertus owns this farm. (Courtesy of Parvin Lambertus.)

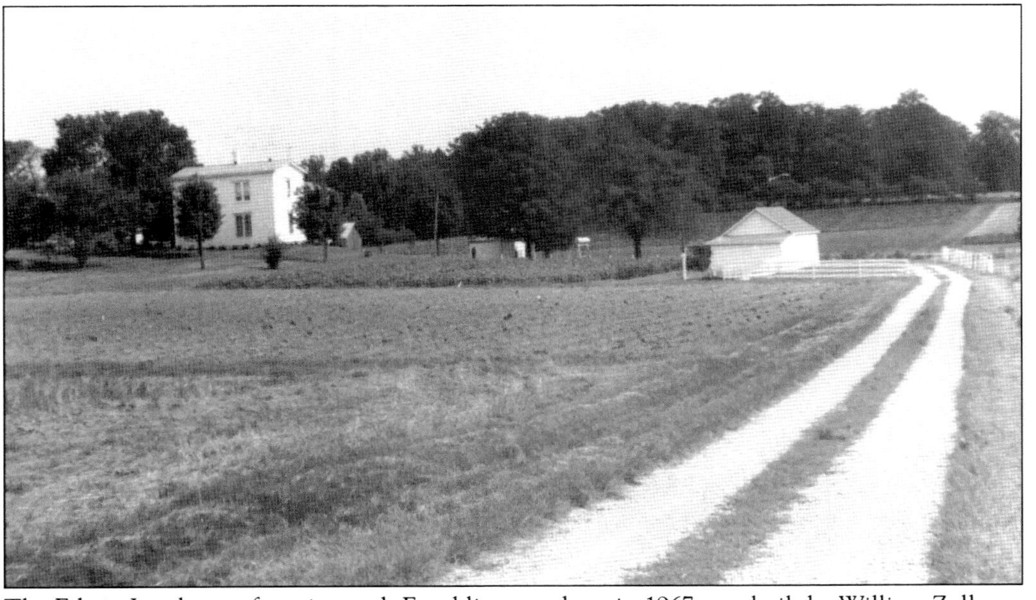

The Edwin Lambertus farm in south Franklin, seen here in 1967, was built by William Zollman in 1896 from the timber on the farm. Today, Maynard and Wilhelmina Lambertus live in the house. The barn, just out of sight behind the house, was built in 1884 and is also still standing. (Courtesy of Maynard Lambertus.)

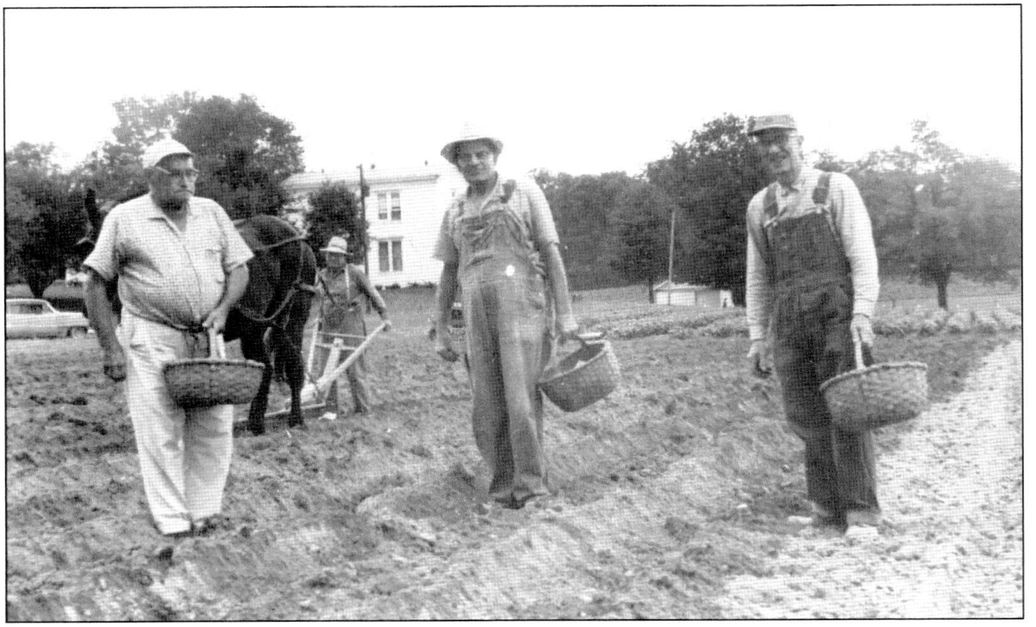

Local farmers (from left to right) Edwin Lambertus(on the plow), Gussie Walther, Julius Blank, and Henry "Pete" Green plant late potatoes in July 1967, hoping to get one more crop for the winter. Notice the horse pulling the plow; even though they had modern tractors, some things are just done better with a horse. (Courtesy of Maynard Lambertus.)

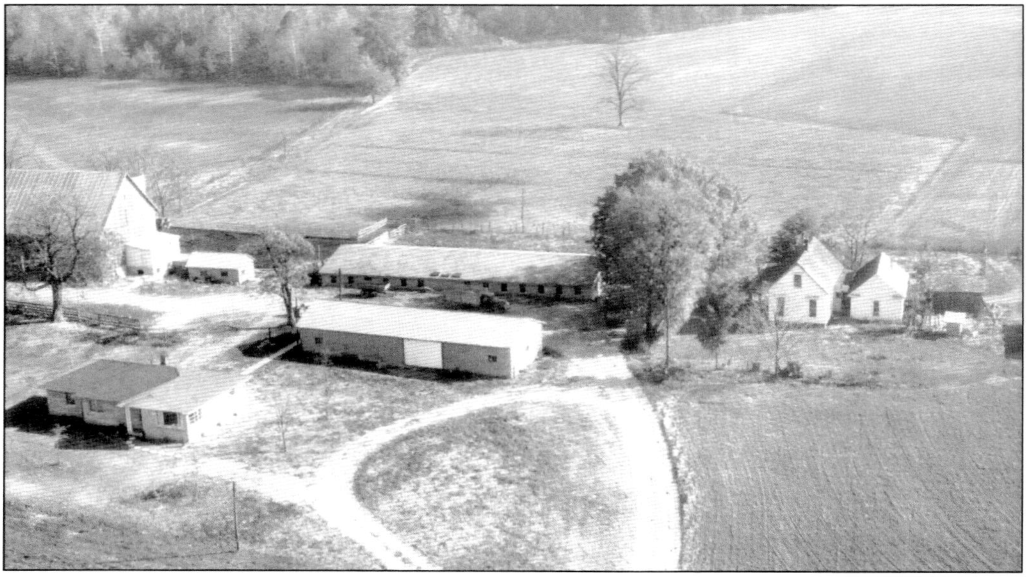

The Busy "B" Farm in south Franklin is seen here in the 1950s when it was owned by David and Norma Blank, who bought it in 1942. The original owner, John Kintner, homesteaded the farm in 1816. The Blanks primarily raised livestock and grain on the 120-acre farm. At one time, they had a 10,000 laying-hen operation with eggs sold to merchants in Louisville. The farm also had the first raised milking parlor in the township and possibly in the state of Indiana. The seventh generation of Blanks still farms it today. (Courtesy of Chris Blank.)

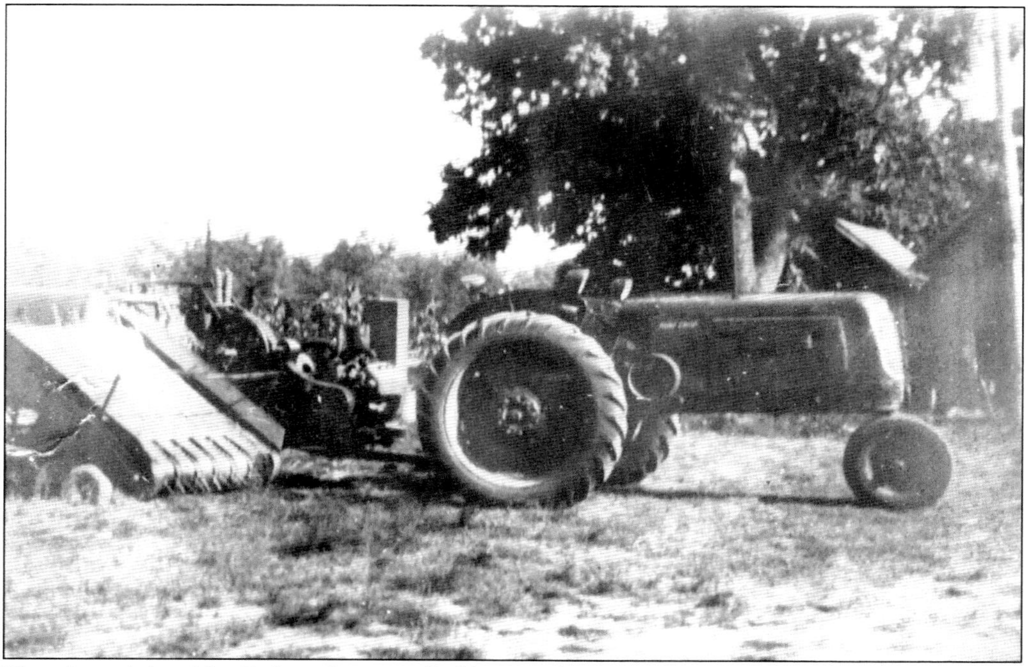

This Ann Arbor Hay Baler is being pulled by an Oliver 70 tractor in 1946 on the Blank farm. As time went on, more modern equipment was developed for the farm, which made bringing in a crop easier and more efficient. (Courtesy of Chris Blank.)

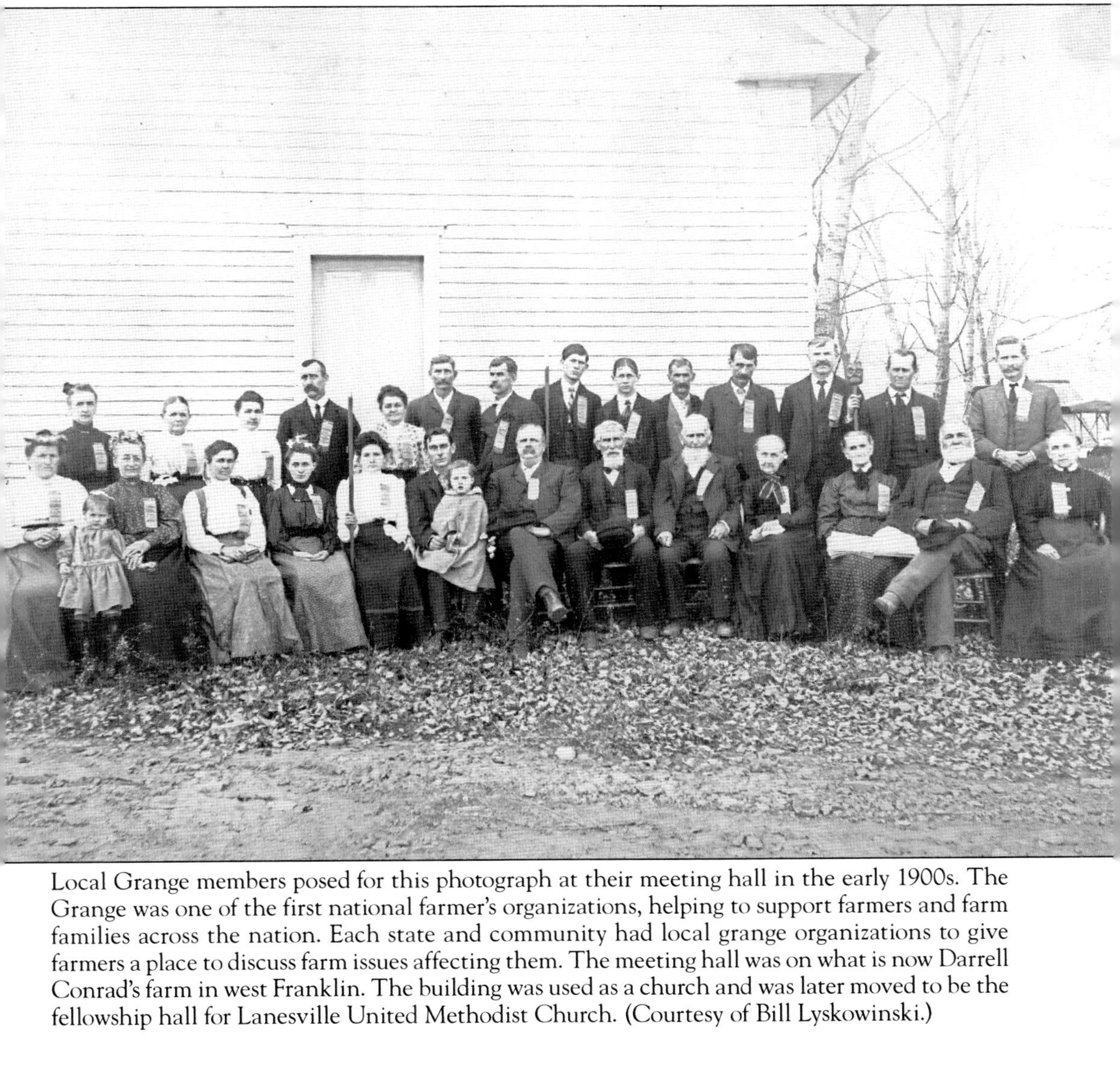

Local Grange members posed for this photograph at their meeting hall in the early 1900s. The Grange was one of the first national farmer's organizations, helping to support farmers and farm families across the nation. Each state and community had local grange organizations to give farmers a place to discuss farm issues affecting them. The meeting hall was on what is now Darrell Conrad's farm in west Franklin. The building was used as a church and was later moved to be the fellowship hall for Lanesville United Methodist Church. (Courtesy of Bill Lyskowinski.)

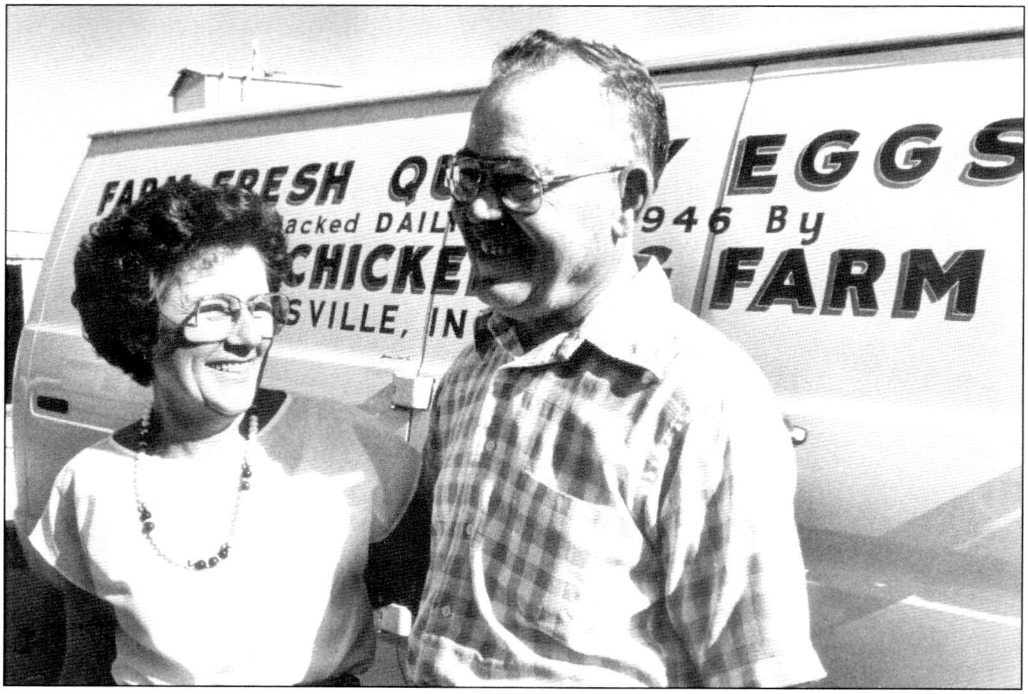

Pete and Joan Schickel are seen here in 1988 when they retired from the egg operation they started in 1946. Their slogan was "Eggs by Schickel is worth every nickel," and they sold quite a few eggs in those 42 years. In retirement, they have been very active in the community and are familiar faces around town. (Courtesy of Peter J. Schickel.)

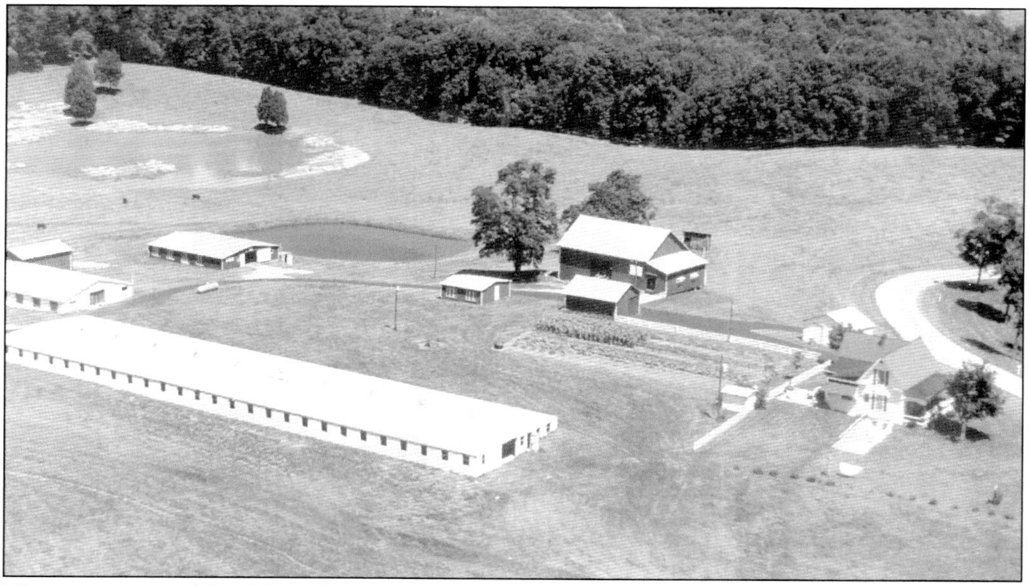

This aerial view of the Schickel farm was taken in 1979. Pete and Joan Schickel obtained the farm from Pete's father, Herman, in 1948. The long chicken house in the center housed the thousands of chickens for the Schickels' egg business. The Schickels still live on the farm. (Courtesy of Peter J. Schickel.)

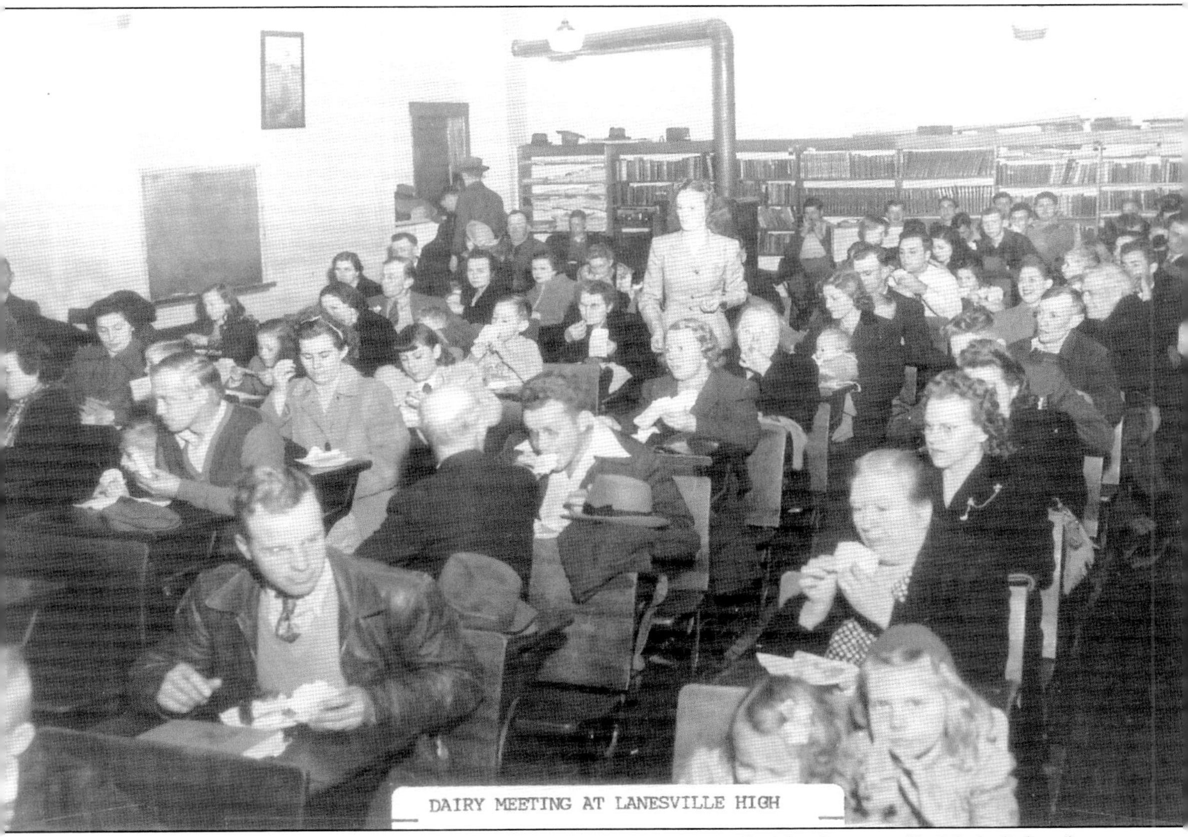

This local gathering of the county-wide Dairyman's meeting was held at Lanesville High School in the 1940s. These meetings were held throughout the school day in one of the classrooms and the young men in the back are giving up their classroom for a few periods while the meeting takes place. At this time, there were many dairy farmers in Franklin Township and throughout Harrison County. (Courtesy of Frederick Porter Griffin Center.)

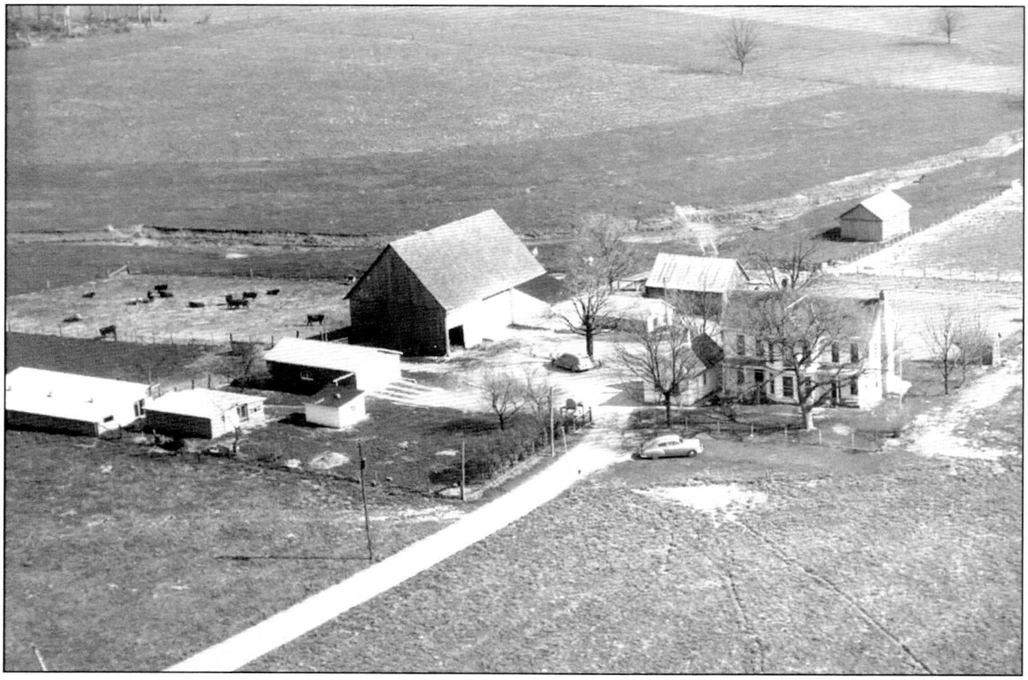

The Jim Felker farm in south Franklin, seen here in the 1950s, has been owned by the Felker family since 1863 and is still being farmed today. Philip C. Felker came from Nassau, Germany, and bought the 80-acre farm from George Foreman for $225 in 1863. Jim Felker's father, Elmer Felker, acquired the farm in 1924, and Jim took over in 1954 and still owns it today. (Courtesy of Jim Felker.)

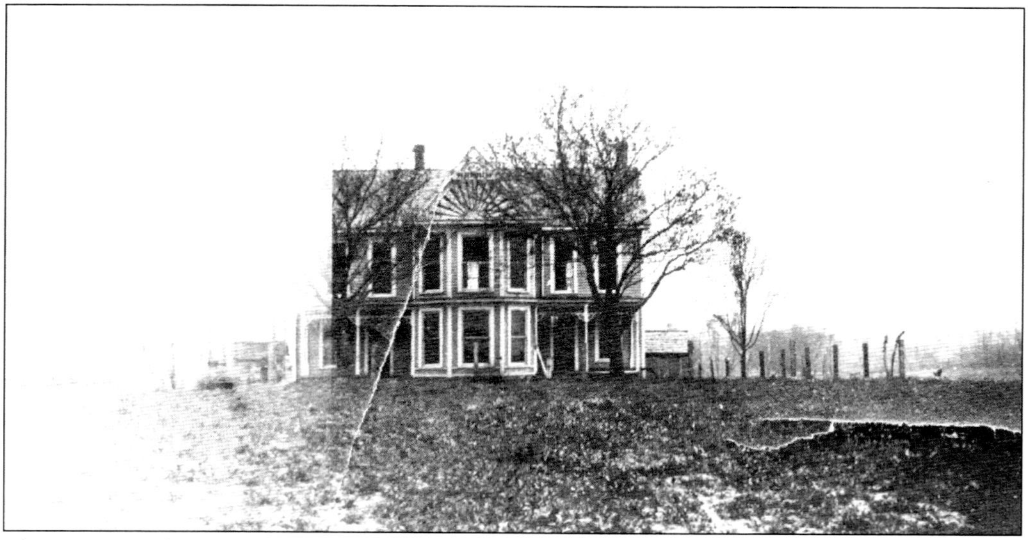

This two-story house was part of the original Felker farm, built in the late 1880s by Jacob Lottick, who was married to Katie Felker, Philip Felker's daughter. The house had hardwood floors and lattice ready for plaster, but the second floor was never finished. The center part of the house was a log cabin from the original homestead, but the house was torn down in 1965, and Jim Felker built a brick home on this site that is still there today. (Courtesy of Jim Felker.)

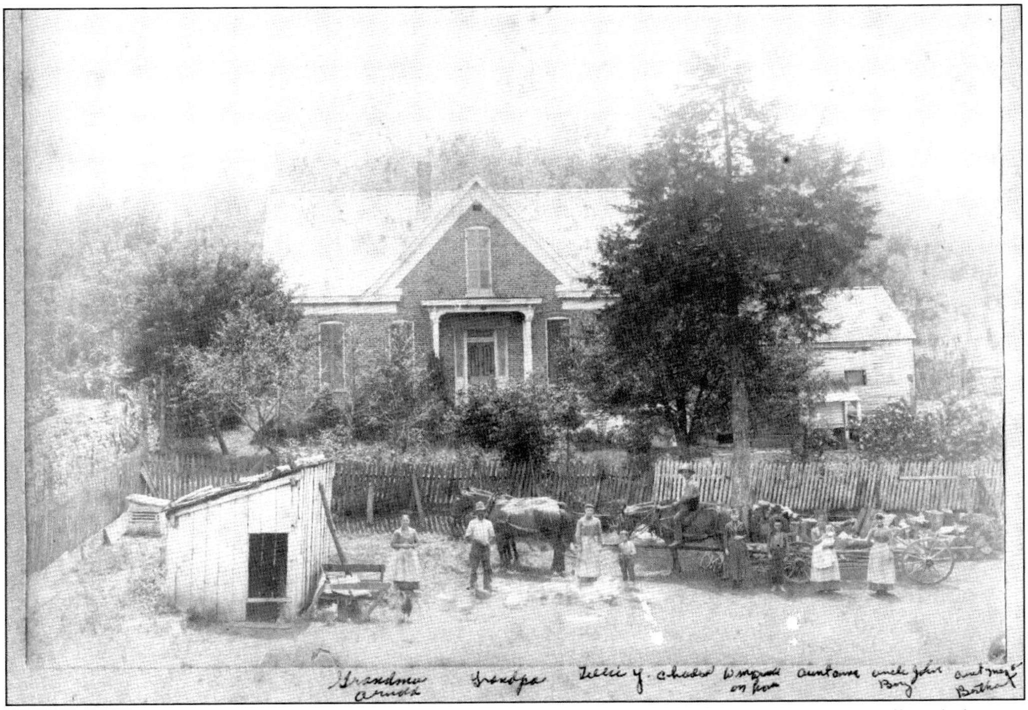

John Arnold stands by his horse in front of his farmhouse around 1900. The redbrick house was pretty extravagant for the time, with bricks made on the farm from the red clay of southern Indiana. It was built in 1881 and the house still stands today just west of Crandall Lanesville Road on Corydon Ridge Road. It is occupied by the great-granddaughter of John Arnold. (Courtesy of Wanda (Arnold) Wright.)

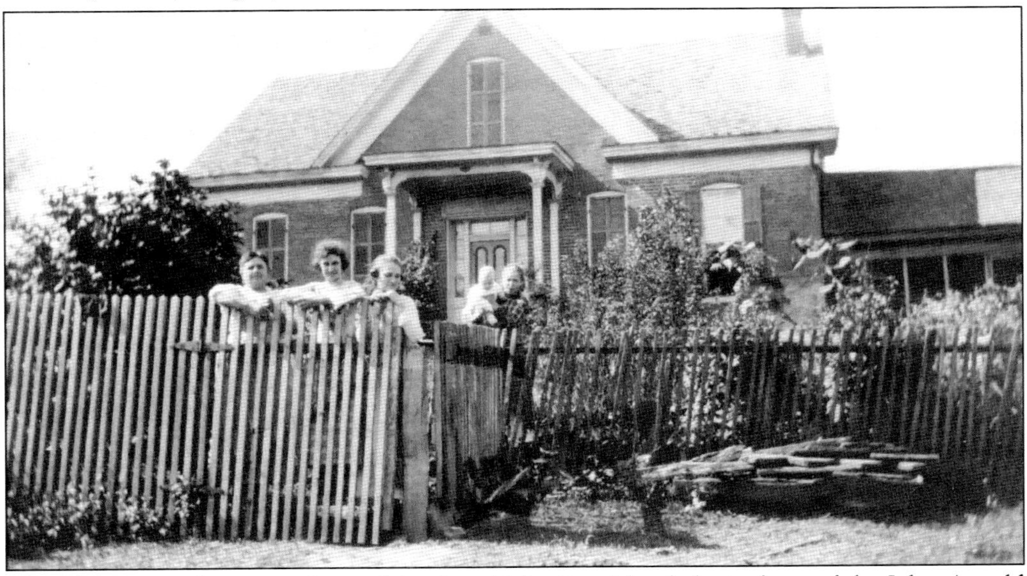

This closer view shows members of the Arnold family with a baby in front of the John Arnold farm in the early 1910s. The original wooden fence was still there at the time. (Courtesy of Wanda (Arnold) Wright.)

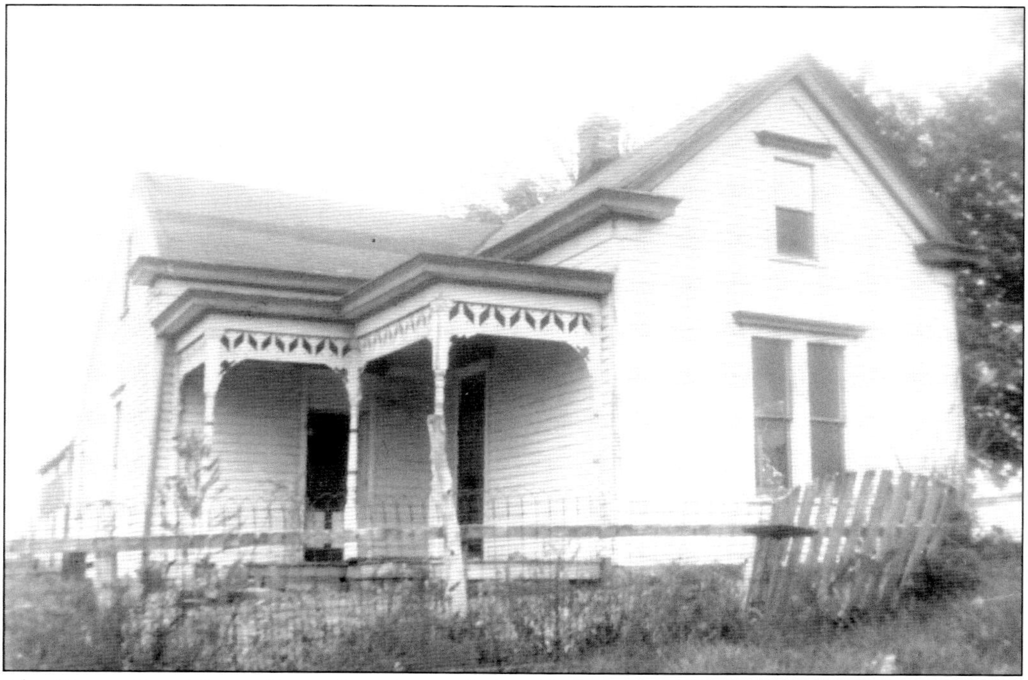

The 82-acre Sam Himmelhaver farm in north Franklin was owned by William and Nancy Bridges when this photograph was taken in 1956. The central section of the house was a two-story log cabin built in 1850 and the house built around it was added in 1904. The author grew up in this house and lived here until he was 23 years old. It was a great old house, and the farm was a great place for kids to grow up. The house stood until 1991 when it was torn down. (Both, courtesy of Allen and Tim Bridges.)

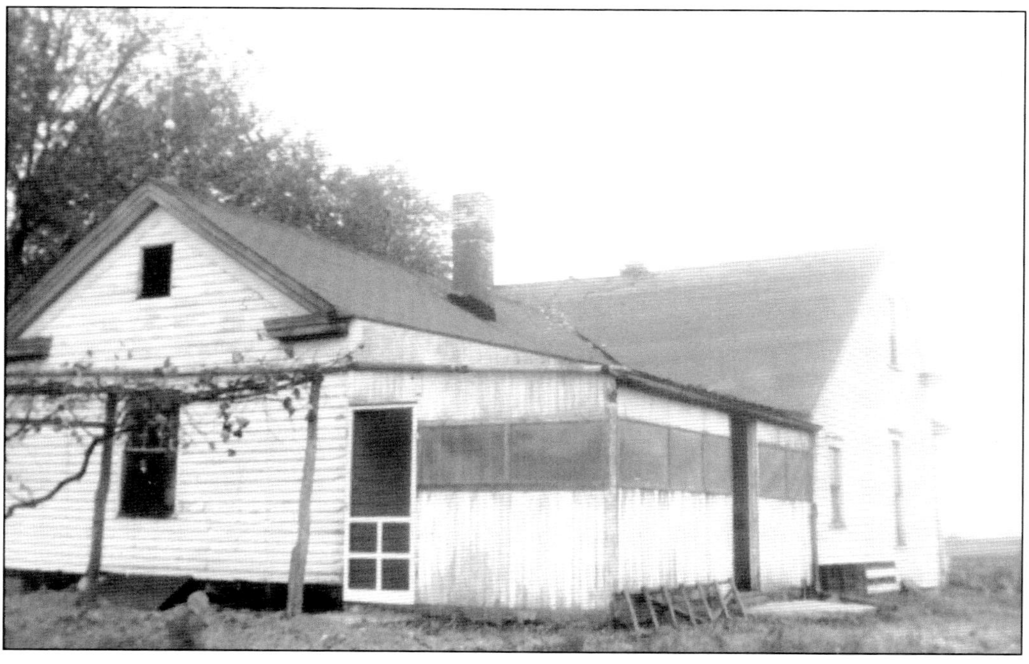

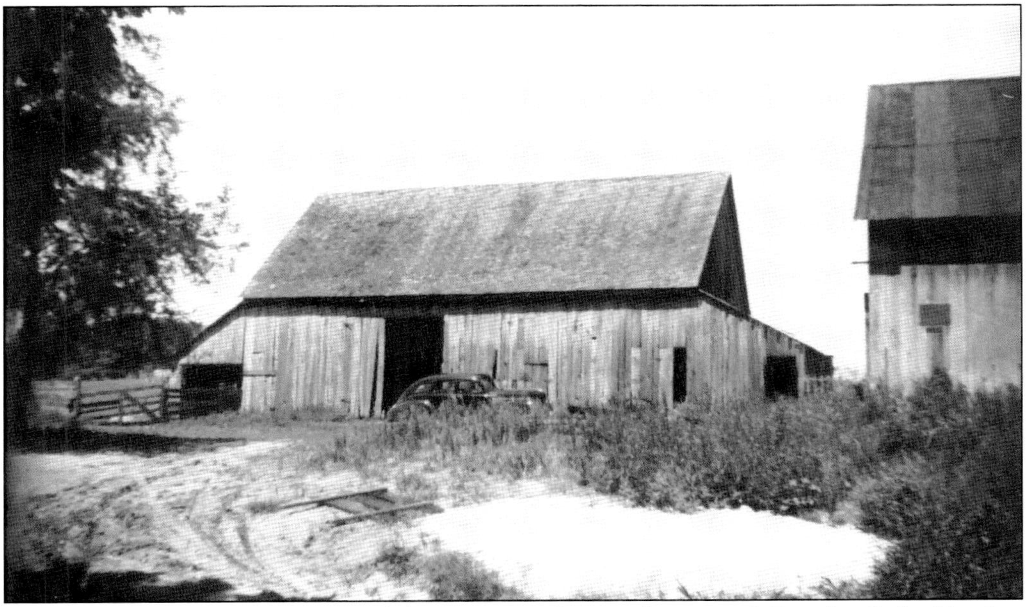

The Joseph Stark place, just west of the Interstate 64 interchange and Corydon Ridge Road, is pictured c. 1930s. This barn stood here until 2010, when it was finally torn down. The Stark family was well known around Lanesville for many years. Brothers Herman, Bob, and Earl Stark lived within walking distance from each other on the farm property, and the community has very fond memories of them. (Courtesy of Kathy Stark.)

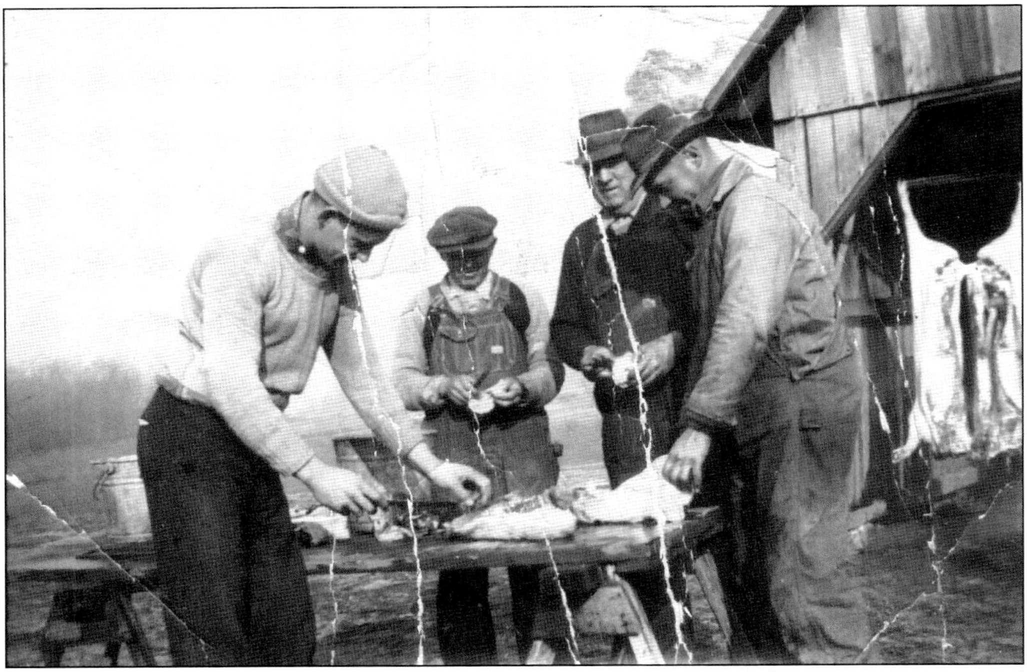

Late fall was the time for hog butchering in Lanesville. Here, from left to right, Sammie and Theodore "Teed" Starke, Sam Himmelhaver, and Clarence Wisman cut up portions of hogs in the fall of 1940. (Courtesy of Kathy Stark.)

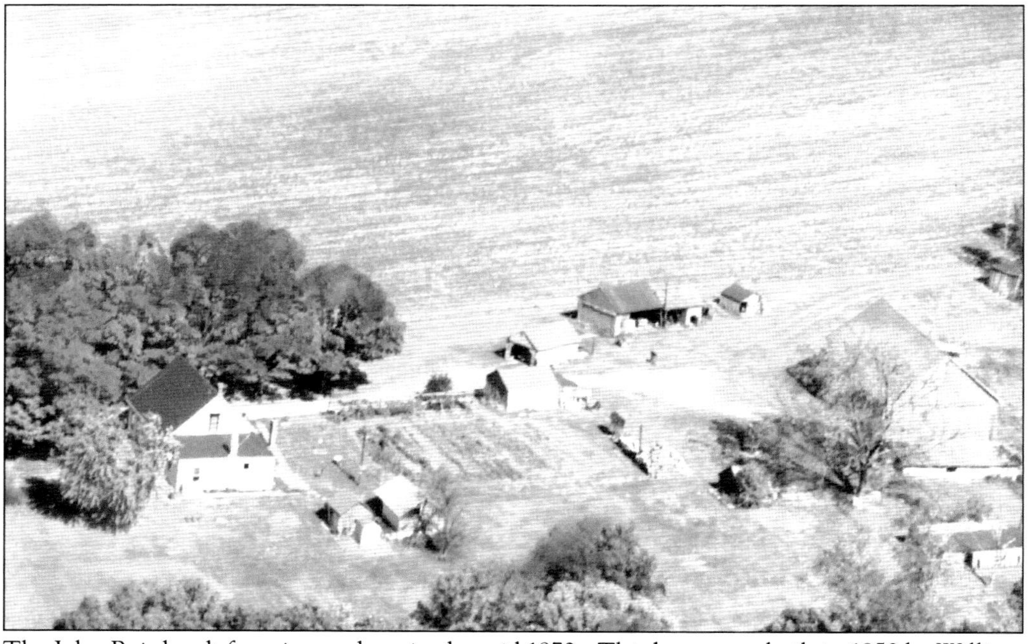

The John Reinhardt farm is seen here in the mid-1970s. This house was built in 1850 by William Benson with wood from the farm and has been in the Reinhardt family since 1871, when Philip Reinhardt bought it. The barns and many of the outbuildings are long gone, but the house stood until it was torn down in 2011. (Courtesy of Lennie Reinhardt.)

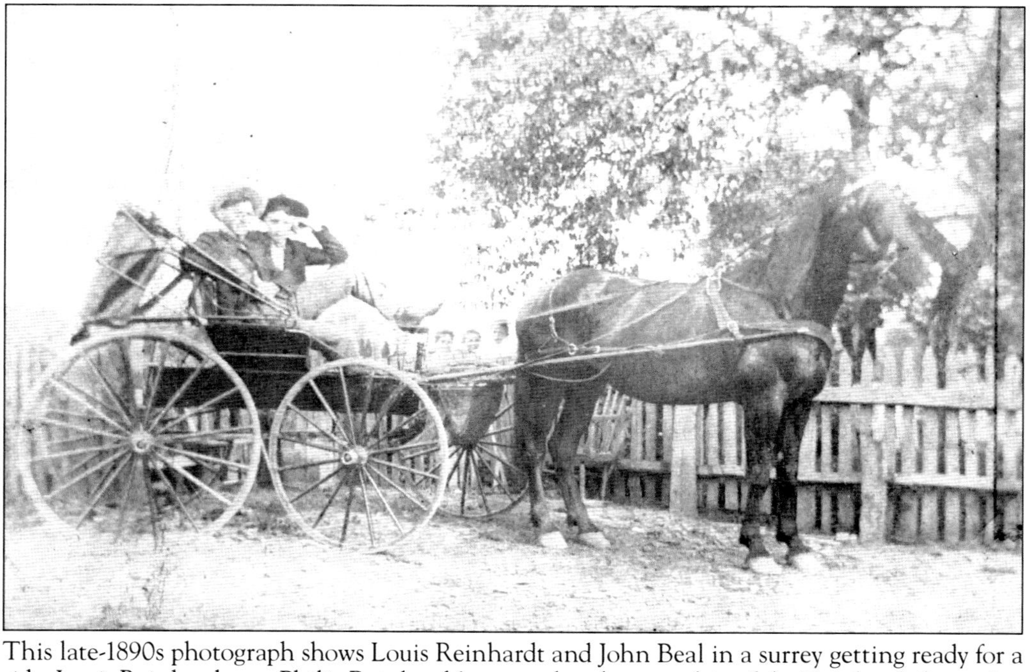

This late-1890s photograph shows Louis Reinhardt and John Beal in a surrey getting ready for a ride. Louis Reinhardt was Philip Reinhardt's son and took ownership of the Reinhardt farm after his father. Louis's son John took over from his father, and John's son Jerry Reinhardt still lives on the farm today. (Courtesy of Lennie Reinhardt.)

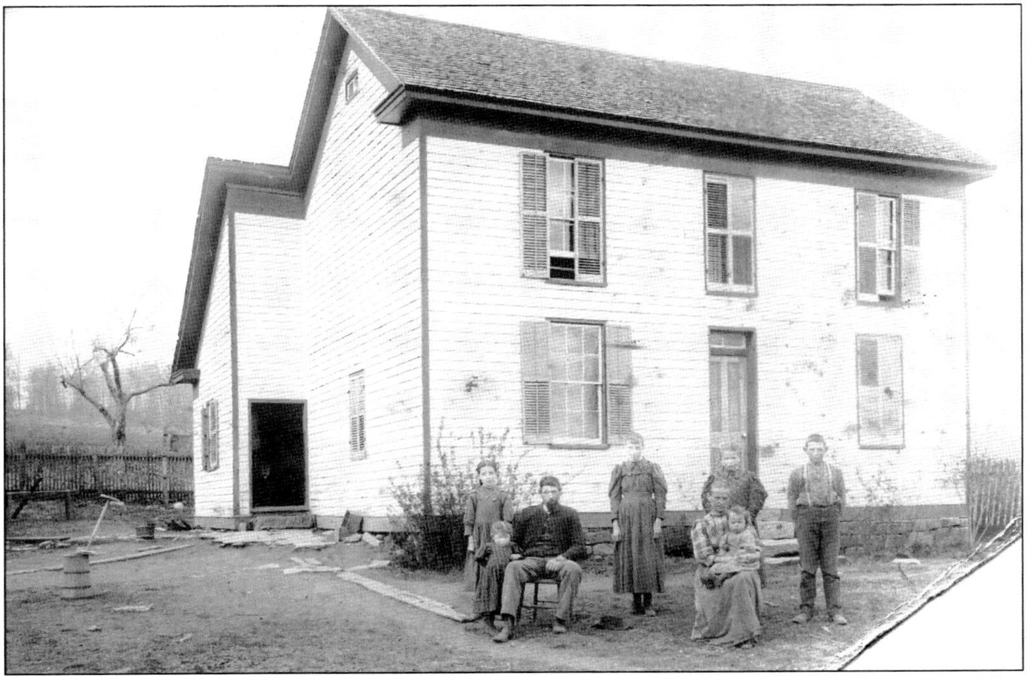

The Zollman family poses in front of the original house on Salt Spring Farm, built in 1886. John Philip Zollman sits on the left with young Mary Zollman Eigelbach, John's wife, Emma Green Zollman, sits with Matilda Zollman. The children standing are, from left to right, Anna Zollman Voelker, Philipena Zollman Day, Louise Zollman Menges, and Christian Zollman. Today, Eugene Gleitz owns the farm. (Courtesy of Sharon Gleitz.)

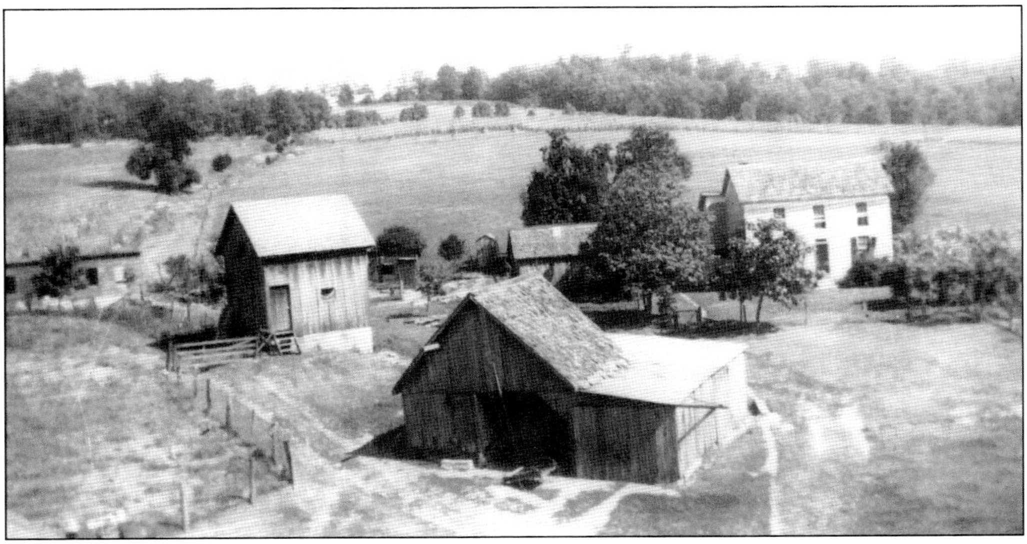

The Salt Spring Farm was named for a famous salt spring bubbling up from Little Indian Creek, which ran through the farm and was one of the reasons families settled here. The farm was purchased by William Henry Harrison, the first governor of the Indiana Territory and the ninth president, at the first government auction on June 10, 1807. The farm has been in the Gleitz family for more than 100 years and is still being farmed today. (Courtesy of Sharon Gleitz.)

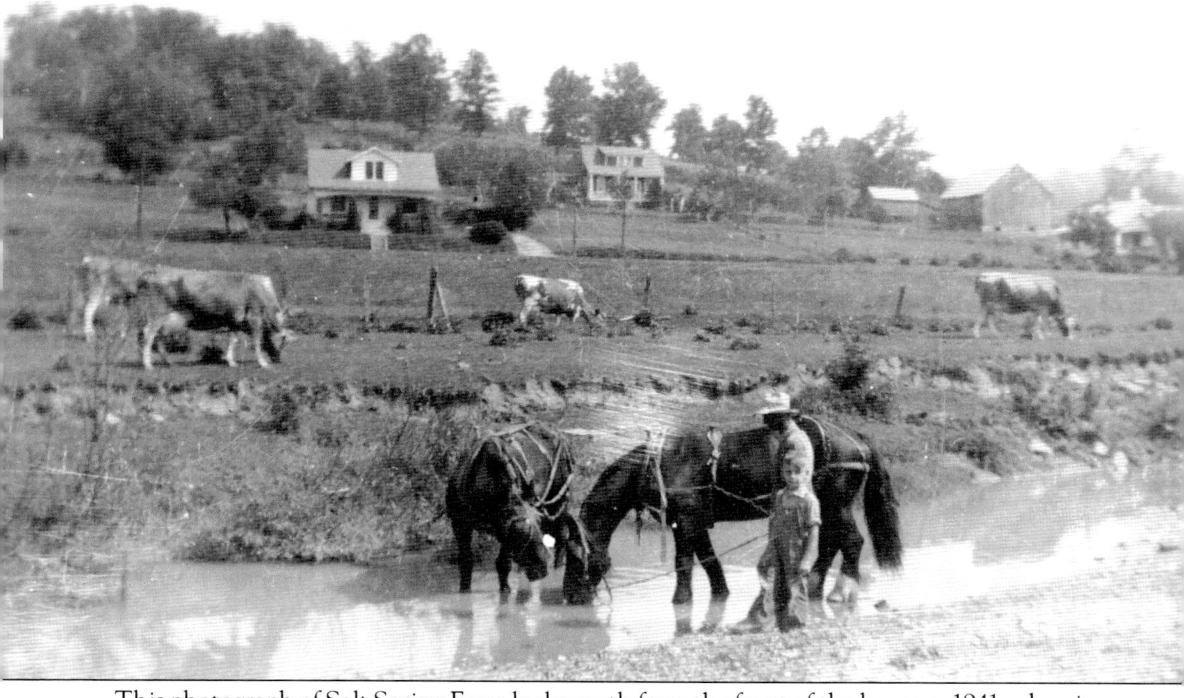

This photograph of Salt Spring Farm looks south from the front of the house c. 1941, when it was owned by Herman Gleitz. Herman and eight-year-old Eugene Gleitz stop on a hot summer day to give their horses, Dave and Doug, a drink. Jake Schuler's house and barn are on the right, and Herman Prage's house is on the left facing State Road 62. (Courtesy of Sharon Gleitz.)

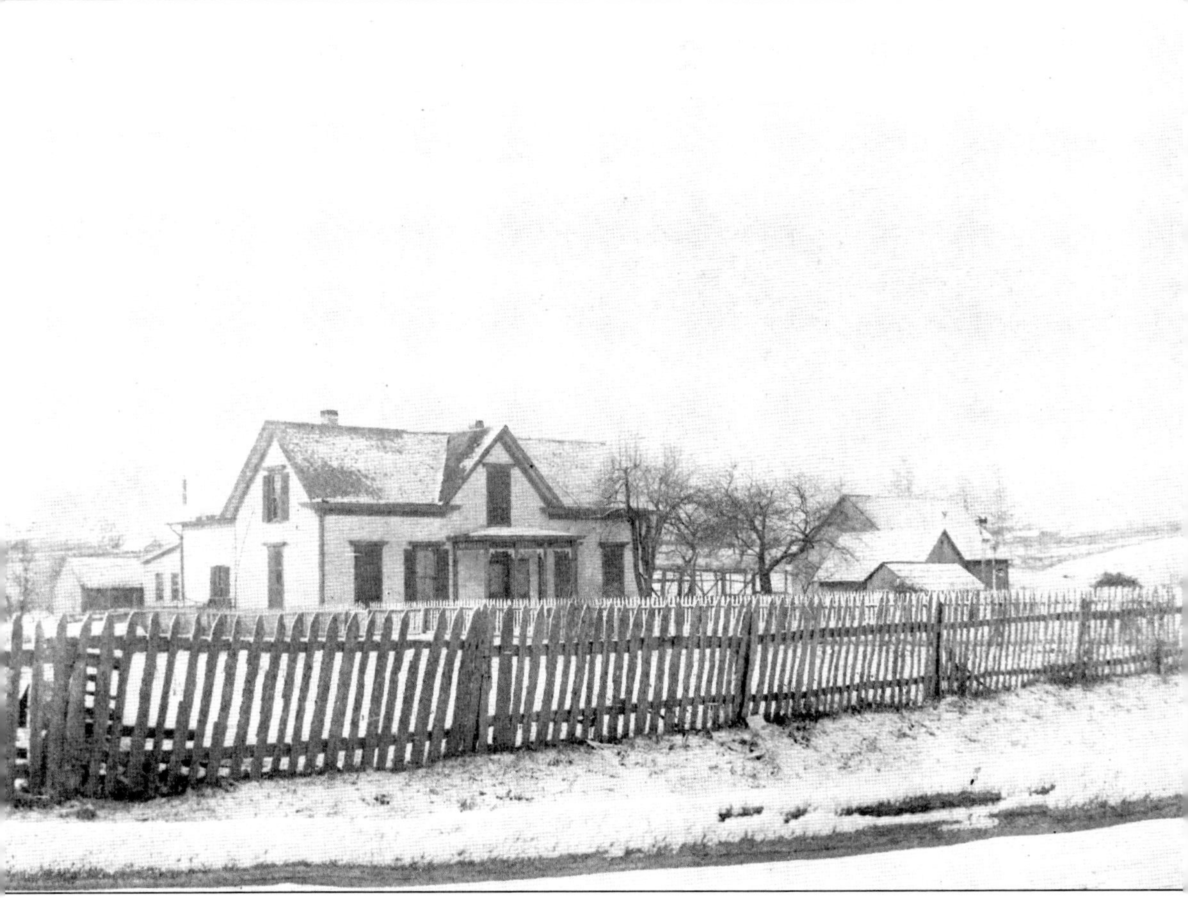

The Anton and Christina (Gehlbach) Voelker farm is seen here in the early 1900s. The farm was on St. John's Church Road, a half-mile south of Hess Jawtak Road. The house and many of the outbuildings are long gone, but the barn (not seen) was standing until just a few years ago. (Courtesy of Sharon Gleitz.)

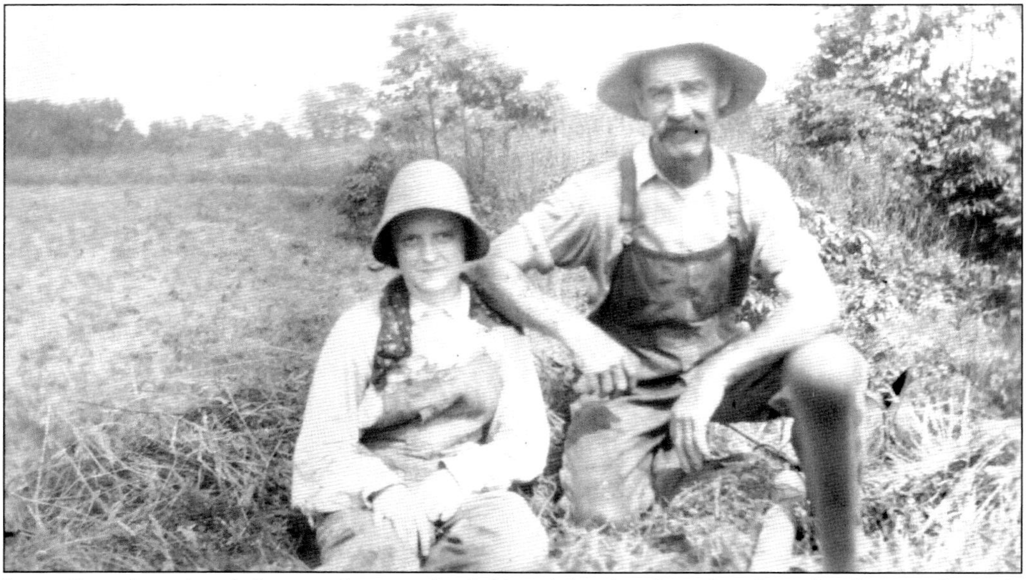

Louis Ott takes a break from working in the field with his daughter Oneda on his farm in the early 1920s. Now owned by Jim Baumgart, the farm sits next to St. John's Lutheran Church south of town. The Otts moved from the farm in the mid-1920s and opened a store in Lanesville. Oneda, about 10 years old here, still lives in town today. (Courtesy of Oneda Ott Ringle.)

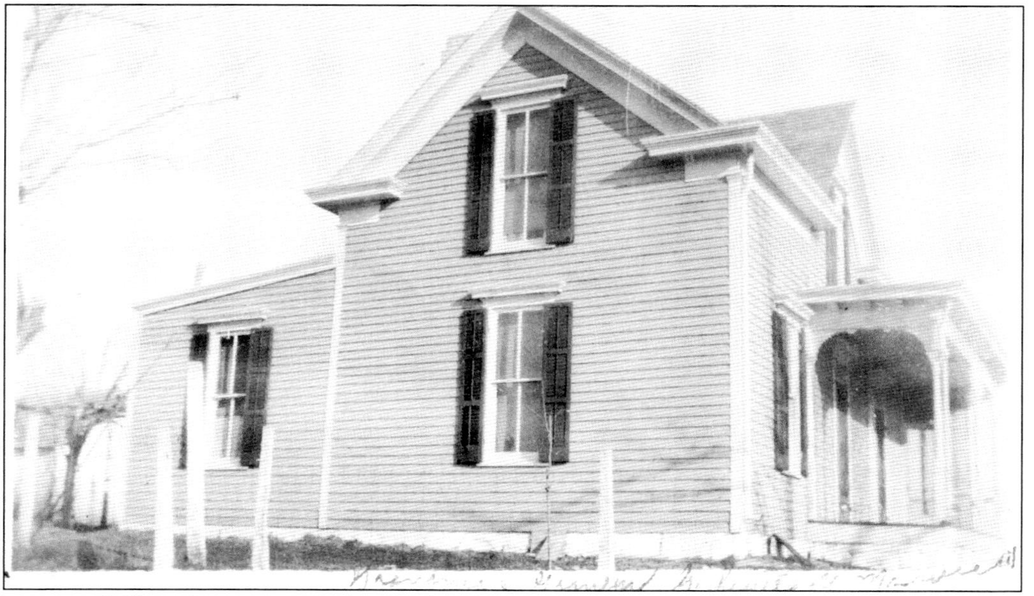

Louis and Clara Geswein moved onto this 115-acre farm (pictured c. early 1900s) in 1923. The farm's picturesque setting east of Lanesville has made it a landmark, and it is still farmed by Louis and Clara's son Maurice and his wife, Anna. (Courtesy of Jane Geswein Berkley.)

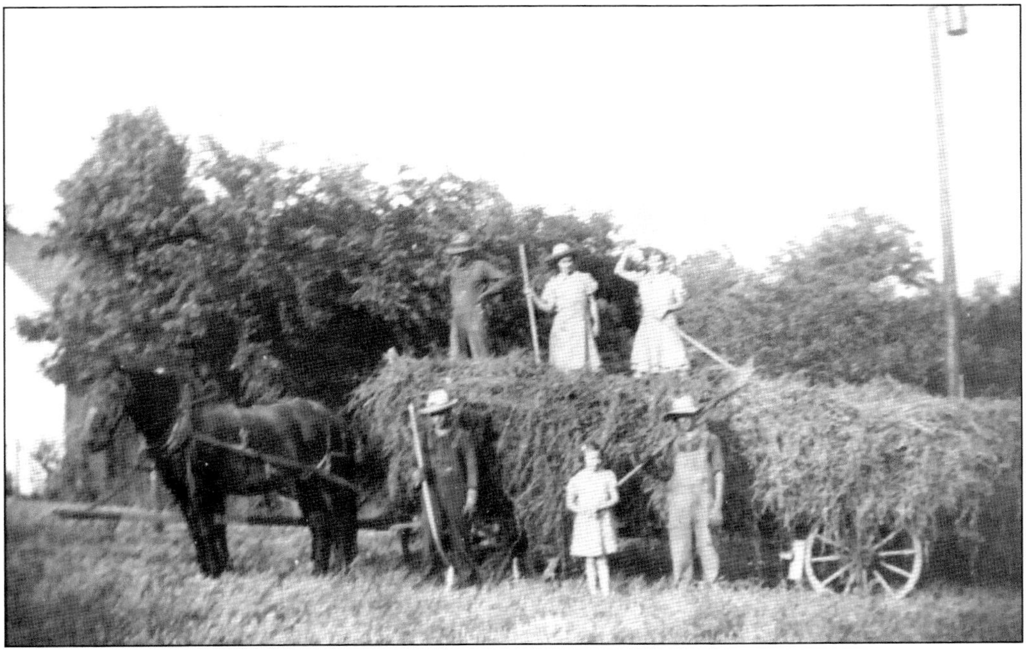

The Blank farm has been in the family since 1904, when it was purchased from Henry Bachman. These two images of the 100-acre farm were taken around the same time in the 1940s. Above, on the hay wagon are, from left to right, Henry Blank and his daughters Christine and Claudine. On the ground are, from left to right, Carl Blank, third daughter Clarice Blank, and Melvin Blank. Clarice and Claudine Blank still live on the farm today. (Both, courtesy of Clarice Blank.)

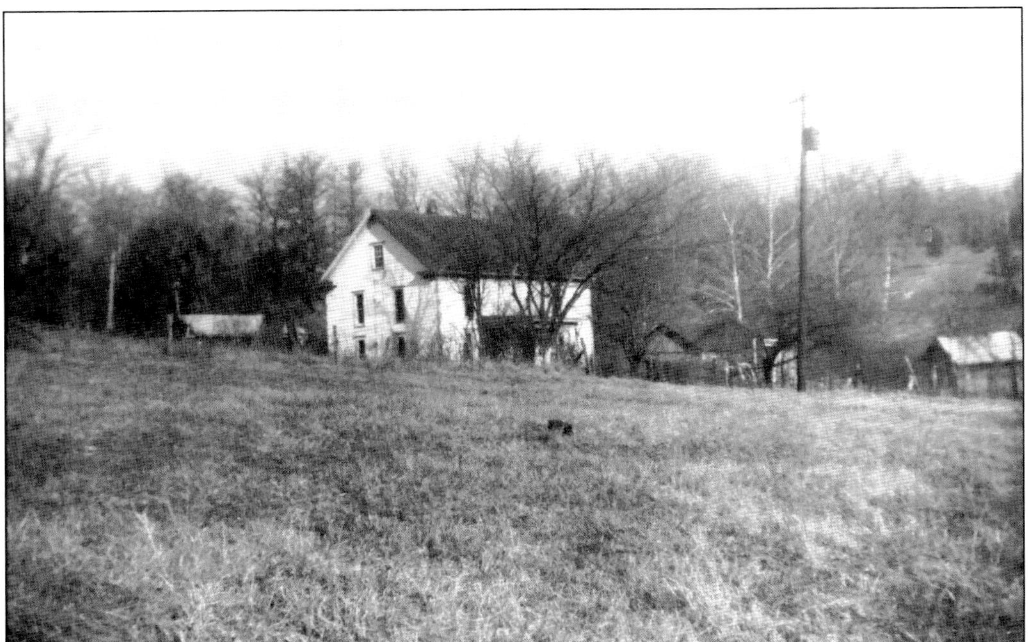

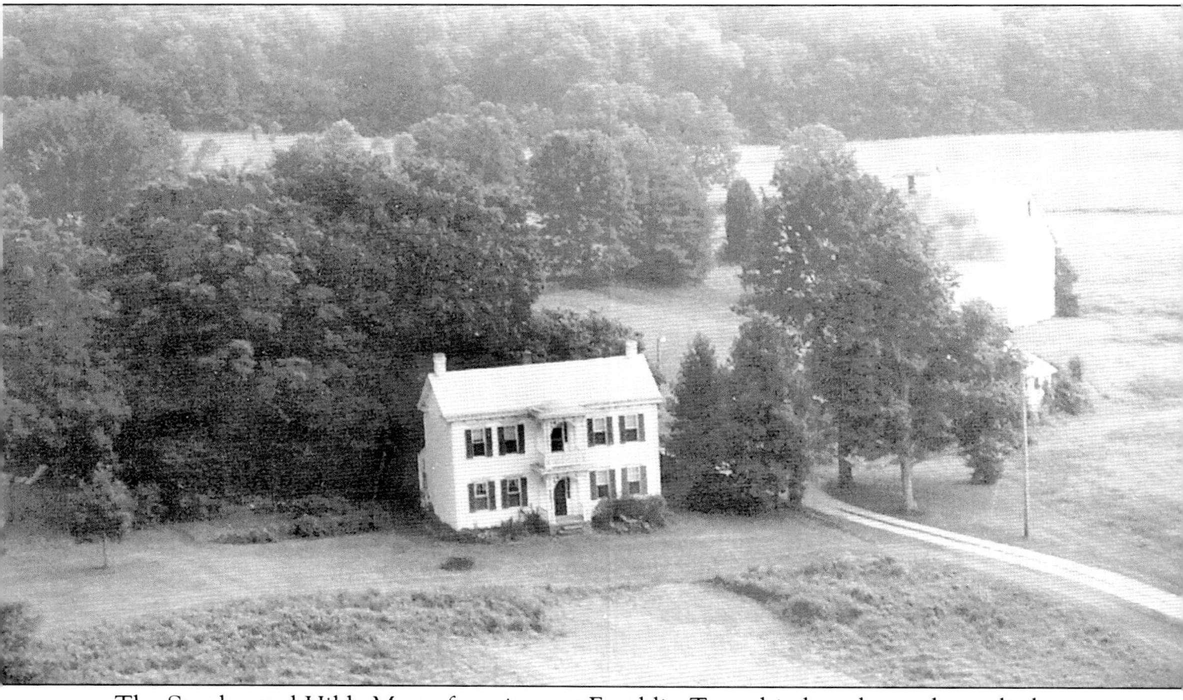

The Stanley and Hilda Meyer farm in west Franklin Township has changed very little since it was built in 1879 by John Deutch. Herman Meyer obtained the farm in 1886, and it has been in the Meyer family ever since. (Courtesy of Marydee Meyer.)

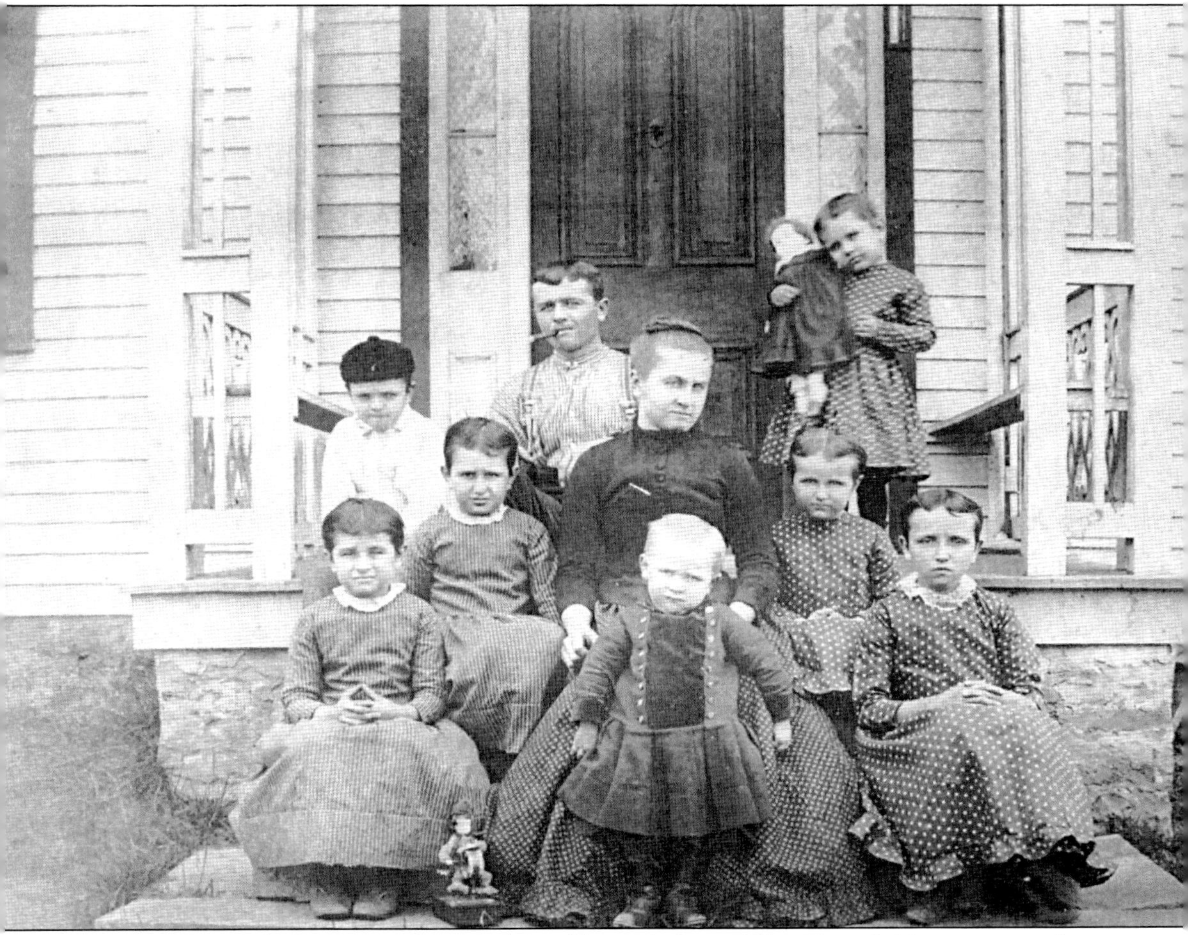

Herman Meyer, with the cigar in his mouth, and his wife, Laura Ellen Deutch Meyer, pose with their family on the front steps of their house in 1886. Herman obtained the farm after marrying Laura, the oldest of seven children who lost their mother. Her father, John, struggled to raise the children without his beloved wife and killed himself but not before willing the farm to Laura with her promise to finish raising her brothers and sisters. Herman and Laura raised her siblings and their own children on the farm. Laura and Herman's son Charlie is in front of Laura. The farm has been in the Meyer family ever since. (Courtesy of Marydee Meyer.)

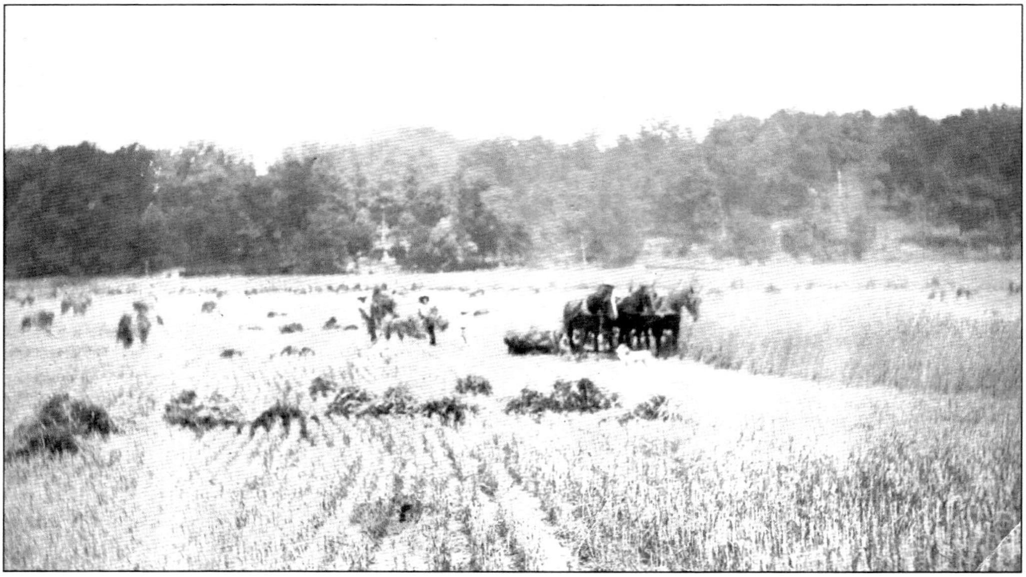

These were typical midsummer scenes on most farms in Franklin Township in the 1920s. Above, a binder is at work putting the wheat into bundles to be picked up, stacked on a wagon by hand, and taken to the barn to be threshed. Below, Herman Meyer, behind the binder, Pfrimmer Faith, left, and Stanley Meyer, right, take a break from their hot and dirty job. (Courtesy of Marydee Meyer.)

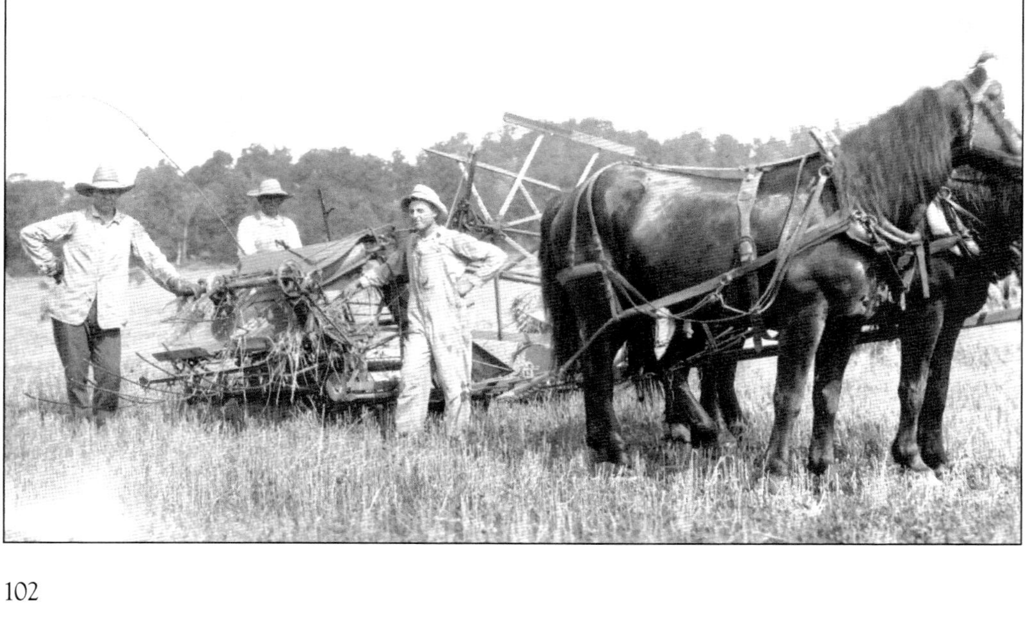

Five

MEMORABLE FACES AND STORIES

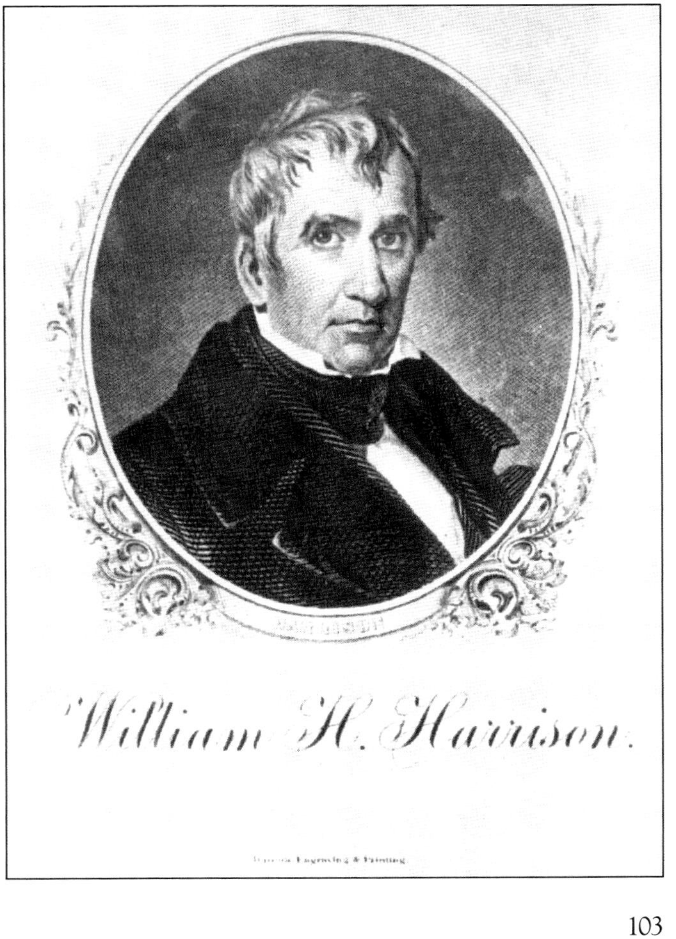

William Henry Harrison, originally from Virginia, was the territorial governor of the Indiana Territory from 1800 to 1812. In that time, Harrison owned much of the property that would later become Harrison County, including most of what would become Lanesville. Harrison became famous as an Indian fighter and went on to be the ninth president of the United States. (Courtesy of the Frederick Porter Griffin Center.)

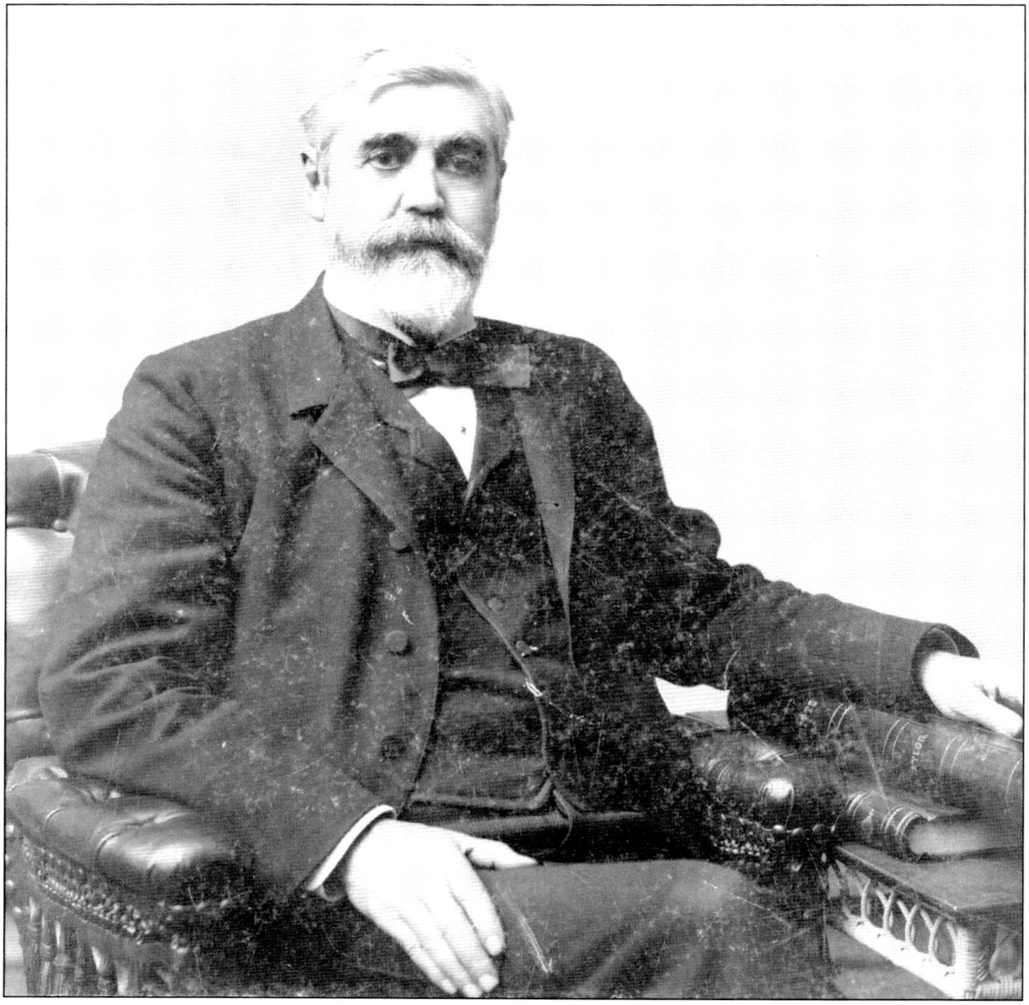

In 1832, a young man named Walter Quintin Gresham was born just a half mile from downtown Lanesville (on the Cletus Zollman farm on St. John's Church Road). Gresham went on to become a lawyer, a Civil War general with close ties Ulysses S. Grant, and a very powerful force in the Republican party in Indiana. He was Postmaster General and Treasury Secretary in the Chester A. Arthur administration in the early 1880s. He was very close to becoming the Republican presidential nominee in the 1884 and 1888 presidential elections. If his aspiration would have driven him in that direction, he very well could have been president of the United States. He was a Federal Circuit Court Judge in the seventh circuit; that appointment came from Grant, his longtime friend. He became Secretary of State in 1893 as a reward for helping Democrat Grover Cleveland get elected to his second term as president. Gresham became disenchanted with the Republican party, and because of his influence with the GOP, many people switched their votes from Republican Benjamin Harrison—who incidentally was Gresham's longtime political enemy—to Democrat Grover Cleveland. As Secretary of State, he was against the annexing of Hawaii to become part of the United States. He was working on relieving a border dispute between Great Britain and Venezuela in British Guyana. He died in the post of Secretary of State in 1895 at the age of 63. He was buried in Arlington National Cemetery in Washington, DC, where he still rests today. (Courtesy of the Library of Congress.)

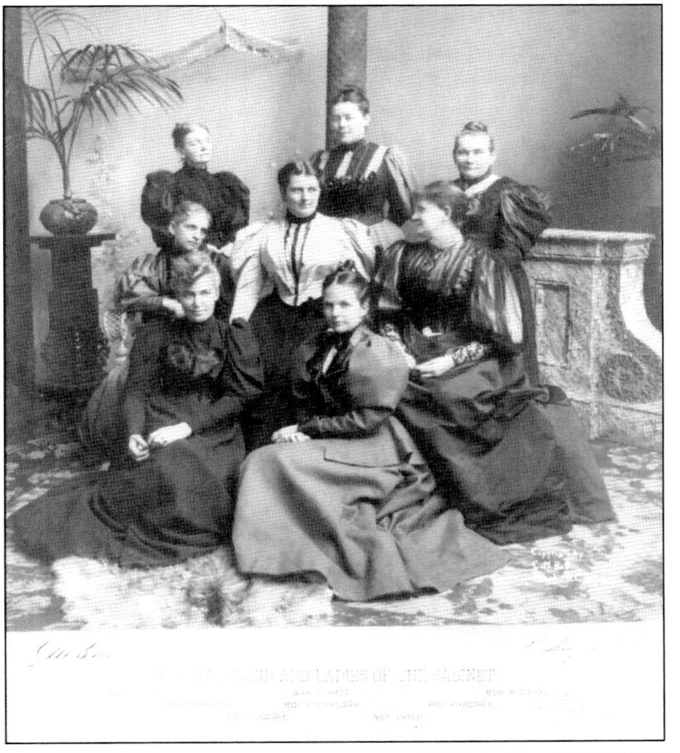

First lady Frances Cleveland and the ladies of President Cleveland's cabin posed for this photograph. Matilda McGrain Gresham, who was known as Tillie, is seated in the second row on the far left, next to Frances. After her husband's death in 1895, Matilda lived to be 90 years old, eventually passing away in Indianapolis in 1930. *The Life of Walter Quintin Gresham*, which she wrote about her husband, was first published in 1910. (Courtesy of the Library of Congress.)

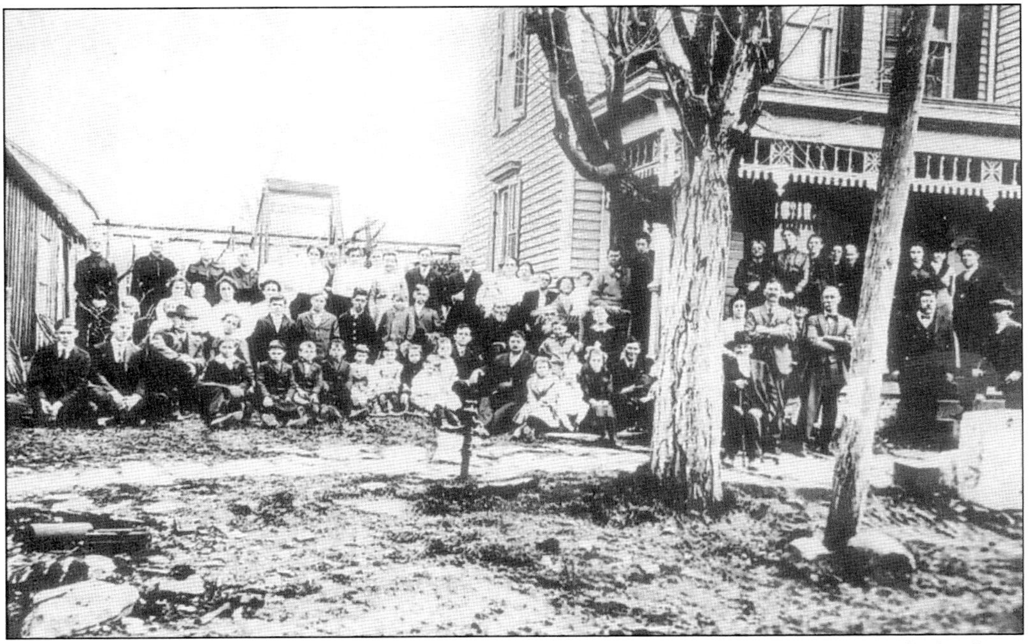

Mr. and Mrs. George Schafer celebrated their golden wedding anniversary in 1919 with this large party. George had a blacksmith shop on the corner of Crestview Avenue and Highway 62, which is just to the left of the large group in this photograph. The house and blacksmith shop are no longer standing. (Courtesy of Bill Baker.)

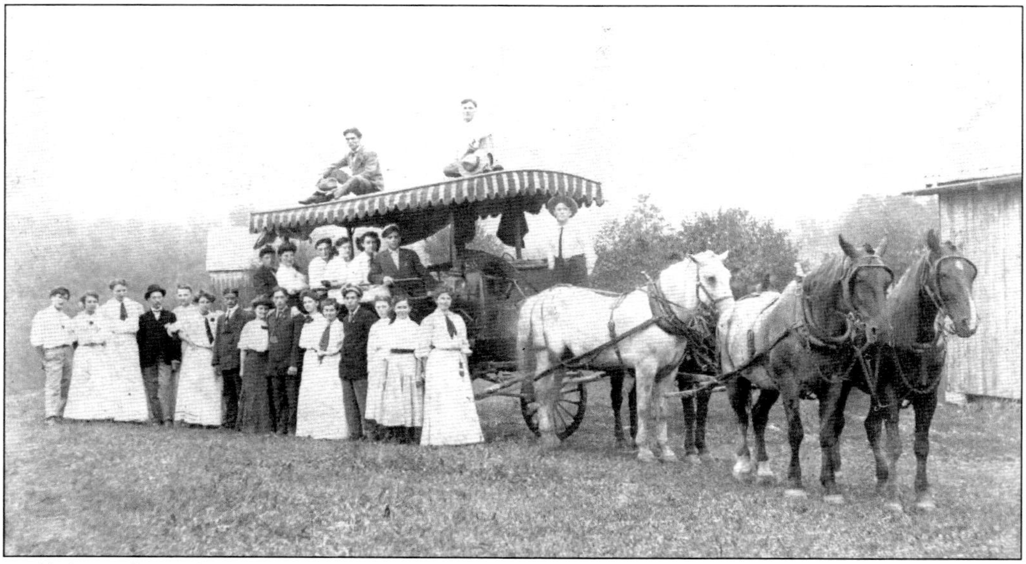

Well-dressed travelers pose in front of their wagon in an early 1900s photograph. In 1851, the New Albany, Lanesville, and Corydon Plank Road Company completed a road connecting Corydon to New Albany, which went straight through Lanesville. In order to pay for the road, many tollhouses were set up, with one on either end of town at different times. The road eventually became State Road 62 in the mid-1920s. (Courtesy of Lennie Reinhardt.)

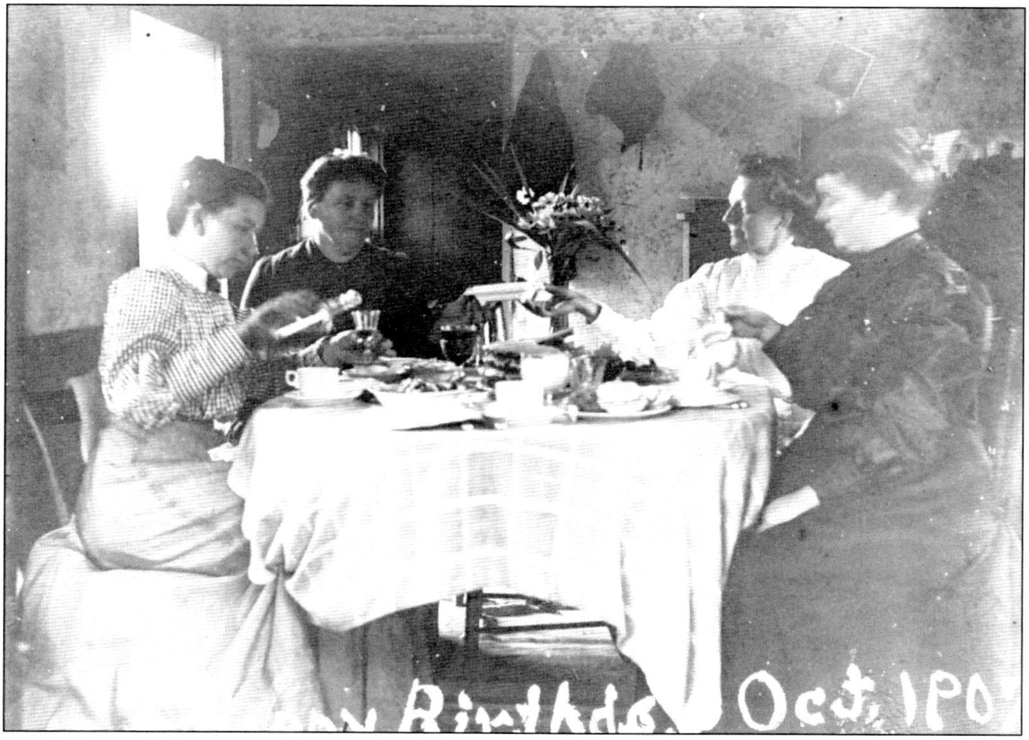

Tillie Green (left, pouring) hosts a birthday party in 1907 with (from left to right) Clara Redick, Kate Zollman, and Lucy Zabel. (Courtesy of Sharon Gleitz.)

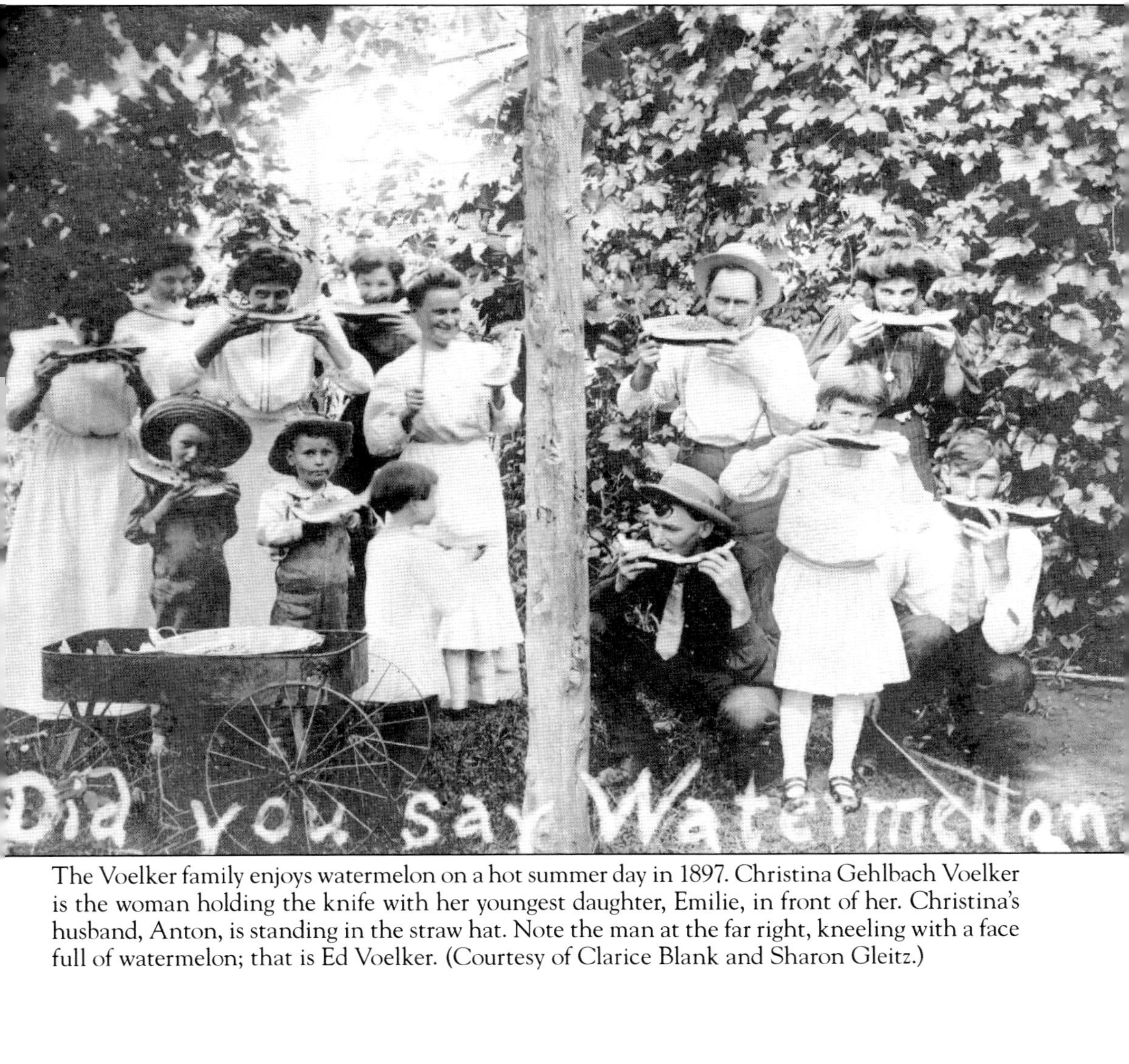

The Voelker family enjoys watermelon on a hot summer day in 1897. Christina Gehlbach Voelker is the woman holding the knife with her youngest daughter, Emilie, in front of her. Christina's husband, Anton, is standing in the straw hat. Note the man at the far right, kneeling with a face full of watermelon; that is Ed Voelker. (Courtesy of Clarice Blank and Sharon Gleitz.)

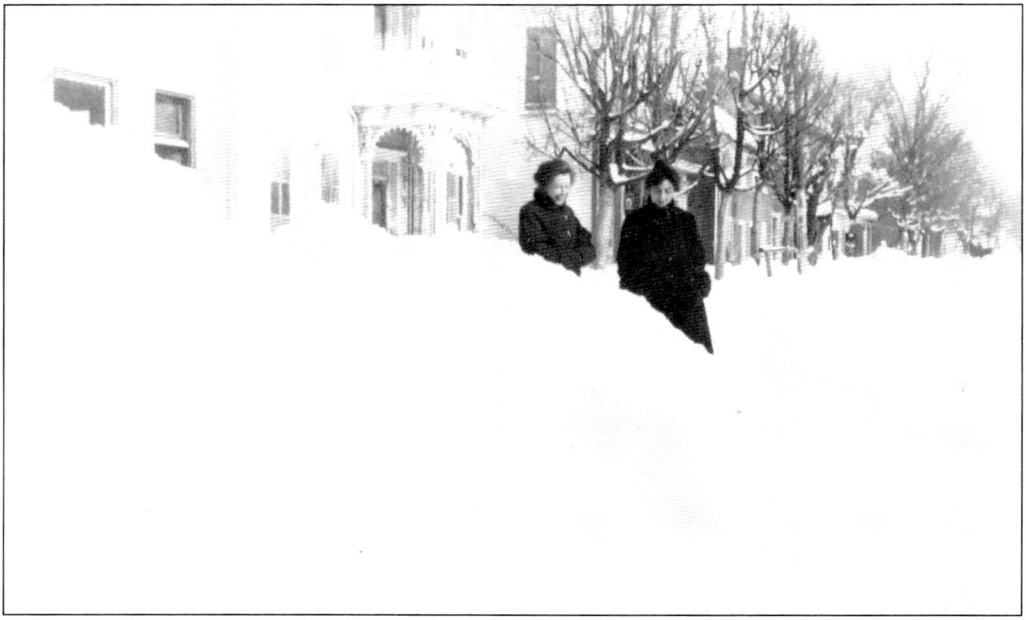

A major snowstorm hit Lanesville and the township in January 1917. The ladies above have a bit of fun in the snow drifts in front of Farmer's State Bank on Main Street. Below, from left to right, Urban Zollman, Andy Voelker, and Julius Zabel stand in front of Zabel's store under the gasoline sign surrounded by snow. (Above, courtesy of Carolyn Baker; below, courtesy of Carolyn Voelker.)

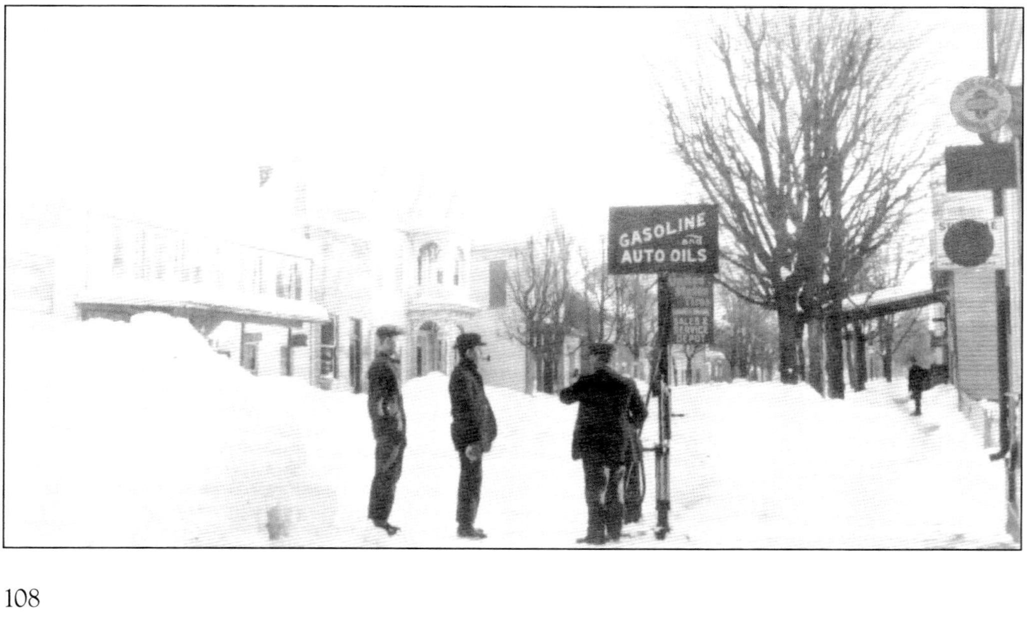

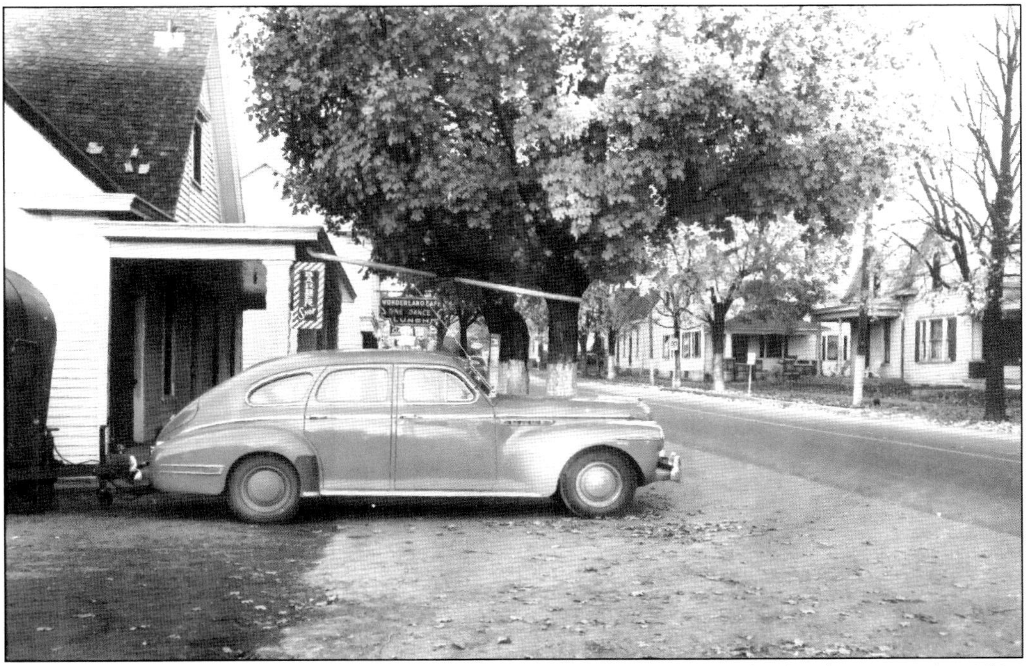

Above, Elias "Pie" Groft's homemade trailer sits in front of Acy Loy's barbershop c. early 1950s. Below, Hazel (Loy) Groft stands proudly by the trailer. Pie built the trailer by hand in his garage just behind the house, and he and Hazel took it to Florida to find a job. In the top image, above the car, is a sign for Wonderland Café, a popular spot in Lanesville in the 1950s. It became the Circle Bar in 1963. (Both, courtesy of Marvin Zabel.)

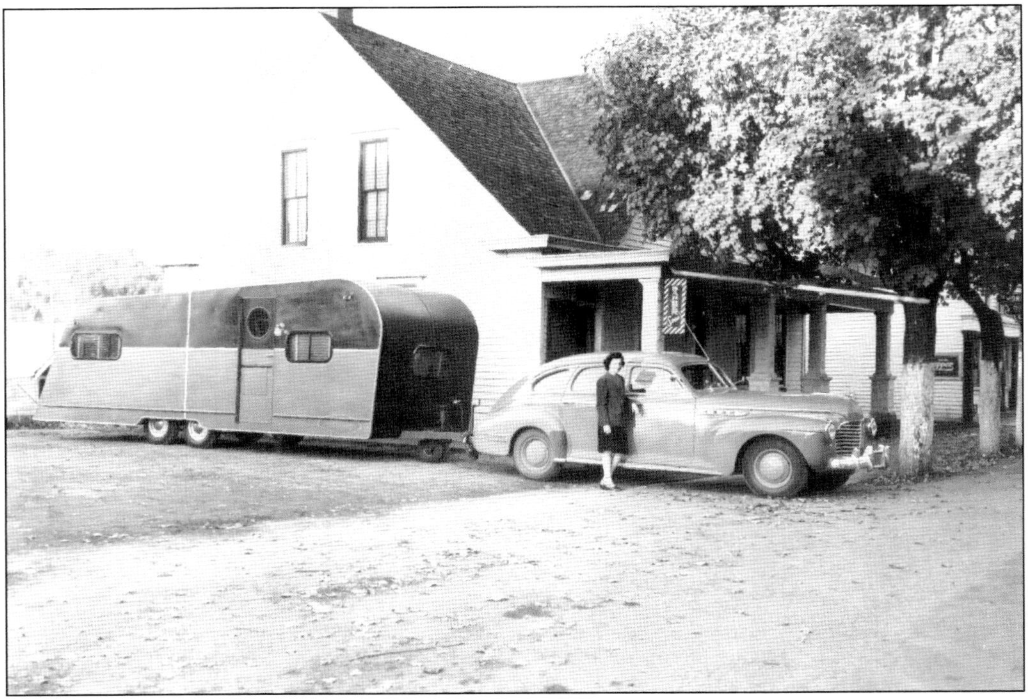

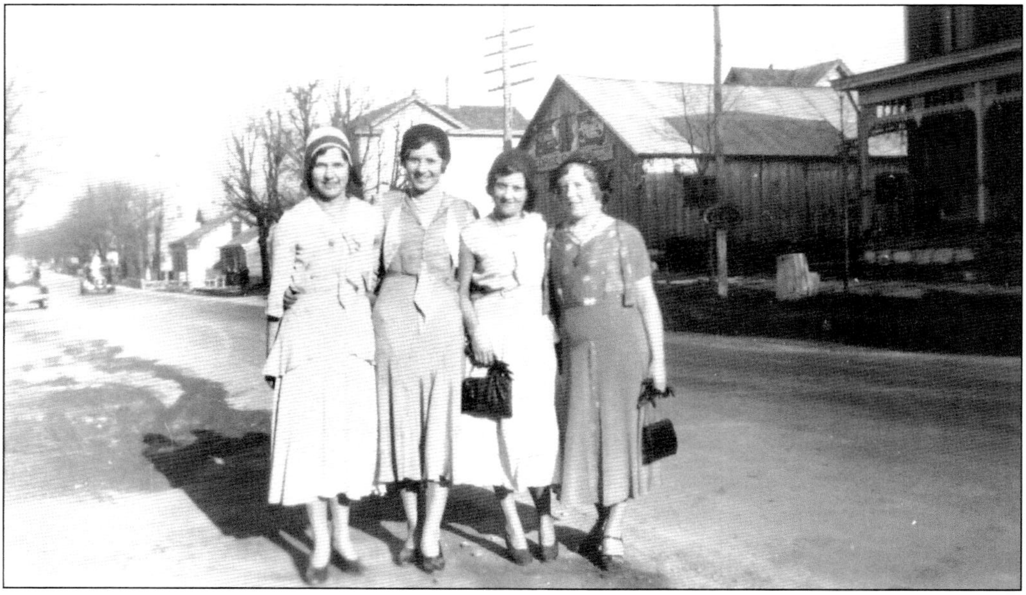

These ladies out for a shopping trip are, from left to right, Marie (Bachman) Day, Jenny (Ringle) Rhodes, Lucille (Day) Kochert, and Hilda (Ringle) Lambertus. The photograph looks east down Main Street. George Schafer's blacksmith shop and house are just to the right of the ladies. (Courtesy of Dolores Dotson.)

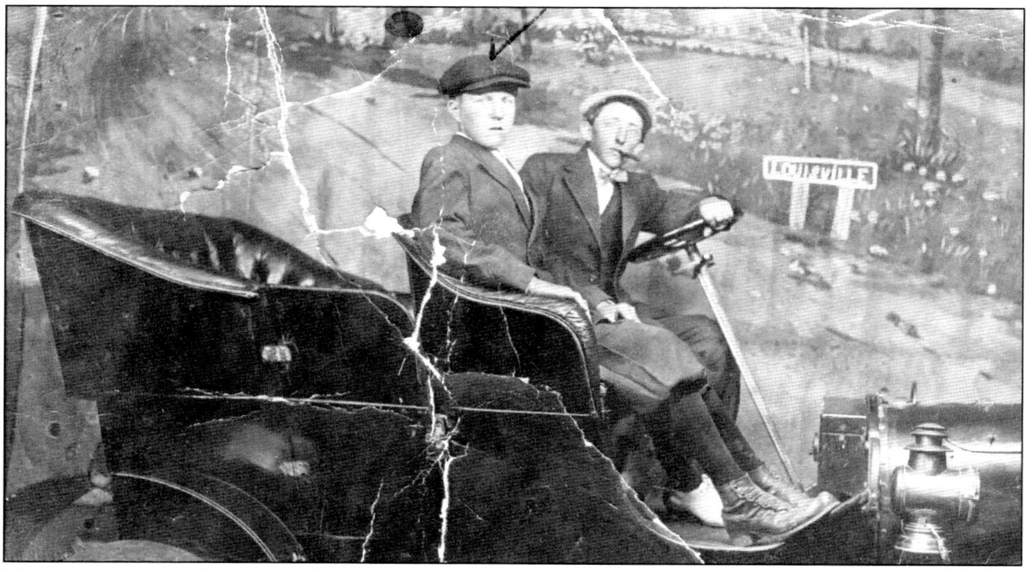

These two young chaps mug for the camera in this 1910s photograph. Charles Stark, the brother of Theodore "Teed" Stark, is in front with an unidentified buddy with a cigar in his mouth. (Courtesy of Kathy Stark.)

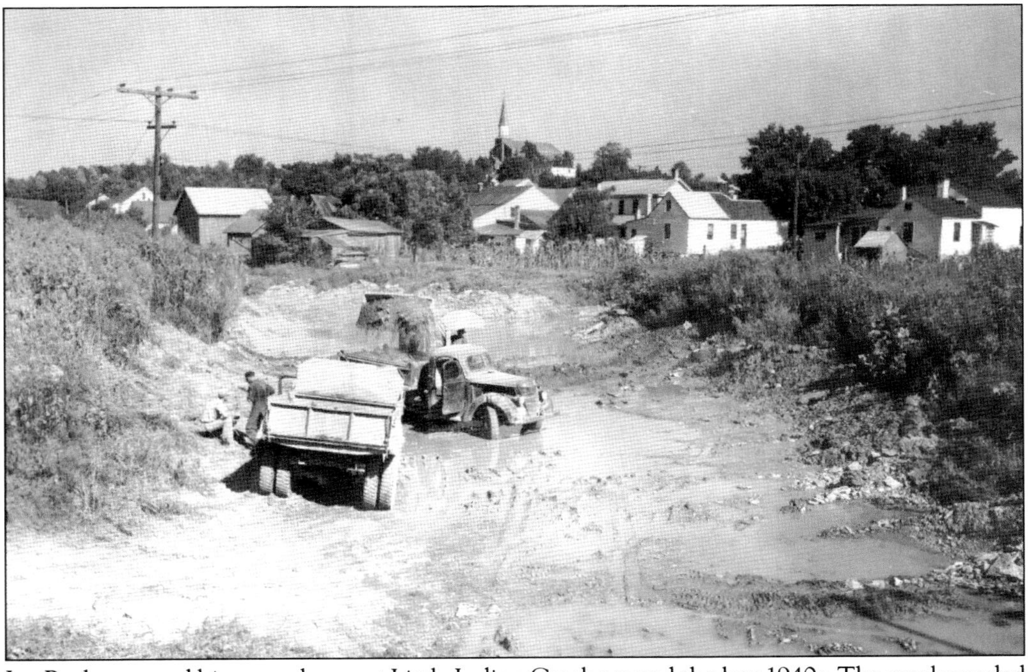

Joe Bachman and his crew clean out Little Indian Creek around the late 1940s. The creek needed cleaned periodically because debris could cause flooding. Bachman made sure to keep the creek neat with the help of his trucks and loaders from the quarry. (Courtesy of Marvin Zabel.)

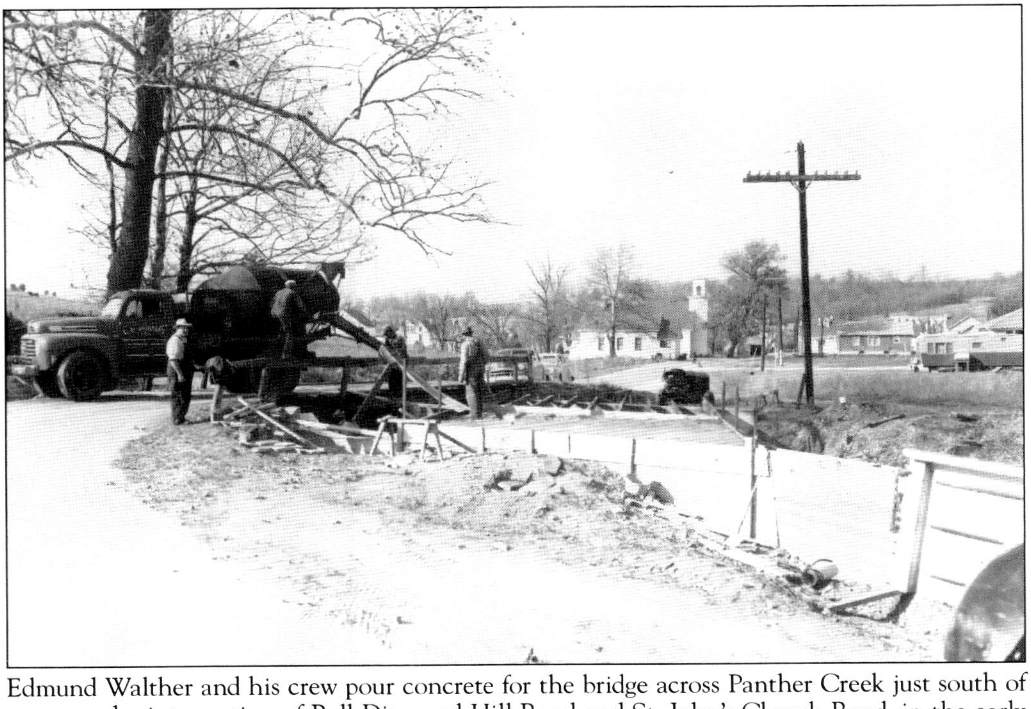

Edmund Walther and his crew pour concrete for the bridge across Panther Creek just south of town, at the intersection of Ball Diamond Hill Road and St. John's Church Road, in the early 1950s. The bridge is still there today. (Courtesy of Marvin Zabel.)

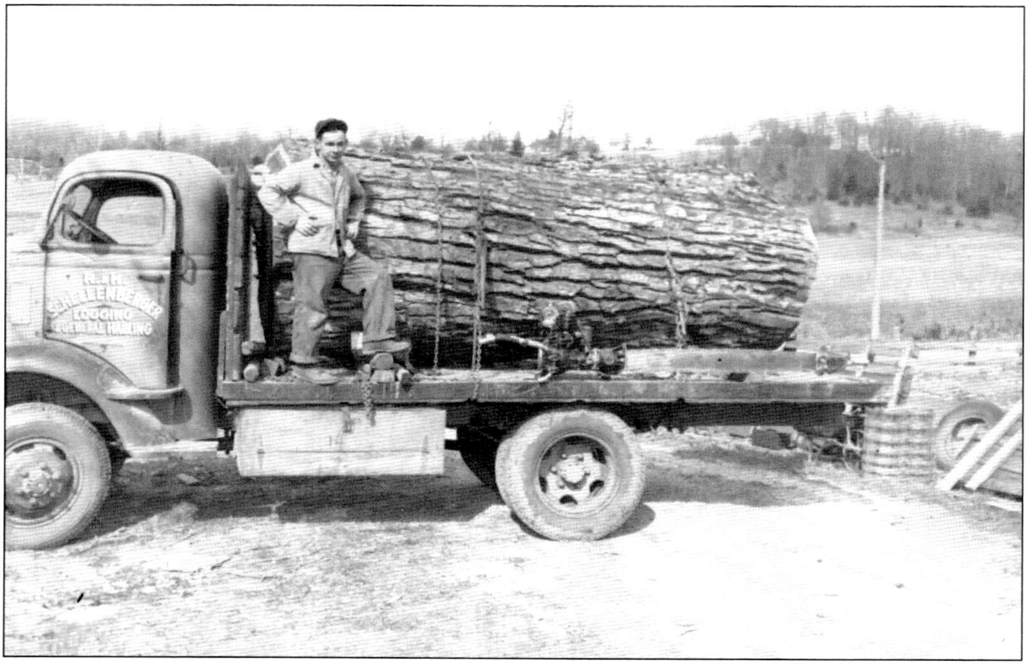

Bob Schellenberger stands on the bed of his logging truck with a huge piece of a cottonwood tree in the late 1940s, when the tree was cut down. The tree was planted by William and Sara Gresham, Walter Gresham's parents, in 1825. It stood for more than 120 years. Bob and his father, Homer, ran a sawmill just east of town on Little Indian Creek. (Courtesy of Marvin Zabel.)

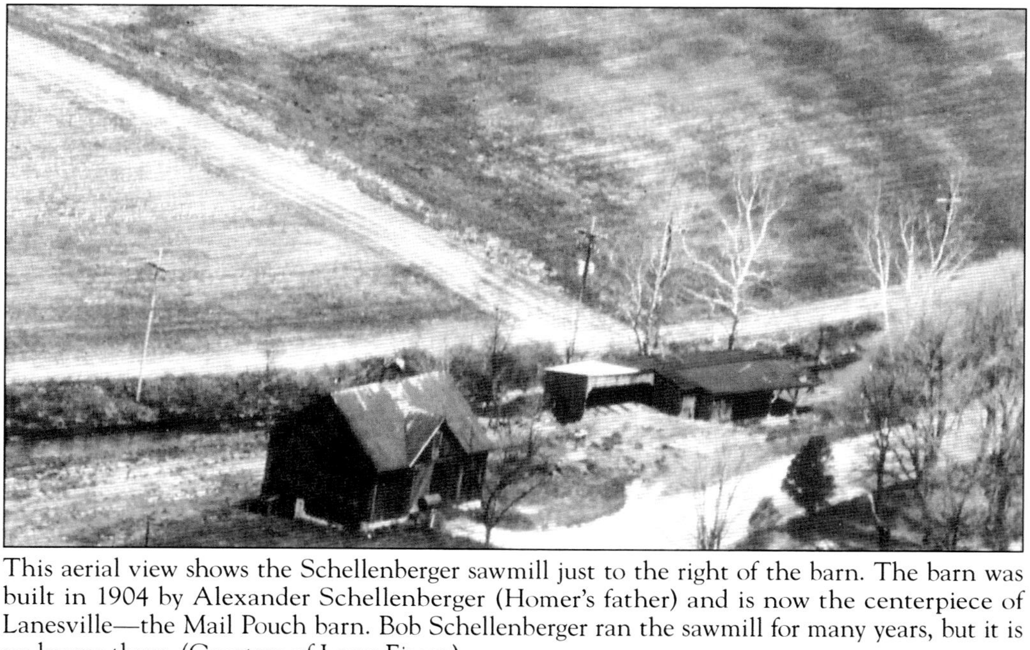

This aerial view shows the Schellenberger sawmill just to the right of the barn. The barn was built in 1904 by Alexander Schellenberger (Homer's father) and is now the centerpiece of Lanesville—the Mail Pouch barn. Bob Schellenberger ran the sawmill for many years, but it is no longer there. (Courtesy of Larry Eisert.)

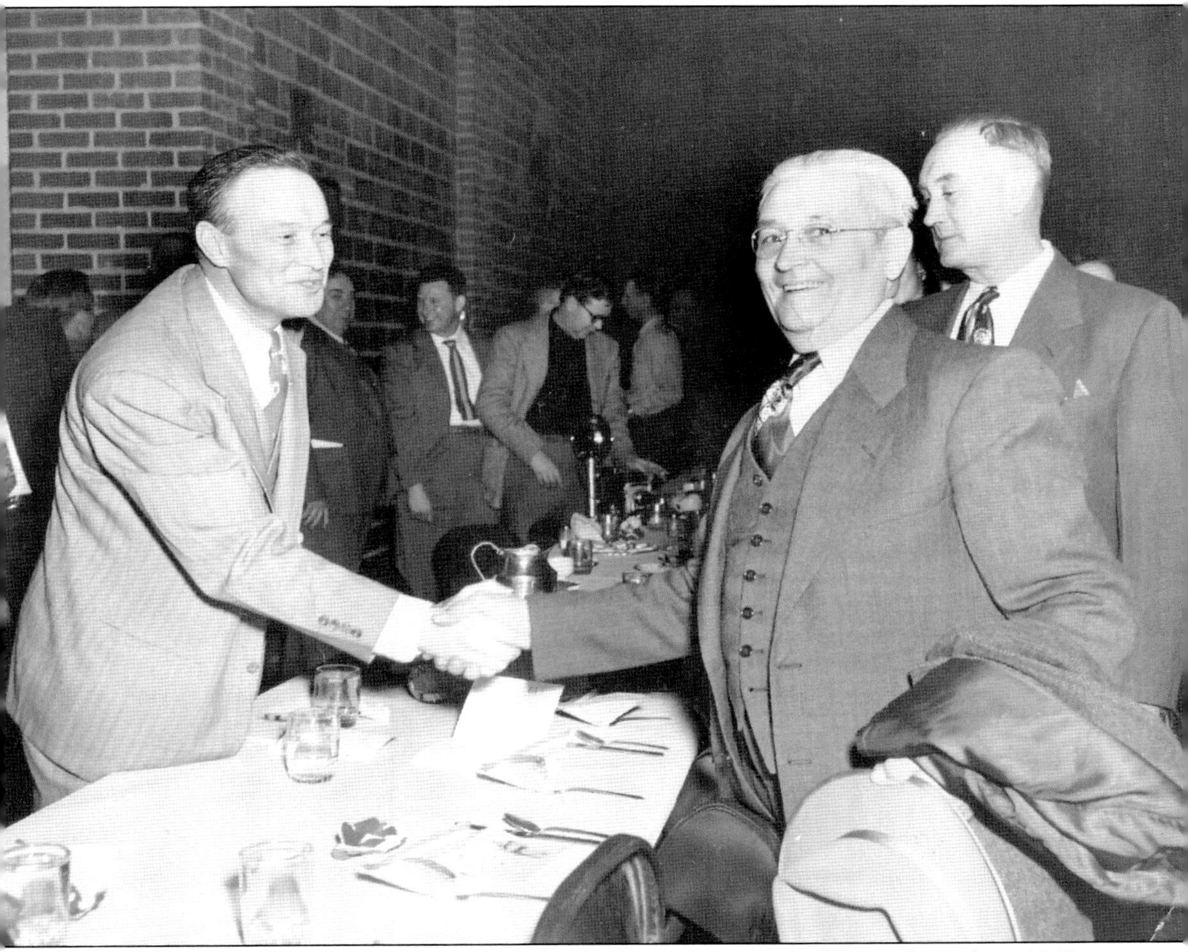

J.G. Zabel (right) shakes hands with William E. Jenner, the US senator from Indiana from 1947 to 1959. Jenner was originally from Marengo, Indiana. Zabel was a Republican leader for many years in Harrison County, and this meeting most likely took place at a party function. (Courtesy of Marvin Zabel.)

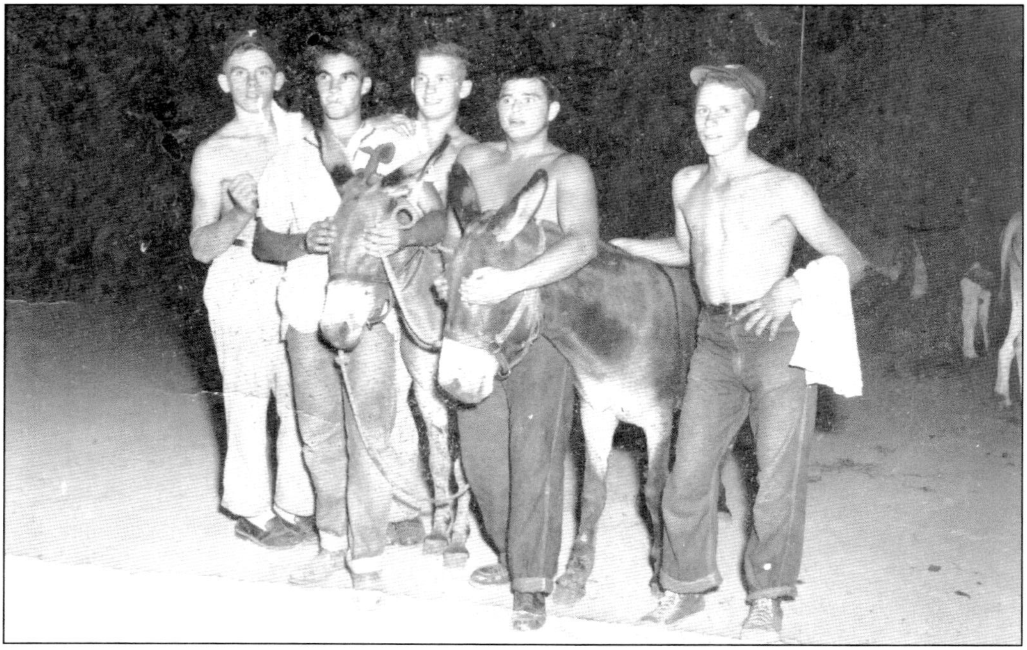

The boys above having fun playing "Donkey Softball" in the mid-1950s are, from left to right, Ed Ullrich, Eddie Miller, Donnie Melton, Marvin Hussung, and Donnie Schueler. The image below was taken the same night, only this time the handler let the girls have some fun sitting on the donkey for the camera. The donkeys could be very calm and gentle, but when their handler whispered in their ear, they would begin to buck and kick whoever was behind them. (Both, courtesy of Marvin Zabel.)

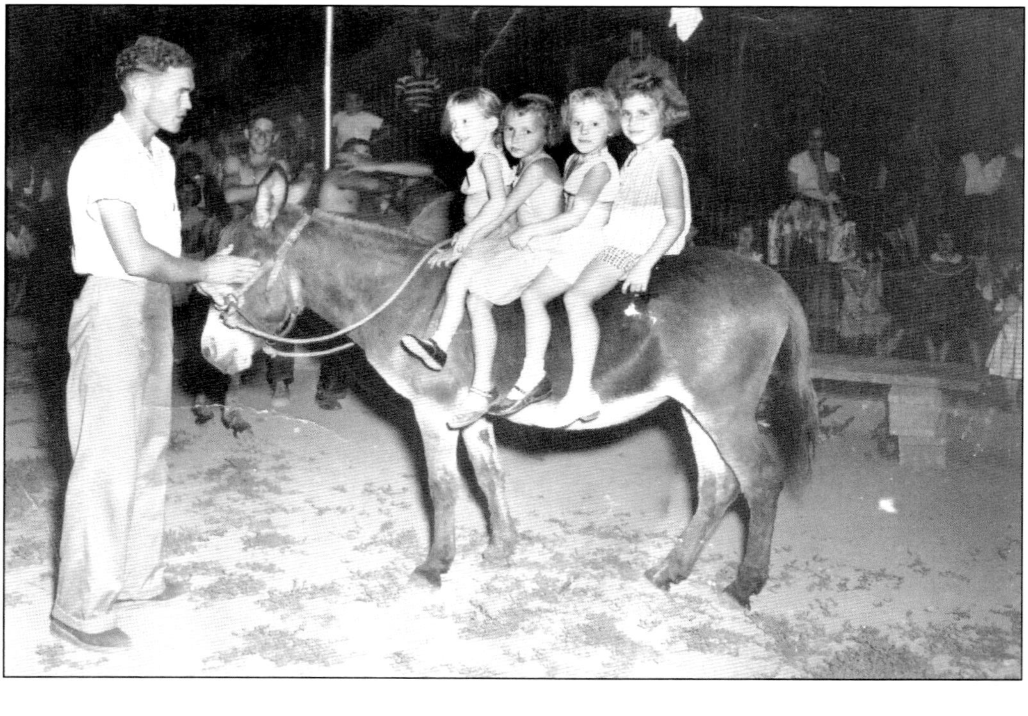

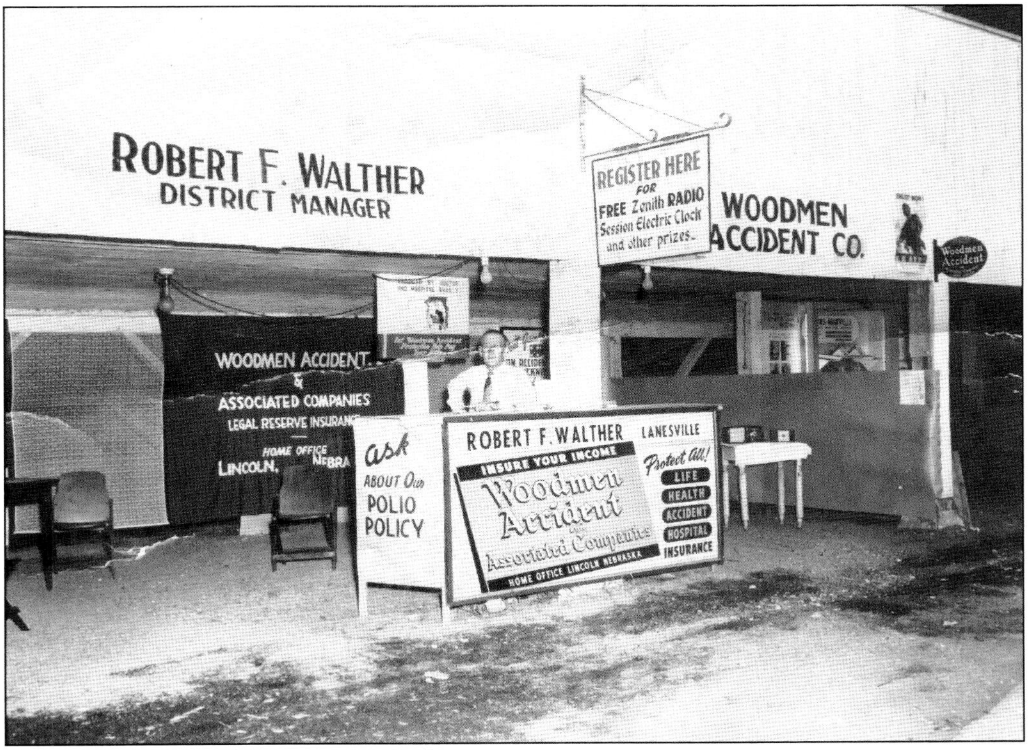

The Woodmen Accident Company had this booth at the Harrison County Fair in the late 1940s. Robert F. Walther, who at one time had been in business with J.G. Zabel, sold insurance for Woodmen Accident Company from the mid-1930s until his death in 1953. (Courtesy of Norbert Walther.)

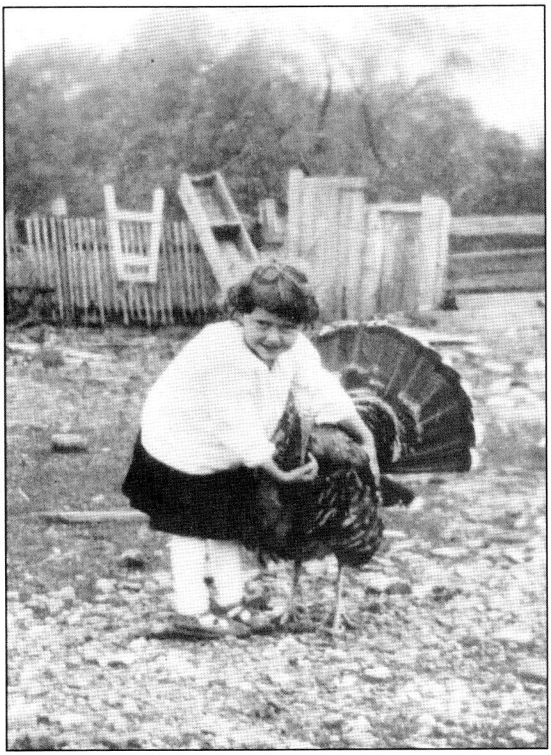

Oneda (Ott) Ringle poses with her pet turkey, Tommy Two Step, in 1916. (Courtesy of Oneda Ringle.)

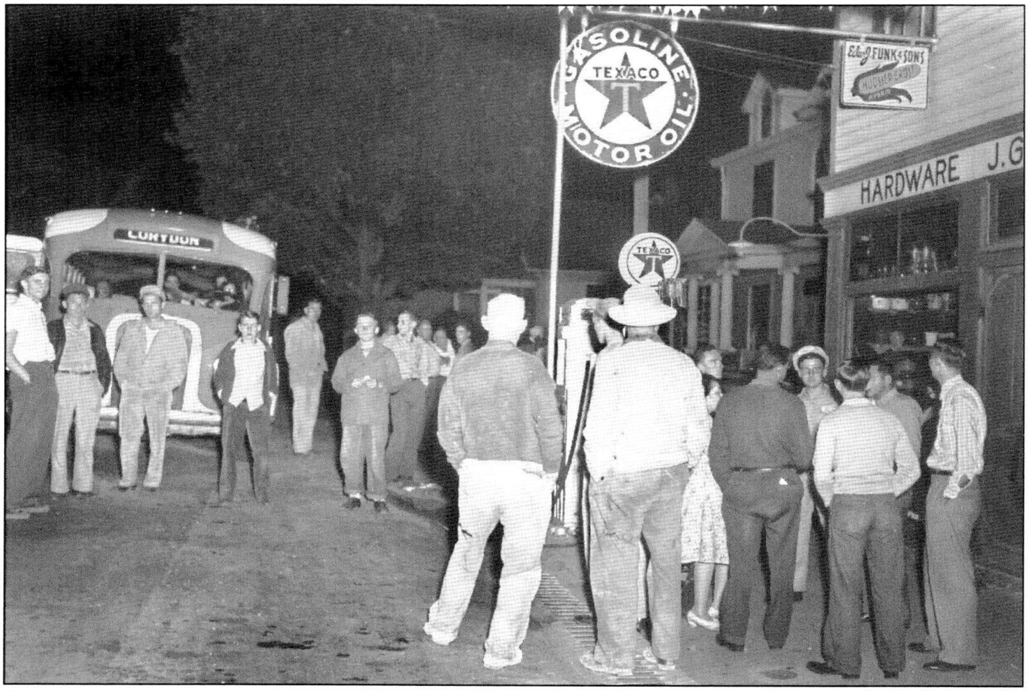

This little accident caused quite a stir in town one evening. Elmer Reinhardt, the driver of the old car, flipped it over and was hit from behind by a Corydon bus. Elmer crawled out of the car, still puffing away at his pipe, to check the damage. No one was hurt, but the wreck caused some excitement. This bus made frequent trips carrying workers from Corydon to and from the munitions plant in Charlestown. (Zabel's hardware store is seen above, and Zollman's store, across the street, is below.) (Both, courtesy of Marvin Zabel.)

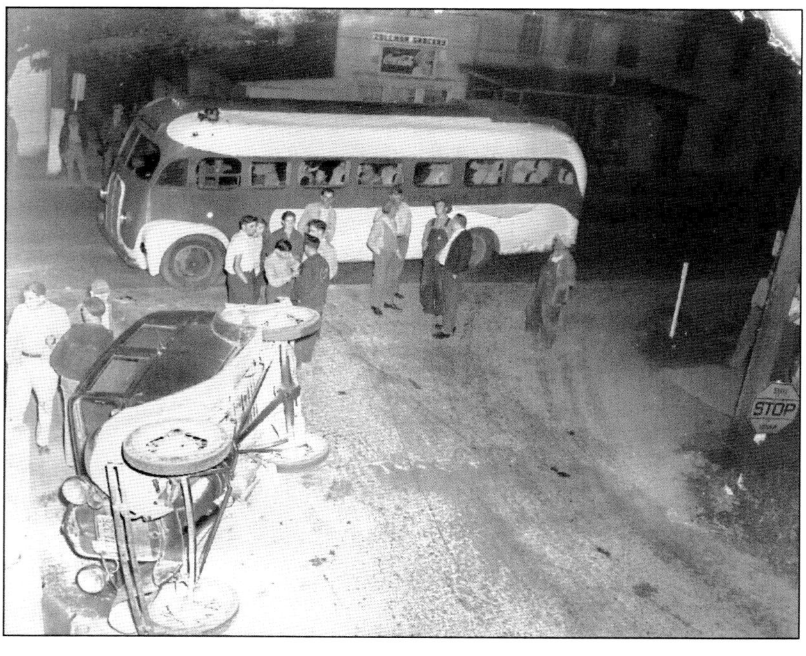

An unidentified member or friend of the Bachman family stands on the snowy hillside overlooking town in the early 1930s. Pennington Street is behind her, as well as houses, St. Mary's Catholic Church, and Lanesville Methodist Church. (Courtesy of Russell Bachman.)

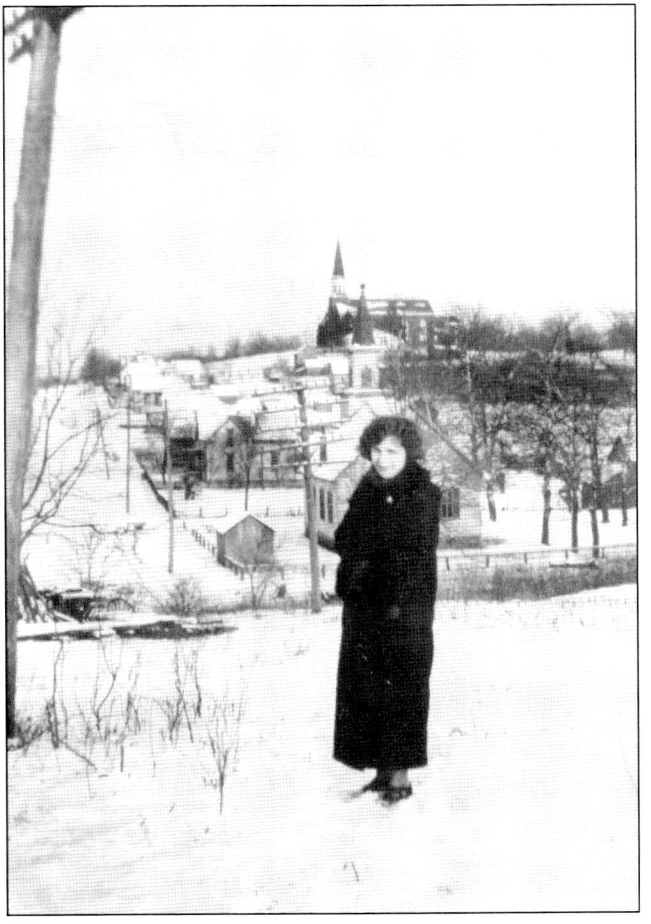

This view of Lanesville looks west from the top of the hill at St. Mary's Catholic Church c. 1915. The high school had not been built yet. Many of these buildings and houses are still visible from the hill today. (Courtesy of Jim Schellenberger.)

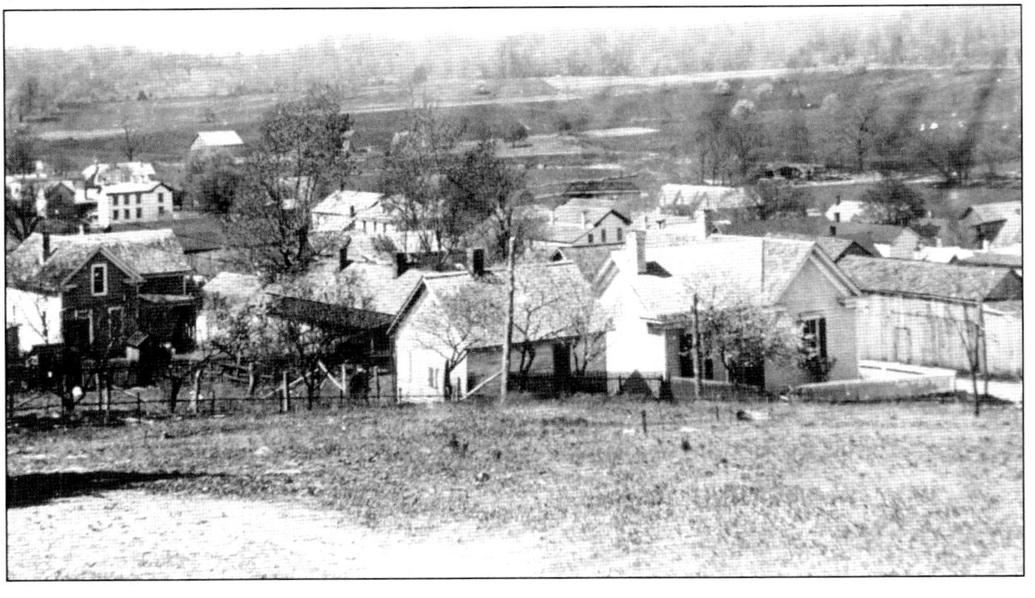

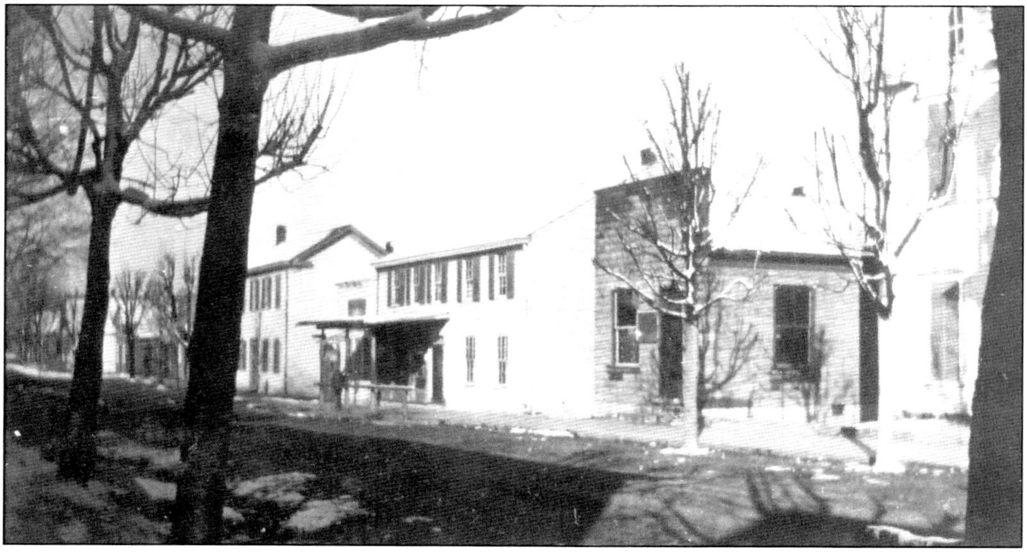

This view looks west down Main Street around the early 1930s. Farmer's State Bank is in the center with Zollman's Store to its left. The two-story house at the left of Zollman's store was the creamery run by Ed Snider, which was a receiving station for Sugar Creek Creamery in Louisville. It was one of two creameries in Lanesville, the other was the Fachinger Creamery just east of town. (Courtesy of Farmer's State Bank.)

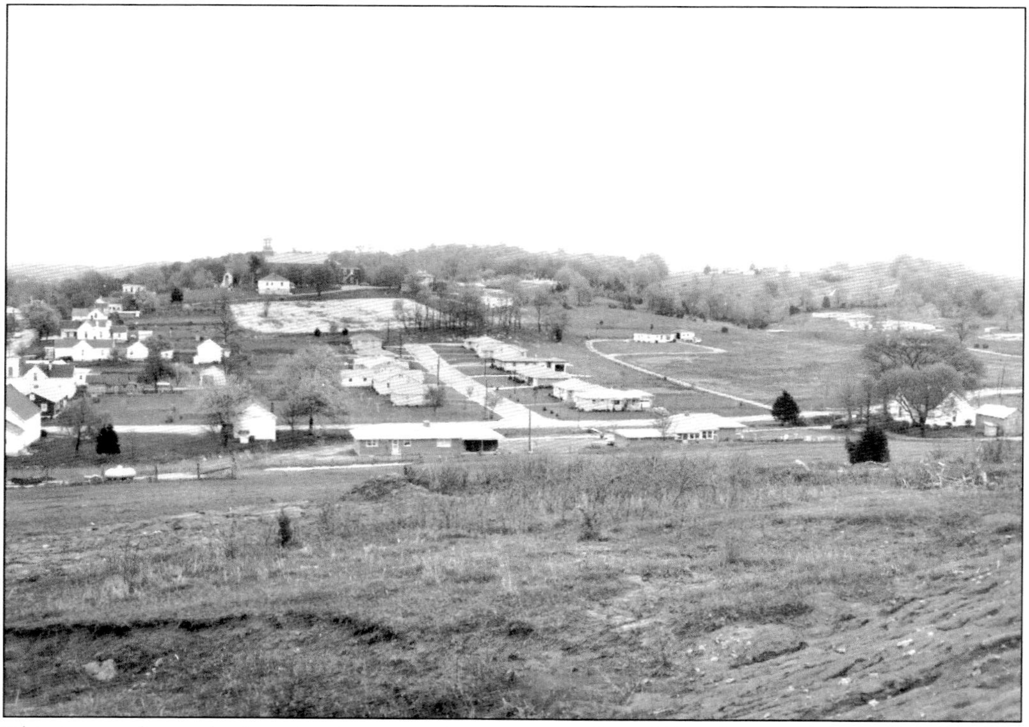

This image shows the housing boom south of town in the 1950s, when homes were built across the country to accommodate growing families after World War II. These houses are still there today, and many of the original families still live in them. (Courtesy of Marvin Zabel.)

Scene Of Attemped Bank Robbery

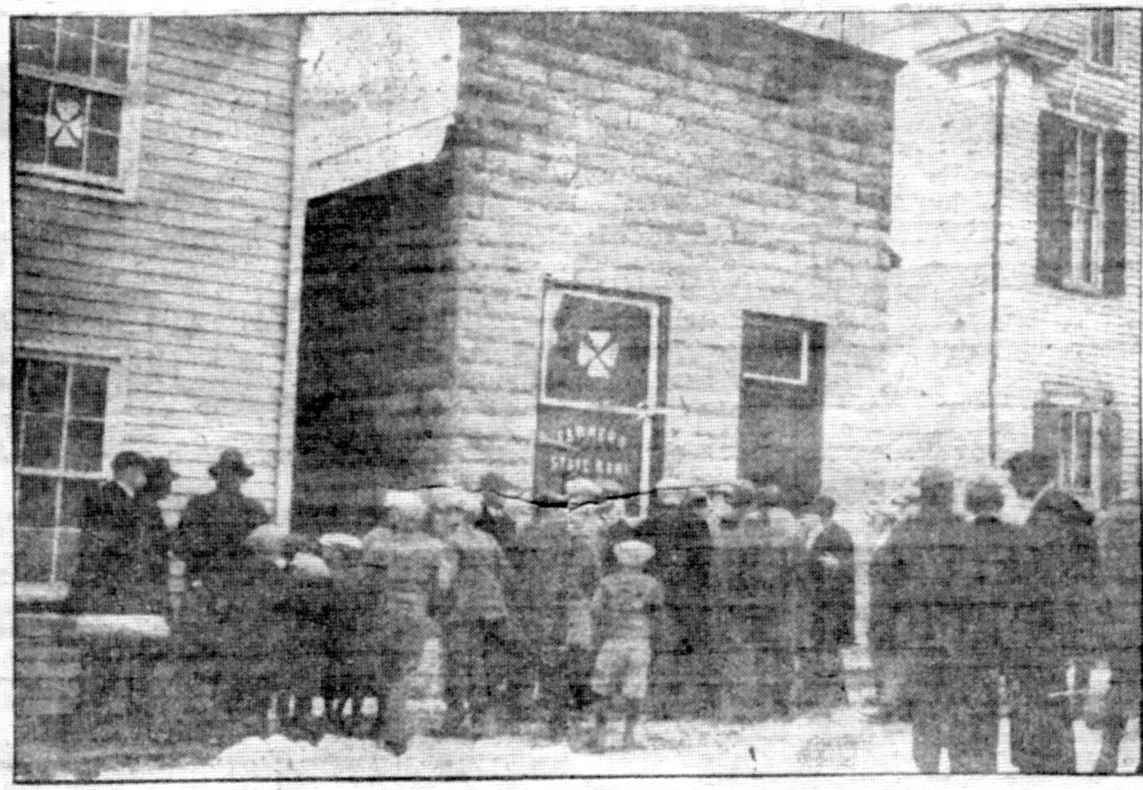

rowds of the curious thronged the streets of the otherwise quiet country village of Lanes-ille in front of the Farmers' State Bank, where six expert cracksmen made an unsuccessful ttempt early Sunday morning to crack the safe. The "X" on the window shows where the obbers entered, only to be frightened away before they had opened the safe. The barking of dog awakened Urban A. Zollman, who lives in the adjoining house, and who watched the ookout for the robbers from the window mark ed "X."

The great bank robbery attempt at Farmer's State Bank was big news. The *Louisville Herald-Post* newspaper reported on January 24, 1926: "At about 3:00 o'clock in the morning of January 24, five men attempted to rob the Farmer's Bank in Lanesville. If it weren't for Urban Zollman's big black Newfoundland watchdog, the robbers may have gotten by with it. The dog's barking at the men alerted Urban to take action. He called the local operator Helen Dietrich who was on duty next door, to alert the several townsmen for a 'call to arms' as the robbers sped off, Urban and several townsmen took shots at the car as it left town. Even though the robbers had cut the phones leading to Corydon and New Albany, quick thinking operator Helen Dietrich called the Crandall operators to warn the New Albany police of the robbers heading their way. They were eventually captured." (Article courtesy of Farmer's State Bank and the *Louisville Herald-Post*.)

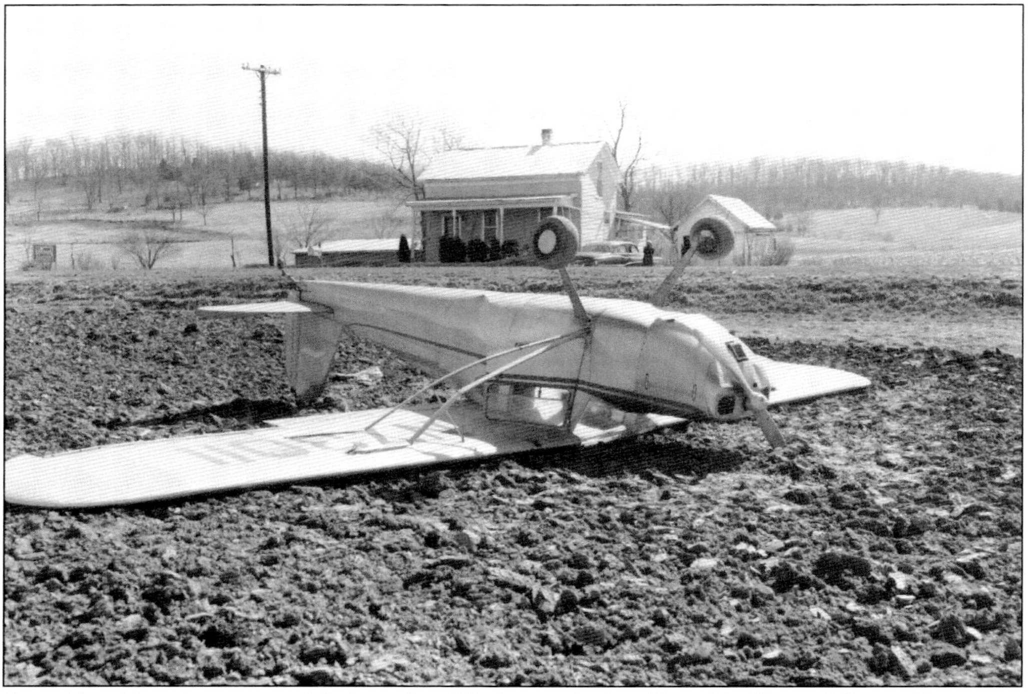

A small malfunction occurred during takeoff for licensed pilots Oscar Voelker and Parvin Baumgart. They were getting ready to go to their jobs as air traffic controllers at Standiford Field in Louisville, when they had a great idea to load 60 dozen eggs in the plane and sell them at Standiford. Once loaded and ready for takeoff, the plane lost power, stopped, and tipped over, dumping all the eggs in the cockpit, mostly all over Baumgart. No one was hurt but there were broken eggs all over the place. The two cleaned up and drove to work. (Both, courtesy of Marvin Zabel.)

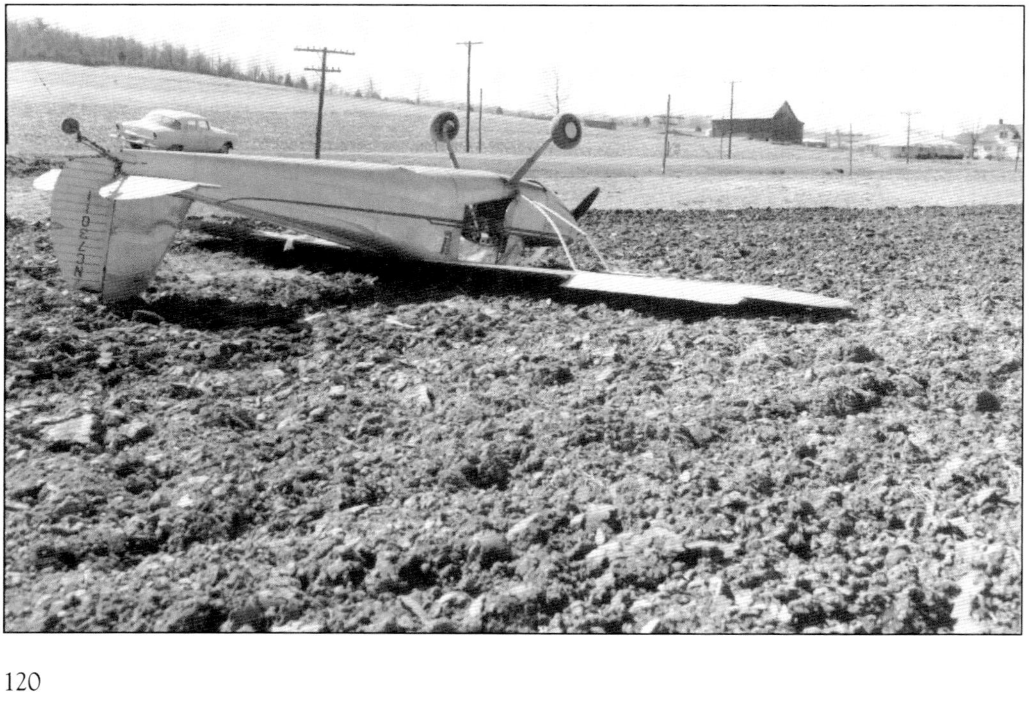

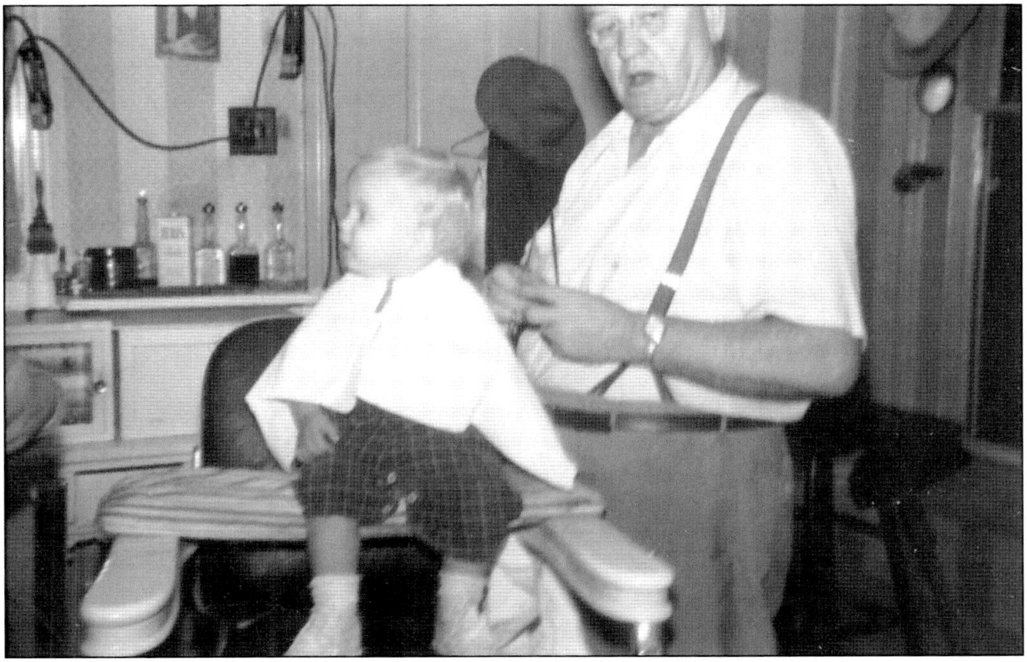

Acy Loy was a barber in Lanesville for many years, cutting hair from the 1930s until 1960, when he sold his shop to Gus Marshall. Here, Loy gives a first haircut to one of Jim Kochert's twin boys, Tony, in 1953. Loy had given Jim his haircuts as a boy as well. (Courtesy of Jim Kochert.)

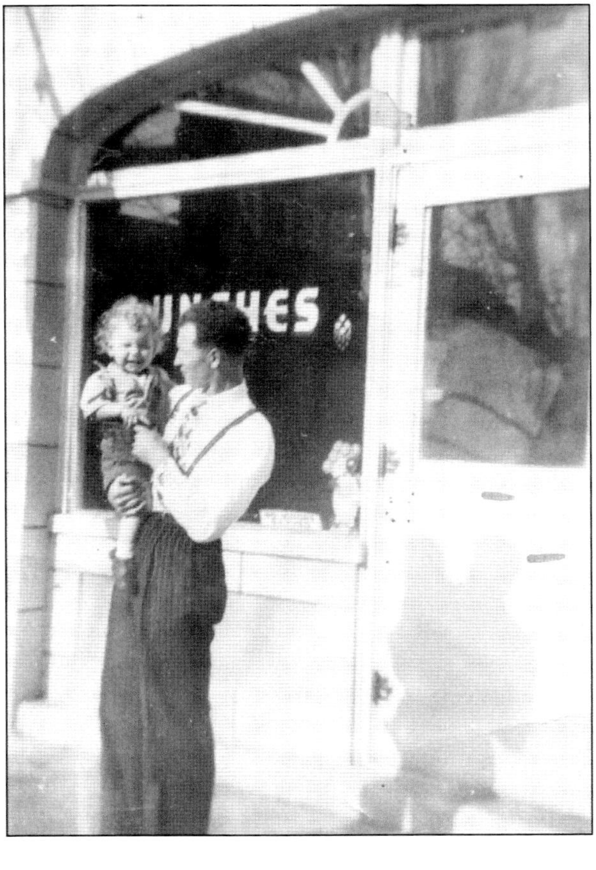

Louis Stilger holds his son Butch outside his bar and restaurant in Lanesville. Stilger operated a tavern and restaurant on Main Street from 1946 to 1960, which he turned into a grocery and laundromat from 1961 to 1975. Today, the building sits between Hog's Tavern and the mill and is still in the Stilger family. (Courtesy of Crystal Stilger.)

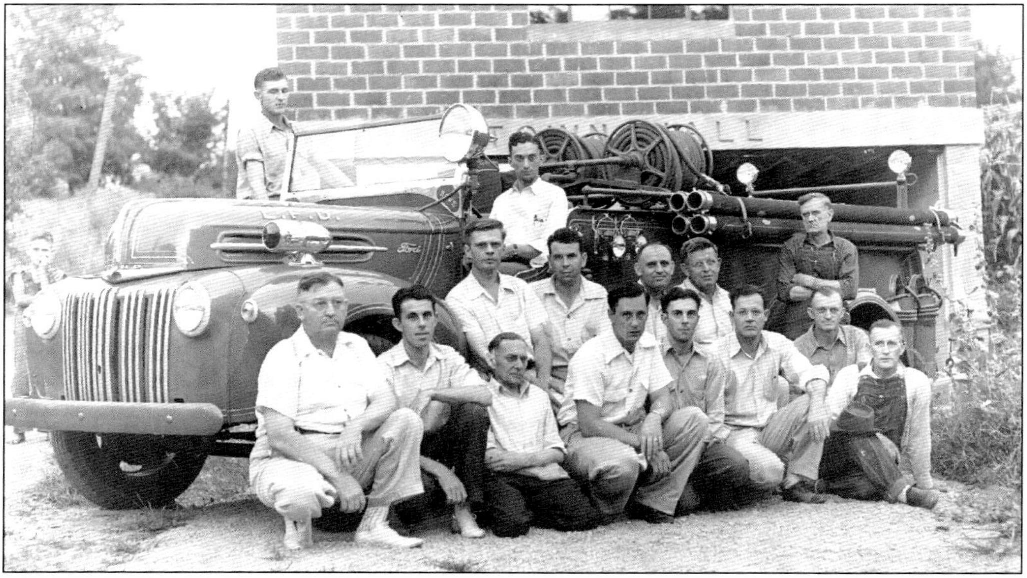

The Lanesville Volunteer Fire Department members sit with their new Ford fire truck in 1941 in front of the town hall, which also housed the fire station. The town hall building was built in 1939. The firefighters included, from left to right, (first row) Acy Loy, Wilford Day, Julius Green, Louis Ott, Wilber Nance, Ed Jaegers, Erwin Baumgart, and Robert Walther; (second row) Orlin Lieber, Byron Baker, George Richmer, Herman Zollman, and Ed Green; (standing) Maurice Kochert (in the driver's seat) and Leonard Jaegers (standing on the left of the truck). (Courtesy of Lennie Reinhardt.)

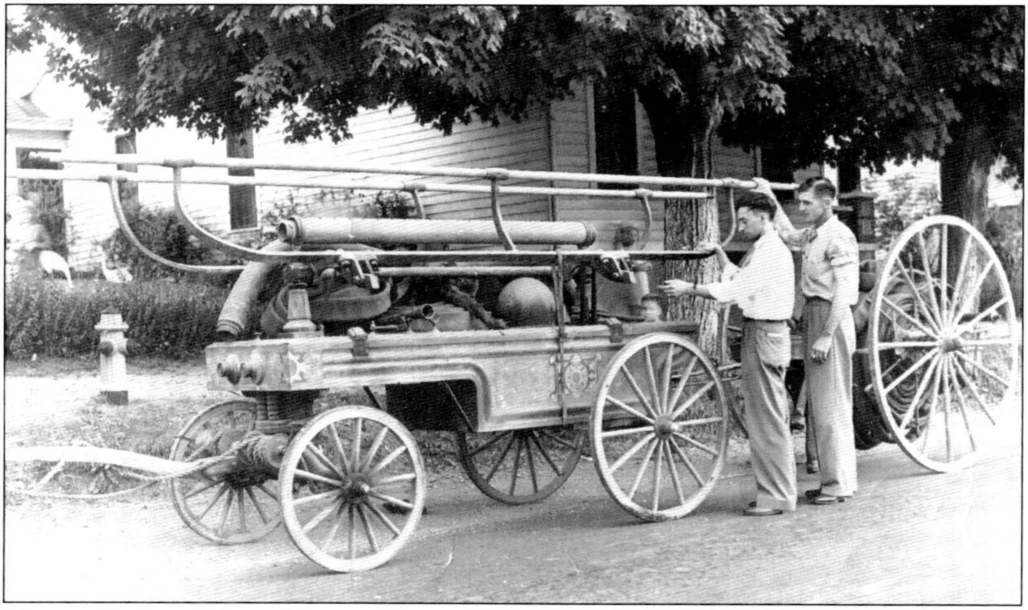

Maurice Kochert (left) and Leonard Jaegers stand in front of the old hand-pumper, the Rumsey Squirrel Tail, produced by Rumsey and Company in Seneca, New York, in 1876. The town bought this pumper in the late 1870s and the fire department still has it today. (Courtesy of Lennie Reinhardt.)

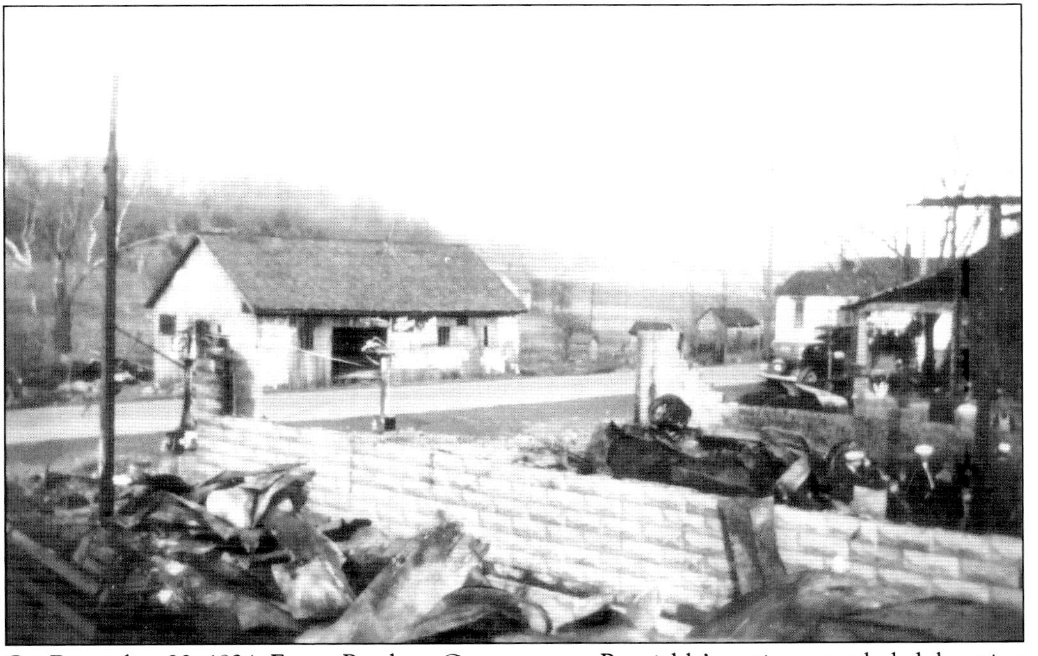

On December 20, 1934, Evans Brothers Garage—now Barnickle's station—exploded, bursting into flames and killing 23-year-old gasoline delivery truck driver Alvin Nieman, who, along with George Sturns of Elizabeth, was transferring gasoline from the truck into metal cans because the truck had broken down. A spark set off the explosion, which destroyed the station and damaged many nearby structures. Owners Asa and Maurice "Hap" Evans were not hurt in the blast. The station was opened by Ed Barnickle in 1937. (Courtesy of Don Schickel.)

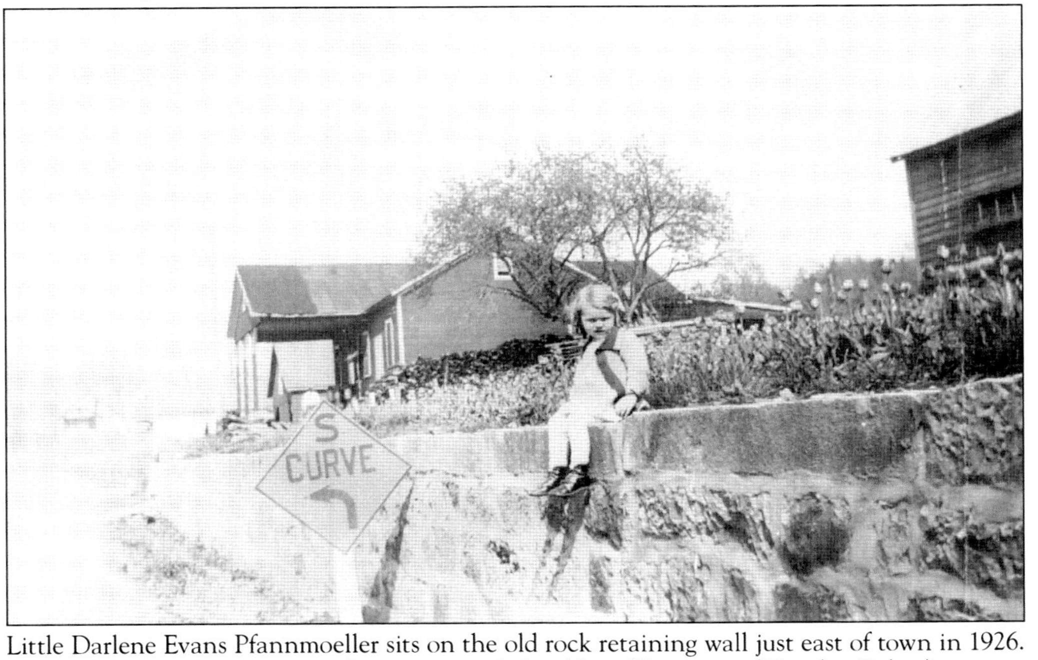

Little Darlene Evans Pfannmoeller sits on the old rock retaining wall just east of town in 1926. The Fachinger Creamery is in plain view just behind her. (Courtesy of Carolyn Baker.)

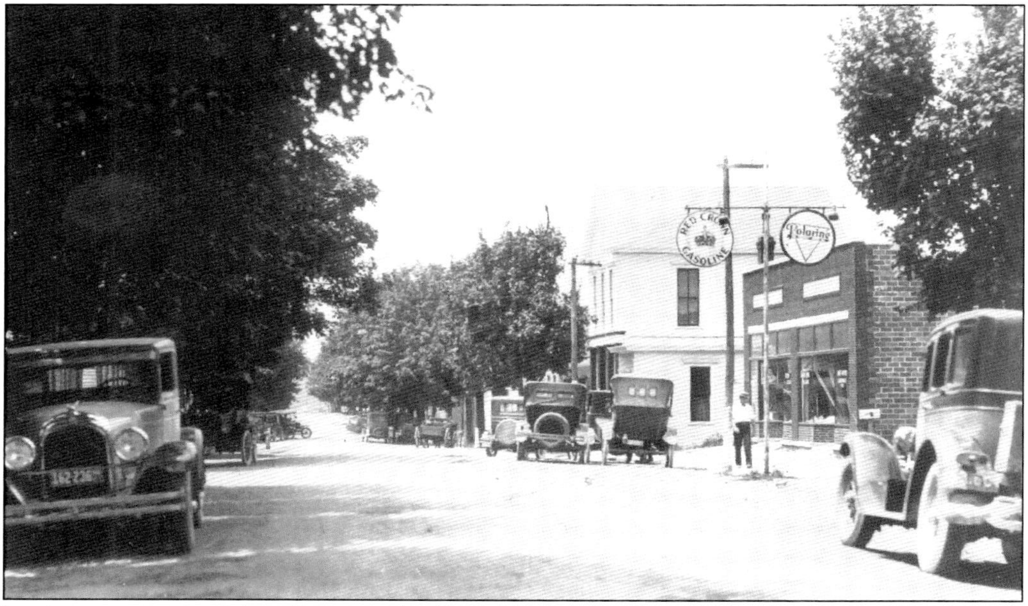

Looking west down Main Street in the late 1920s, Morris Baker's store is on the right with its sign for Red Crown Gasoline and Polarine, which made automobile oil and lubricants. While many of the trees are long gone, the store is still in business, and many of the buildings still exist today. (Courtesy of Carolyn Baker.)

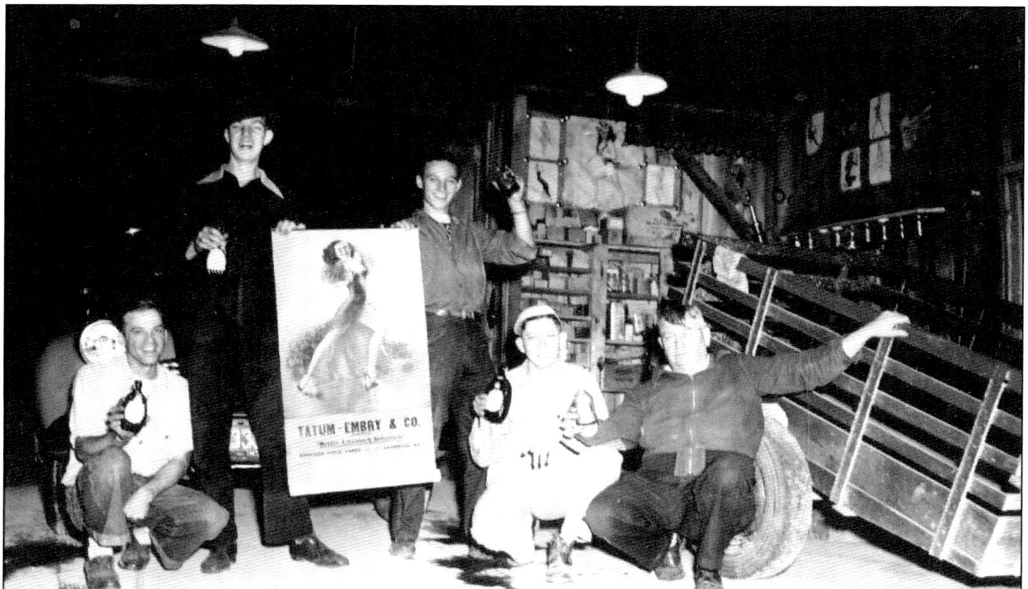

Barnickle's station was a gathering place where folks sat around and caught up on the news. From left to right, Darrell Harbeson, Joe Barnickle, Bob Harbeson, Everitt Day, and Acy Loy joke around at the station. The poster advertised Tatum-Embry & Co., a meatpacking plant. (Courtesy of Marvin Zabel.)

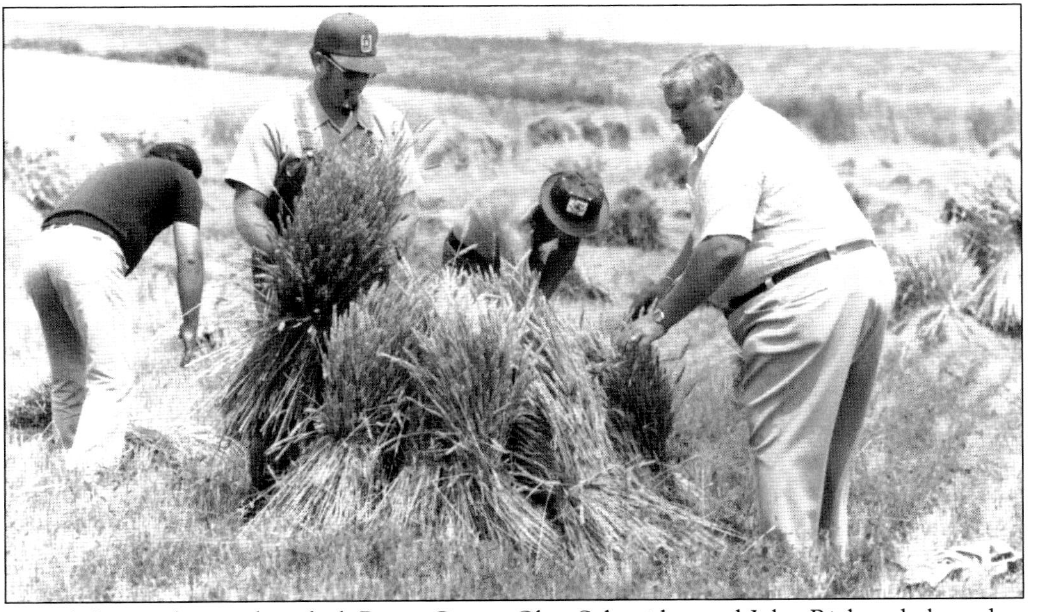

From left to right, unidentified, Bruce Green, Glen Schneider, and John Richert help gather wheat shocks for the Lanesville Heritage Weekend Festival, which occurs every September. Green and Richert started the festival in 1976 as a school project for the nation's bicentennial, and it became one of the biggest festivals in the state of Indiana. Bruce Green and John Richert were great teachers at Lanesville High School and were great people. They have both passed away, and the community misses them dearly. (Courtesy of Maynard Lambertus.)

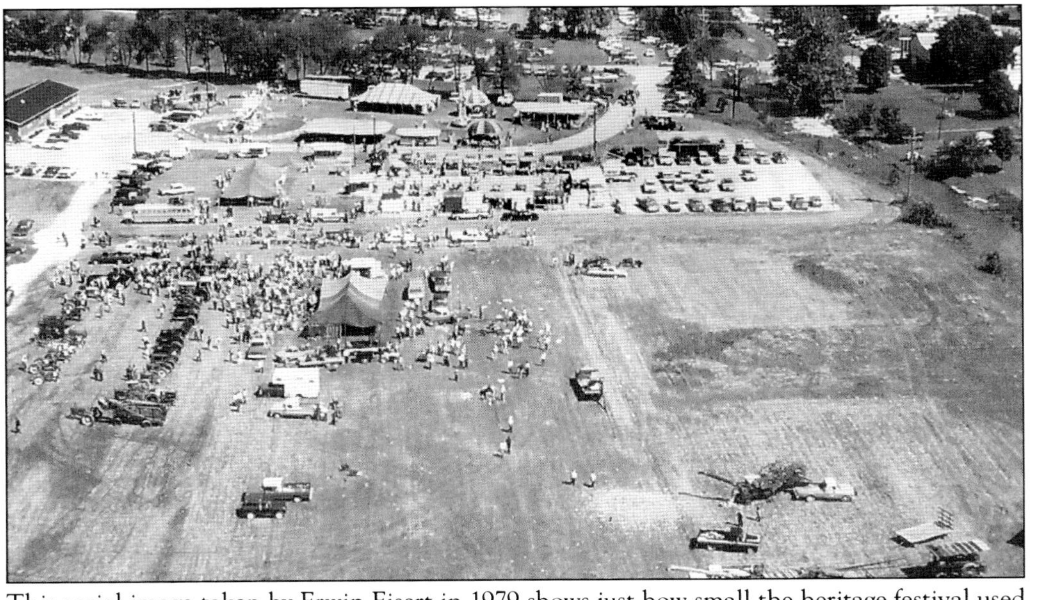

This aerial image taken by Erwin Eisert in 1979 shows just how small the heritage festival used to be. Today, the three-day festival takes up about three times the space and has several hundred exhibits. In the past few years, attendance has been estimated at 50,000 or more over three days. What was started as a small project blossomed into a festival known statewide. (Courtesy of Larry Eisert.)

Vol. 114 No. 43 CORYDON, INDIANA, WEDNESDAY, DECEMBER 10, 1969

Good-bye 5! Hello (812) 952-2555

The switch-over of the Lanesville Telephone Company became effective last Sunday morning at 2:01; however, a number of Lanesville Telephone users found that they could dial direct to Corydon and other Eureka Telephone exchanges during Saturday.

The sweep of electronic improvements did not pass without a touch of nostalgia.

With the departure of the personable telephone operators and the move from the fancy, colorful office (lower left picture) to the stark, modern control center (lower picture), gone are the days when the friendly operator tells you that you sound like you've got a bad cold, when the doctor leaves the number where he can be reached, and when the number of the high school was a simple, unadorned "5."

Now that number is 952-2555, and conversations like this, overheard last week, will no longer take place:

Lanesville operator to metropolitan operator: "Operator, that number is 5. No, operator, just 5. (Pause) That's all there is to it, just 5."

(Corydon Democrat photos by Parker Sams)

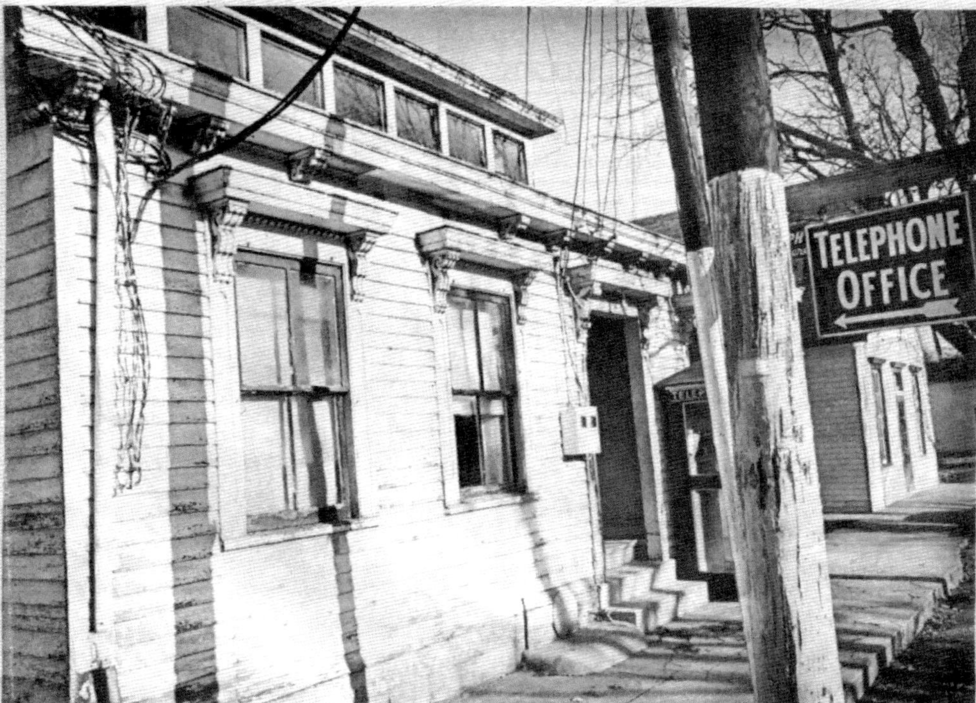

The Lanesville exchange was an important part of life for the residents of Lanesville and Franklin Township. The phone company sat on the corner of Crestview Avenue and State Road 62 for many years, but it came to an end in 1969. This *Corydon Democrat* article was a nice tribute to the ladies who worked the switchboards for many years. (Courtesy of Saundra Conrad and the *Corydon Democrat*.)

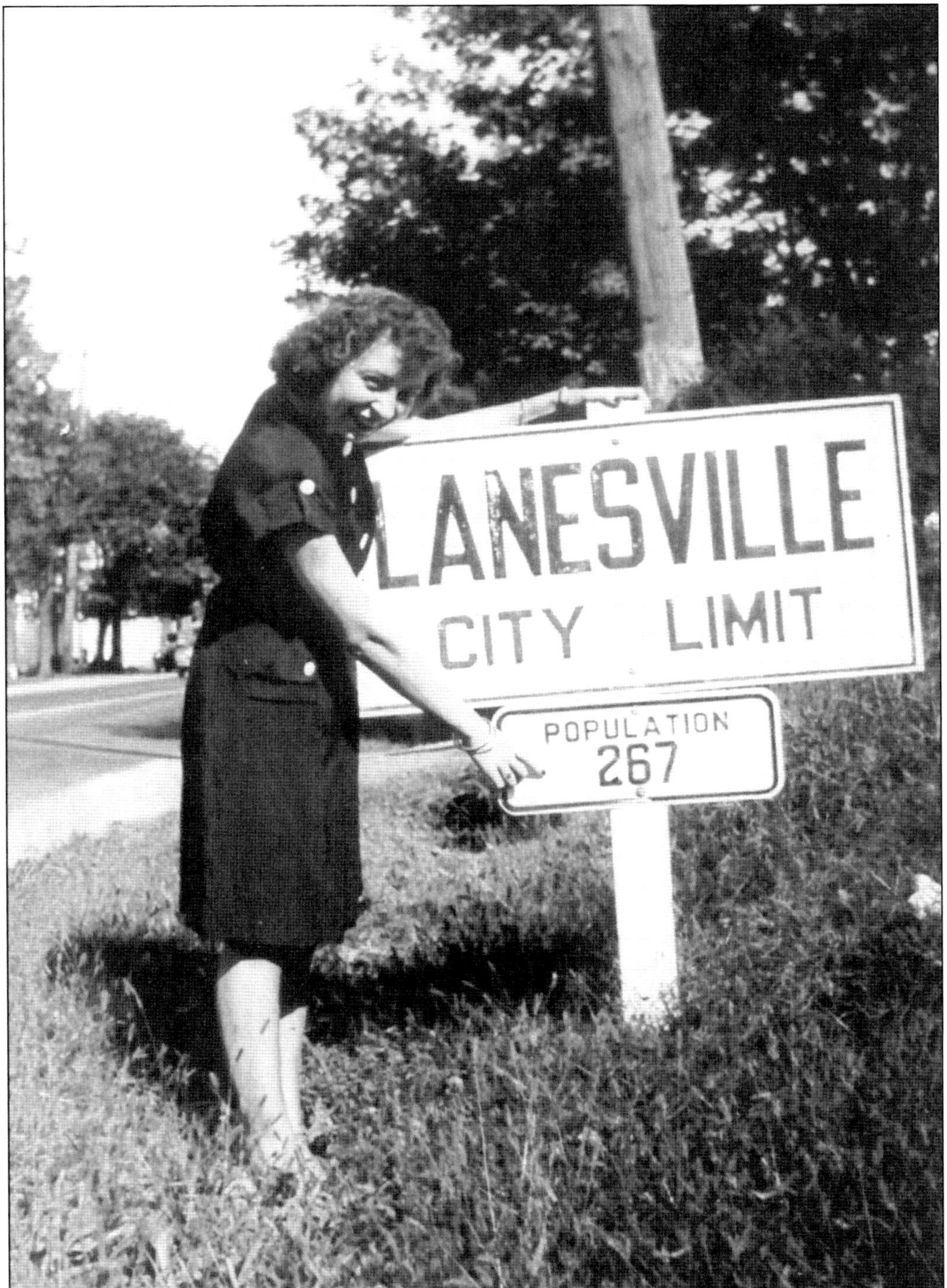

A friend of Bernice (Zollman) Barnickle visited Lanesville on a summer afternoon in 1945 and posed next to the town sign. This is a fitting end to the book, which shares the history of this small American town with the rest of the world. (Courtesy of Bernice Barnickle.)

Consistent with our mission to preserve history on a local level, this book was printed in South Carolina on American-made paper and manufactured entirely in the United States. Products carrying the accredited Forest Stewardship Council (FSC) label are printed on 100 percent FSC-certified paper.